Fourth Workshop on Computational Linguistics and Clinical Psychology: From Linguistic Signal to Clinical Reality (CLPsych 2017)

Held at ACL 2017

Vancouver, Canada
3 August 2017

ISBN: 978-1-5108-4581-7

Fourth Workshop on Computational Linguistics and Clinical Psychology: From Linguistic Signal to Clinical Reality (CLPsych 2017)

Held at ACL 2017

Vancouver, Canada
3 August 2017

CLPsych 2017

The Fourth Workshop on
Computational Linguistics and Clinical Psychology —
From Linguistic Signal to Clinical Reality

Proceedings of the Workshop

August 3, 2017
Vancouver, Canada

Gold Sponsors:

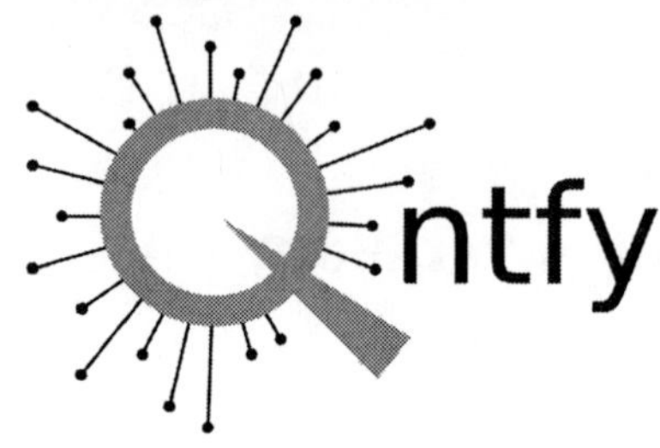

Bronze Sponsor:

Introduction

In the United States, mental and neurological health problems are among the costliest challenges we face. Depression, Alzheimer's disease, bipolar disorder, and attention deficit hyperactivity disorder (ADHD) are only a handful of the many illnesses that contribute to this cost. The global cost of mental health conditions alone was estimated at $2.5 trillion in 2010, with a projected increase to over $6 trillion in 2030. Neurological illnesses and mental disorders cost the U.S. more than $760 billion a year. The World Health Organization (WHO) estimates one out of four people worldwide will suffer from a mental illness at some point in their lives, while one in five Americans experience a mental health problem in any given year. Mental, neurological, and substance use disorders are the leading cause of disability worldwide, yet most public service announcements and government education programs remain focused on physical health issues such as cancer screening, influenza vaccines, and obesity. Despite the substantial and rising burden of such disorders, there is a significant shortage of resources available to prevent, diagnose, and treat them; thus technology must be brought to bear—in particular, language technology.

For clinical psychologists, language plays a central role in diagnosis, and many clinical instruments fundamentally rely on manual coding of patient language. Applying language technology in the domain of mental and neurological health could lead to inexpensive screening measures that may be administered by a wider array of healthcare professionals. Researchers had begun targeting such issues prior to this workshop series, using language technology to identify emotion in suicide notes, analyze the language of those with autistic spectrum disorders, and aid the diagnosis of dementia.

The series of Computational Linguistics and Clinical Psychology (CLPsych) workshops began at ACL 2014 with lively discussions about the advantages and disadvantages of diagnostic language tools and language-based interventions. NAACL 2015 and 2016 hosted the second and third such workshop with a near-doubling of attendance. The 2015 workshop also hosted the first CLPsych Shared Task, and the 2016 Shared Task saw a near-quadrupling of participants, with 15 submissions aiming to identify forum posts requiring immediate moderator attention an online peer-support forum hosted by ReachOut.com. The CLPsych workshops diverge from the conventional "mini-conference" workshop format by inviting clinical psychologists and researchers to join us at the workshop as discussants, to provide real-world points of view on the potential applications of NLP technologies presented during the workshop. We hope to continue building the momentum towards releasing tools and data that can be used by clinical psychologists, and as such, the ability to communicate relevant computational methods and results clearly, connecting the work to clinical practice, is as important as the quality of the work itself, and more important than research novelty.

ACL 2017 hosts the fourth CLPsych workshop, with another shared task. Published papers in this proceedings propose methods for automatically detecting and explaining psychological crisis, assessing depression and anxiety, analyzing language of murderers and dreams, and tracking affect patterns in social media of mental illness and suicide groups. The 2017 CLPsych Shared Task once again centered on the classification of posts from a mental health forum to assist forum moderators in triaging and escalating posts requiring immediate attention. We received 21 submissions for the workshop, 8 of which were abstracts submitted for the new non-archival track. Of the workshop submissions, 16 (76%) were accepted: 4 for oral presentation, 4 for a new 'mini oral' presentation format, and 6 for poster presentation; 2 were withdrawn. Oral presentations will be followed by discussions led by several experts on working in the fields of behavioral and mental health and with clinical data: Dr. Rebecca Resnik and Dr. Andrew Littlefield.

We wish to thank everyone who showed interest and submitted a paper, all of the authors for their contributions, the members of the Program Committee for their thoughtful reviews, our clinical discussants for their helpful insights, and all the attendees of the workshop. We also wish to extend thanks to the Association for Computational Linguistics for making this workshop possible, and to Microsoft Research, Qntfy, and RealComm Global for their generous sponsorships.

– Kristy, Molly, and Kate

Table of Contents

Conference Program

Thursday August 3, 2017

9:00–9:20 **Opening Remarks**
Chairs: Kristy Hollingshead, Molly E. Ireland and Kate Loveys

9:20–10:30 **Session: Oral Presentations 1**

A Cross-modal Review of Indicators for Depression Detection Systems
Michelle Morales, Stefan Scherer and Rivka Levitan

In Your Wildest Dreams: The Language and Psychological Features of Dreams
Kate Niederhoffer, Jonathan Schler, Patrick Crutchley, Kate Loveys and Glen Coppersmith

11:00–12:15 **Session: Poster Presentations**

A Corpus Analysis of Social Connections and Social Isolation in Adolescents Suffering from Depressive Disorders
Jia-Wen Guo, Danielle L Mowery, Djin Lai, Katherine Sward and Mike Conway

Monitoring Tweets for Depression to Detect At-Risk Users
Zunaira Jamil, Diana Inkpen, Prasadith Buddhitha and Kenton White

Examining Sentiment and Depression in Survivors of Intimate Partner Violence.
Joseph Costello, Catherine Kothari, Duncan Vos, Richard Brandt and Angie Moe

Ethical Challenges in Algorithmic Inference of Mental Illness with Large-Scale Social Data
Stevie Chancellor, Vincent Silenzio, Eric Caine and Munmun De Choudhury

Validation of Twitter Self-Stated Models of Mental Health against Patient Medical Records
Glen Coppersmith, Patrick Crutchley, Raina M. Merchant and H. Andrew Schwartz

Language Style Matching in Subclinically Depressed and Anxious Participants' Responses to Social Media-Style Posts
Taleen Nalabandian and Molly Ireland

1:45–2:30   **Session: Mini-Oral Presentations**

Investigating Patient Attitudes Towards the use of Social Media Data to Augment Depression Diagnosis and Treatment: a Qualitative Study
Jude Mikal, Samantha Hurst and Mike Conway

Natural-language Interactive Narratives in Imaginal Exposure Therapy for Obsessive-Compulsive Disorder
Melissa Roemmele, Paola Mardo and Andrew Gordon

Detecting Anxiety through Reddit
Judy Hanwen Shen and Frank Rudzicz

Detecting and Explaining Crisis
Rohan Kshirsagar, Robert Morris and Samuel Bowman

2:30–3:30   **Session: Oral Presentations 2**

A Dictionary-Based Comparison of Autobiographies by People and Murderous Monsters
Micah Iserman and Molly Ireland

Small but Mighty: Affective Micropatterns for Quantifying Mental Health from Social Media Language
Kate Loveys, Patrick Crutchley, Emily Wyatt and Glen Coppersmith

4:00–5:00   **CLPsych2017 Shared Task: Results & Open Discussion**
Chair: David Milne

5:00–5:30   **Closing Remarks**

A Cross-modal Review of Indicators for Depression Detection Systems

Michelle Renee Morales
Linguistics Department
The Graduate Center, CUNY
New York, NY 10016
mmorales@gradcenter.cuny.edu

Stefan Scherer
USC Institute for
Creative Technologies
Los Angeles, CA 90094
scherer@ict.usc.edu

Rivka Levitan
Computer Science Department
Brooklyn College, CUNY
Brooklyn, NY 11210
levitan@sci.brooklyn.cuny.edu

Abstract

Automatic detection of depression has attracted increasing attention from researchers in psychology, computer science, linguistics, and related disciplines. As a result, promising depression detection systems have been reported. This paper surveys these efforts by presenting the first cross-modal review of depression detection systems and discusses best practices and most promising approaches to this task.

1 Introduction

Given advancements in hardware and software, coupled with the explosion of smartphone use, the forms of potential health care solutions have begun to change and interest in developing technologies to assess mental health has grown. Among the latest technologies are depression detection systems, which use indicators from an individual in combination with machine learning to make automated depression level assessments. Researchers have made significant progress, but challenges remain. One major challenge is the existing disconnect between language technology subfields: approaches to depression assessment from natural language processing (NLP), speech processing, and human-computer interaction (HCI) tend to silo by subfield, with little discussion about the utility of combining promising approaches. This existing disconnect necessitates a bridge to facilitate greater collaboration and cooperation across subfields and modalities.

Experts across several fields are attempting to build valid tools for depression assessment. Each subfield tends to approach the task from a unique perspective, with slightly different goals, and completely different data sources. Due to these experimental differences, it is difficult to compare approaches and even more difficult to combine promising approaches. For example, if we consider data sources alone, NLP research has aimed to detect depression from writing, both formal and informal (i.e. online text), speech processing research has aimed to assess depression level from audio while HCI and related fields try to assess depression level from video. Each data source is then labeled for depression through different approaches, including rating scales, self-report surveys, manual annotation, etc. As a result, we see various definitions of how depression is defined across studies. Regardless of the existing differences, every study and system share the common goal of discovering a way to use technology to help assess depression.

This survey paper aims to serve as a bridge between the subfields by providing the first review of depression detection systems across subfields and modalities. This paper focuses on the following research questions, how has depression been defined and annotated in detection systems? What kinds of depression data exists or could be obtained for depression detection systems? What (multimodal) indicators have been used for the automatic detection of depression? How do we evaluate depression detection systems? Each research question could serve as the main focus of an entire paper. Therefore, this review briefly touches upon each question and dedicates the most focus to reviewing indicators of depression and subsequently features for depression detection systems. We cover numerous features across modalities, including visual, acoustic, linguistic, and social. We briefly review approaches to defining and annotating depression, existing data sources, and how to evaluate depression detection systems. Lastly, we end our discussion with the practical or ethical issues that require attention when building systems for depression detection.

Proceedings of the Fourth Workshop on Computational Linguistics and Clinical Psychology, pages 1–12,
Vancouver, Canada, August 3, 2017. © 2017 Association for Computational Linguistics

2 Defining and Labeling Depression

2.1 Clinical Definition and Diagnostics

According to the Diagnostic and Statistical Manual of Mental Disorders (APA, 2013), the most widely used resource in diagnosing mental disorders in the United States, most people will experience some feelings of depression in their lifetime, although it does not meet the criteria of an illnesss until a person has experienced, for longer than a two-week period, a depressed mood and/or a markedly diminished interest/pleasure in combination with four or more of the following symptoms: significant unintentional weight loss or gain, insomnia or sleeping too much, agitation or psychomotor retardation noticed by others, fatigue or loss of energy, feelings of worthlessness or excessive guilt, diminished ability to think or concentrate, indecisiveness, or recurrent thoughts of death. In addition, diagnosis requires that the symptoms cause clinically significant distress or impairment in social, occupational, or other important areas of functioning.

Commonly used assessment tools for depression include clinical interviews or self-assessments. The Hamilton Rating Scale for Depression (HAM-D) (Hamilton, 1960) is a widely used assessment tool and is often regarded as the most standard assessment tool for depression for both diagnosis and research purposes (Cummins et al., 2015a). The HAM-D is clinician-administered, includes 21 questions, and takes 20 to 30 minutes to complete. The interview assesses the severity of symptoms associated with depression and gives a patient a score, which relates to their level of depression. Some symptoms included are depressed mood, insomnia, agitation, and anxiety. Each of the questions has 3 to 5 possible responses which range in severity, scored between 0-2, 2-3, or 4-5 depending on the importance of the symptom. All scores are then summed and the total is arranged into 5 categories (normal-severe).

There also exist commonly used self-report measures, including the the Beck Depression Inventory (BDI-II) (Beck et al., 1961). The BDI-II is a self-report questionnaire that consists of 21 items and takes 5 to 10 minutes to complete. The question items aim to cover important cognitive, affective, and somatic symptoms associated with depression. Each question receives a score on a scale from 0-3 depending on how severe the symptom was over the previous week. Similar to HAM-D, all scores are summed and the final score is categorized into 4 different levels (minimal-severe). Other diagnostic tools include the Montgomery-Åsberg Depression Rating Scale (Montgomery and Asberg, 1979), the Patient Health Questionnaire (Kroenke et al., 2001), and the Quick Inventory of Depressive Symptomology (Rush et al., 2003).

2.2 Scalable Approaches to Annotation

When working with datasets, it is not always feasible to acquire clinical ratings for depression level. As a result, researchers have come up with innovative ways of acquiring depression labels at scale, notably from social media sources. Given the explosion of social media, this domain is especially rich in data for mental health research. However, any research in this domain must take into account the ability of online users to be anonymous or even deceptive.

Coppersmith et al. (2015) looked for tweets that explicitly stated "I was just diagnosed with depression". Moreno et al. (2011) evaluated Facebook status updates using references to depression symptoms such as "I feel hopeless" to ultimately determine depression label. Choudhury et al. (2013) used crowdsourcing, via the Amazon Mechanical Turk platform, to collect Twitter usernames as well as labels for depression. Reece and Danforth (2016) used a similar crowdsourcing approach to collect both depression labels and Instagram photo data. In some approaches to annotation, depression is subsumed into broader categories like distress, anxiety, or crisis. For example, Milne et al. (2016) used judges to manually annotate how urgently a blog post required attention, using a triage system of green/amber/red/crisis.

These innovative approaches to data annotation highlight the potential of social media data. This domain offers a very rich data source which can be used to build, train, and test models to automatically perform mental health assessments at a large scale.

3 Datasets

The task of depression detection is inherently interdisciplinary and all disciplines—psychology, computer science, linguistics—bring an essential set of skills and insight to the problem. However, it is not always the case that a team is fortunate enough to have collaborators from all disciplines. One way to promote collaboration is to

Dataset	Modality	Depression Label Annotation	Reference
AVEC 2013	Video/audio	Self-report survey (BDI-II)	Valstar et al. (2013)
AVEC 2014	Video/audio	Self-report survey (BDI-II)	Valstar et al. (2014)
Crisis Text Line	Text	Crisis counselor judgment	Lieberman and Meyer
DAIC	Video/audio/text	Self-report survey (PHQ-8)	Gratch et al. (2014)
DementiaBank Database	Video/audio/text	Clinical diagnosis of depression (HAM-D)	Becker et al. (1994)
ReachOut Triage Shared Task	Text	Expert judged for crisis/green/amber/red	Milne et al. (2016)
SemEval-2014 Task 7	Text	Hand labeled for depression	Pradhan et al. (2014)

Table 1: Datasets for depression detection systems.

organize challenges and publicly release data and code. Public datasets are invaluable resources that can give new researchers the ability to work on the task while connecting accomplished researchers across disciplines. The Computational Linguistics and Clinical Psychology (CLPsych) Shared Task (2013-2017) and the Audio/Visual Emotion Recognition (AVEC) Workshop Depression Sub-challenge (2013-2016) are examples of depression detection system challenges that spurred interest, promoted research, and built connections across the research community. In this section, we describe the kinds of depression data that exist, listed in Table 1. We focus solely on datasets that are publicly available to download. For a detailed list of databases both private and public that have been used in speech processing studies see (Cummins et al., 2015a).

Both the AVEC 2013 and 2014 corpora are available to download[1]. The AVEC challenges are organized competitions aimed at comparing multimedia processing and machine learning methods for automatic audio, video and audiovisual emotion and depression analysis, with all participants competing under strictly the same conditions. The AVEC 2013 corpus (Valstar et al., 2013) includes 340 video clips in German of subjects performing a HCI task while being recorded by a webcam and a microphone. The video files each contain a range of vocal exercises, including free and read speech tasks. The level of depression is labeled with a single value per recording using the BDI-II. The AVEC 2014 corpus (Valstar et al., 2014) is a subset of the AVEC 2013 corpus. In total, the corpus includes 300 videos in German; the duration ranges from 6 seconds to 4 minutes. The files include a read speech passage (Die Sonne und der Wind) and an answer to a free response question.

The Crisis Text Line [2] is a free 24/7 crisis support texting hot line where live trained crisis counselors receive and respond quickly to texts. The main goal of the organization is to support people with mental health issues through texting. The organization includes an open data collaboration. In order to gain access, researchers must complete an Institutional Review Board application with their own university and an application with Crisis Text Line, which gives researchers access to a vast amount of text data annotated by conversation issue, including but not limited to depression, anger, sadness, body image, homelessness, self-harm, suicidal ideation, and more.

The Distress Analysis Interview Corpus (DAIC) (Gratch et al., 2014) contains clinical interviews in English designed to support the diagnosis of psychological distress conditions such as anxiety, depression, and post-traumatic stress disorder. The interviews were conducted by an animated virtual interviewer called Ellie. The DAIC interviews were meant to simulate the first step in identifying mental illness in health care settings, which is a semi-structured interview where health care providers ask a series of open-ended questions with the intent of identifying clinical symptoms. The corpus includes audio and video recordings and extensive questionnaire responses. Each interview includes a depression score from the PHQ-8 (Kroenke et al., 2009). A portion of the corpus was released during the AVEC 2016 Depression Sub-challenge and is available to download[3]. The publicly-available dataset also includes transcripts of the interview.

The DementiaBank Database[4] represents data collected between 1983 and 1988 as part of the Alzheimer Research Program at the University of Pittsburgh (Becker et al., 1994). DementiaBank is a shared database of multimedia interactions for the study of communication in dementia. A subset of the participants from the dataset also have HAM-D depression scores.

The ReachOut Triage Shared Task dataset[5] consists of 65,024 forum posts written between July 2012 and June 2015 (Milne et al., 2016). A subset

---

[1] https://avec2013-db.sspnet.eu/

[2] www.crisistextline.org

[3] http://dcapswoz.ict.usc.edu/

[4] http://dementia.talkbank.org/

[5] http://clpsych.org/shared-task-2016/

of the corpus (1,227 posts) is manually annotated by three separate expert judges indicating how urgently a post required a moderators attention. Labels included crisis, red, amber, and green.

The SemEval-2014 Task 7 (Pradhan et al., 2014) dataset[6] represents clinical notes which are annotated for disorder mentions, including mental disorders such as depression.

4 Indicators of Depression

Ideally, machine learning tools for depression detection should have access to the same streams of information that a clinician utilizes in the process of forming a diagnosis. Therefore, features used by such classifiers should represent each communicative modality: face and gesture, voice and speech, and language. This section provides a review of each modality highlighting markers that have had success in systems.

4.1 Visual Indicators

Visual indicators have been widely explored for depression analysis, including body movements, gestures, subtle expressions, and periodical muscular movements.

Girard et al. (2014) investigated whether a relationship existed between nonverbal behavior and depression severity. In order to measure nonverbal behavior they used the Facial Action Coding System (FACS) (Ekman et al., 1978). FACS is a system used to taxonomize human facial movements by their appearance on the face. It is a commonly used tool and has become standard to systematically categorize physical expressions, which has proven very useful for psychologists. FACS is composed of facial Action Units (AUs), which represent the fundamental actions of individual muscles or groups of muscles. Girard et al. (2014) found that participants with high levels of depression made fewer affiliative facial expressions, more non-affiliative facial expressions, and diminished head motions. Scherer et al. (2013b) also investigated visual features using FACS and found that depression could be predicted by a more downward angle of the gaze, less intense smiles, shorter average durations of smile, longer self-touches, and fidgeting.

In addition to FACS features for video analysis, others have considered Space-Time Interest Points (STIP) features (Cummins et al., 2013; Joshi et al., 2013), which capture spatio-temporal

changes including movements of the face, hands, shoulder, and head. Using STIP features, Joshi et al. (2013) found that they could detect depression with 76.7% accuracy. Their results showed that body expressions, gestures, and head movements can be significant visual cues for depression detection.

4.2 Speech Indicators

Recent research has shown the promise in using speech as a diagnostic and monitoring aid for depression (Cummins et al., 2015b,a, 2014; Scherer et al., 2014; Williamson et al., 2014a). The speech production system of a human is very complex and as a result slight cognitive or physiological changes can produce acoustic changes in speech. This idea has driven the research on using speech as an objective marker for depression. Depressed speech has consistently been associated with a wide range of prosodic, source, formant and spectral indicators. For a thorough review of speech processing research for depression detection see (Cummins et al., 2015a).

Many researchers have provided evidence for the robustness of prosodic indicators to capture depression level, specifically noting the promise of speech-rate (Mundt et al., 2012; Hönig et al., 2014). Cannizzaro et al. (2004) examined the relationship between depression and speech by performing statistical analyses of different acoustic measures, including speaking rate, percent pause time, and pitch variation. Their results demonstrated that speaking rate and pitch variation had a strong correlation with the depression rating scale. Moore et al. (2008) investigated the suitability for a classification system formed from the combination of prosodic, voice quality, spectral, and glottal features and reported maximum accuracy of 91% for male speakers and 96% accuracy for females speakers when classifying between absence/presence of depression.

Stassen et al. (1998) found for 60% of patients in their study that speech pause duration was significantly correlated with their HAM-D score. Alpert et al. (2001) also found significant differences in speech pause duration between spontaneous speech of their depressed group versus their control group. Cannizzaro et al. (2004) found a significant correlation between reduced speaking rate and HAM-D score. Mundt et al. (2012) found six prosodic timing measures to be significantly correlated with depression severity, includ-

---

[6]http://alt.qcri.org/semeval2014/task7/index.php?id=data-and-tools

ing total speech time, total pause time, percentage pause time, speech pause ratio, and speaking rate. Hönig et al. (2014) reported a positive correlation with increasing levels of speaker depression and average syllable duration. Trevino et al. (2011) found that changes in speech rate are stronger at the phoneme level, finding stronger relationships between speech rate and depression severity when using phone-duration and phone-specific measures instead of a global speech rate. Cohn et al. (2009) investigated vocal prosody and found that variation in fundamental frequency and latency of response to interviewer questions achieved 79% accuracy in distinguishing participants with moderate/severe depression from those with no depression.

Low et al. (2011) investigated various acoustic features, including spectral, cepstral, prosodic, glottal and a Teager energy operator based feature. In their best performing systems, using sex-dependent models, they achieved 87% accuracy for males and 79% for females. In Cummins et al. (2011) spectral features, particularly mel-frequency cepstral coefficients (MFCCs) were found to be useful, distinguishing 23 depressed participants from 24 controls with an accuracy of 80% in a speaker-dependent configuration. Scherer et al. (2013a) found glottal features (normalized amplitude quotient and quasi-open quotient) differed significantly between depressed and control groups. When used to detect depression they found glottal features to differentiate between the 2 groups with 75% accuracy. Alghowinem et al. (2013) investigated a number of feature sets for detecting depression from spontaneous speech and found loudness and intensity features to be the most discriminative.

4.3 Linguistic and Social Indicators

While most literature concerning depression detection systems has focused on the speech signal, there is a related body of work on detecting depression from writing using linguistic cues. For clinical psychologists, language plays a central role in diagnosis. Therefore, when building language technology in the domain of mental health it is essential to consider both the acoustic and linguistic signal. For an in-depth review of NLP applications for mental health assessment see Calvo et al. (2017).

Features derived from the speech signal are motivated by ways in which the cognitive and physical changes associated with depression can lead to differences in speech. Similarly, psychological and sociological theories suggest that depressed language can be characterized by specific linguistic features. Aaron Beck's (1967) cognitive theory of depression posits that people prone to depression possess a depressive schema, leading them to see themselves and the world in pervasively negative terms. When activated, these schema give rise to depressive thinking. A stressful event can then trigger these schema, leading an individual to perceive the event in a negative way and, as a result, cause an episode of depression. Pyszczynski and Greenberg (1987) speculated that depressed individuals think a great deal about themselves, stressing the role of self-focused attention and extreme self-criticism. Also related is the social integration model by Durkheim (1951), which posits that the perception of oneself as not integrated into society (detached from social life) is key to suicidality and is also relevant to the depressed persons' perceptions of self.

These theories have motivated empirical studies of depressed language which have in turn provided support for their validity. Stirman and Pennebaker (2001) provided evidence consistent with both the self-focus and social integration perspectives by studying the word usage of suicidal and non-suicidal poets. They conducted a comparison of 300 poems from the early, middle, and late periods of nine poets who committed suicide and nine who did not. They used the Linguistic Inquiry and Word Count (LIWC) dictionary (Pennebaker et al., 2007), which is a text analysis tool that can be used to count words in psychologically meaningful categories. Using LIWC, they found that suicidal poets used more first-person singular (I, me, my) words, and fewer first-person plural (we, us, our) words. In related work, Poulin et al. (2014) used medical records and a text analysis approach to predict suicide risk with an accuracy of 65%, finding that certain words were predictive of suicide.

Later work by Rude et al. (2004) analyzed narratives written by currently-depressed, formerly-depressed, and never-depressed college students. In the context of an essay task, they examined linguistic patterns using LIWC, including the use of first person singular, first person plural, social references, and negatively/positively valenced words. As hypothesized based on Pyszcynski and Greenberg's model of self-focus, depressed students used significantly more first person singular words than did never-depressed individuals. They also found that depressed students used more negatively valenced words and fewer positive emotion words, supporting both the negative focus predicted by Beck's cognitive theory of depression and the self-preoccupation predicted by Psyzcynski and Greenberg's control theory of depression. Given the success of LIWC in Rude et al.'s work, many other researchers have incorporated LIWC into depression detection systems with encouraging results. Nguyen et al. (2014) found LIWC to be useful in capturing topic and mood which showed good predictive validity in depression classification between clinical and control groups in blog post texts. Morales and Levitan (2016b) incorporated LIWC into a depression detection system and found certain LIWC categories to be useful in measuring specific depression symptoms, including sadness and fatigue.

Various approaches to modeling word usage have had much success in detecting depression. Coppersmith et al. (2015) accurately identified depression with high accuracies using n-gram models in Twitter text. Althoff et al. (2016) presented a large-scale quantitative study on the discourse of counseling conversations. They developed a set of discourse features to measure how correlated linguistic aspects of conversations were with outcomes. Features in their study included: sequence-based conversation models, language model comparisons, message clustering, and psycholinguistics-inspired word frequency analyses. Their results were also consistent with Psyzcynski and Greenberg's theory of depression, in that texters with a smaller amount of self-focus were associated with more successful conversations. In addition, Schwartz et al. (2014) showed that regression models based on Facebook language can be used to predict an individuals degree of depression.

In addition to considering word usage, researchers have also explored syntactic characteristics of depressed language. Zinken et al. (2010) investigated whether an analysis of a depressed patients' syntax could help predict improvement of symptoms. This work built upon previous findings that showed the health benefit of expressive writing (Pennebaker, 1997). Building upon this work, Zinken et al. considered the psychological relevance of syntactic structures of language use. Word use and syntactic structure were analyzed to explore whether the degrees to which a participant constructs relationships between events in a brief text can inform the likelihood of successful participation in depression treatment. They also used LIWC and targeted 2 categories: causation words and insight words. In addition, they manually coded eight different syntactic structures (ranging from simple to complex) in the patients' narratives. They found that certain structures were correlated with patients' potential to complete a self-help treatment. Zinken et al.'s findings demonstrate the promise in investigating syntactic characteristics of an individual's language use. Moreover, related work has found that differences in frequencies of part-of-speech (POS) tags were useful in detecting depression from writing (Morales and Levitan, 2016b).

Resnik et al. (2015) explored the use of supervised topic models in the analysis of detecting depression from Twitter. They use 3 million tweets from about 2,000 twitter users, of whom roughly 600 self-identify as having been diagnosed with depression. This work provided a more sophisticated model for text-based feature development for detecting depression, yielding promising results using supervised Latent Dirichlet Allocation (LDA). LDA uncovers underlying structure in a collection of documents by treating each document as if it were generated as a mixture of different topics. Qualitative examples confirmed that LDA models can uncover meaningful and potentially useful latent structure for the automatic identification of important topics for depression detection.

With the rise of social media, posts on sites such as Twitter and Facebook provide an interesting domain to investigate depression. Not only do these domains provide rich text data but also social metadata which captures important social behaviors and characteristics, like number of friends/followers, number of likes, retweets, etc. De Choudhury et al. (2014) studied Facebook data shared voluntarily by 165 new mothers. Their work aimed to detect and predict onset of postpartum depression (PPD). They considered multiple behavioral features including activity (frequency of status updates, media items, and wall posts), social capital (likes and comments on status updates or media), emotional expression and linguistic style measured through LIWC. They found that experiences of PPD were best predicted by increased isolation, which was modeled by reduced social activity and interaction on Facebook and decreased access to social capital.

Wang et al. (2013) constructed a model to detect depression from online blog posts. The features they extracted included first person singular and plural pronouns, polarity of each sentence using their polarity calculation algorithm, ratio of first person singular pronouns to first person plural pronouns, use of emoticons, user interactions with others (@username mentions), and number of posts. Using 180 users, the features given above, and three different kinds of classifiers Wang et al. (2013) report a a precision of 80% when classifying between depressed versus non-depressed users.

4.4 Multimodal Indicators

Researchers have also investigated multimodal indicators for depression detection. Scherer et al. (2013a), investigated visual signals and voice quality in a multimodal system, finding that they were able to distinguish interviewees with depression from those without depression with an accuracy of 75%.

Morales and Levitan (2016b) provided a comparative investigation of speech versus text-based features for depression detection systems, finding that a multimodal system leads to the best performing system. In addition, Morales and Levitan investigated using an automatic speech recognition system (ASR) to automatically transcribe speech and found that text-based features generated from ASR transcripts were useful for depression detection.

Fraser et al. (2016) extracted a large number of textual features and acoustic features. Textual features included POS tags, parse tree constituents, psycholinguistic measures, measures of complexity, vocabulary richness, and informativeness. Acoustic features include fluency measures, MFCCs, voice quality features, and measures of periodicity and symmetry. Using these multimodal features, Fraser et al. were able to detect depression with 65.8% accuracy. Related work on suicide risk assessment found that multimodal indicators were able to discriminate between suicidal and non-suicidal patients (Venek et al., 2016).

5 Evaluation

Depression detection can be divided into three different prediction tasks: presence (depressed vs. not depressed), severity (normal, mild, moderate, severe, and very severe), and score level prediction. With each task comes a set of evaluation metrics. In regards to the first two groups, performance is usually reported in terms of classification accuracy (Acc.). Given that accuracy is heavily affected by skewness in datasets, often times sensitivity (Sens.), specificity (Spec.), precision (Prec.), and F1-score (harmonic mean of precision and recall) are also reported. For score level prediction, performance is usually reported as a measure of differences between values predicted and the values actually observed, such as Mean Absolute Error (MAE) and Root Mean Square Error (RMSE). In Table 2 we report, to our knowledge, the best performing depression detection systems from 2016.

As Table 2 highlights, it is very difficult to make systematic comparisons across studies. Data, task, label, and experimental set-up tend to vary across study. Therefore, it is hard to understand which approach is most promising. However, in regards to features, it tends to be the case that combining features from multiple modalities leads to improvements (Morales and Levitan, 2016a; Scherer et al., 2013a; Fraser et al., 2016; Williamson et al., 2016; Valstar et al., 2016). In many cases, researchers may only have access to certain labels. However, when data sources do contain score labels reporting both error for regression as well as classification performance metrics will help facilitate comparisons across systems. Given that each feature or subset of features are meant to measure specific depression indicators or symptoms, it is also extremely important to understand how well each feature is performing. Therefore, it is best to always include correlation experiments, such as Pearson correlation tests, in order to make it transparent which features are important.

5.1 Confounding Factors

Specific variability factors have been shown to be strong confounding factors for depression detection systems (Cummins et al., 2015a, 2014, 2013, 2011; Sturim et al., 2011). Variability factors include traits like gender, age, emotion, or personality of the speaker. Therefore, it is important to keep these factors in mind when building a detection system. For example, in many studies systems have achieved better results using sex-dependent classifiers (Moore et al., 2008; Low et al., 2011; Yang et al., 2016; Scherer et al., 2014). Oth-

Reference	Task	Features	MAE	Acc.	Spec.	Sens.	Prec.	F1
Fraser et al. (2016)	Binary	MFCCs/lexical/syntax		0.66	0.61	0.71		
Milne et al. (2016)	4 classes	N-grams		0.78				
Kim et al. (2016)	4 classes	TF-IDF n-gram/post embedding		0.85				
Malmasi et al. (2016)	4 classes	Lexical/syntax/metadata		0.83				
Brew (2016)	4 classes	TF-IDF unigrams/metadata		0.79				
Valstar et al. (2016)	Binary	Visual				0.78	0.47	0.58
		Acoustic				0.89	0.27	0.41
		All				0.78	0.47	0.58
	PHQ-8	Visual	6.12					
		Acoustic	5.72					
		All	5.66					
Williamson et al. (2016)	PHQ-8	Visual	5.33					0.53
		Acoustic	5.32					0.57
		Semantic	3.34					0.84
		All	4.18					0.81
Yang et al. (2016)	PHQ-8	Visual/acoustic	6.70			0.67	0.50	0.57

Table 2: Best performing depression detection systems. F1 score, precision, and sensitivity are reported for the *depressed* class.

ers (Morales and Levitan, 2016a) have used unsupervised clustering prior to depression detection, finding that this approach could tease out participant differences and in turn lead to performance improvements. However, these approaches to dealing with variability factors usually mean a reduction in training data, which at times can be a substantial trade-off.

Another factor to consider, is comorbidity. Comorbidity refers to the simultaneous presence of two chronic diseases or conditions. For example, Alzheimer's disease (AD) and depression frequently co-occur. Fraser et al. (2016) found that their depression detection system performed considerably lower on patients with comorbid depression and AD than on those patients with only depression. Therefore, comorbidity can lead to a more difficult task given the wide overlap of symptoms in the two conditions. Factors such as gender, age, and comorbidity, can have substantial effects on system performance. In order to better understand performance across studies and the effect of variability factors more transparency is necessary, in regards to dataset details and descriptions. In addition, researchers should begin to consider more diverse populations in their studies. Thus far, most research and data collection efforts have focused on detecting depression from young and otherwise healthy participants. In order to generalize detection systems, datasets representing other populations need to be considered.

6 Discussion

As with any technology or tool there is always risk of misuse and therefore it is important to discuss general ethical considerations with pursuing this line of research. It is especially important to define and outline appropriate use of these systems. Mental health professionals should view language technology for depression detection as a mechanism to complement current diagnoses by giving them access to a novel and rich non-intrusive data source. It is understandable that mental health professionals as well as the general population may be uncomfortable with the possibility that technologies might have to predict psychological states, especially when relatively accurate predictions can be made. To be clear, these systems are not proposed as standalone diagnostic tools that could replace current approaches to diagnosing mental health issues, but instead proposed as part of a broader awareness, detection, and support system. These technologies provide numerous advantages, including large-scale and remote assessment, which in turn could help a broader population. These methods could also provide a lower cost complement to traditional depression assessments. In addition, these tools could help health professionals manage current patients more efficiently, allowing clinicians to monitor their patients continuously. Determining how machines should augment and assist in diagnosis is a complicated issue. However, there exists evidence that mechanical prediction (statistical, algorithmic, etc.) is typically as accurate or more accurate than clinical prediction (Grove et al., 2000). Moreover, mechanical predictions do not require an expert judgment and are completely reproducible. Although there are general ethical considerations, it is important to highlight the potential of mental health assessment tools to enhance the quality of life for society.

7 Conclusion

In this paper, we present a review of the latest work on depression detection systems. We provide a cross-modal review of indicators for depression detection systems, covering visual, acoustic, linguistic, and social features. We also outline approaches to defining and annotating depression, existing data sources, and how to evaluate depression detection systems. This paper serves as a bridge between the subfields by providing the first review across subfields and modalities. Given that depression detection is inherently a multimodal problem, this paper is an important contribution to the research community as it serves as a great resource for understanding multimodal features as well as what factors to consider when designing a depression detection system. Lastly, in order for the research community to progress together researchers should begin to follow the best practices (Stodden and Miguez, 2013). Best practices lead to communication standards, which will help disseminate reproducible research, facilitate innovation by enabling data and code re-use, and enable broader communication of the output of computational research. Without the data and code that underlie scientific discoveries, is is all but impossible to verify published findings. We urge researchers to focus on reproducible research, through the dissemination, availability, and accessibility of data and code.

References

Sharifa Alghowinem, Roland Goecke, Michael Wagner, Julien Epps, Tom Gedeon, Michael Breakspear, and Gordon Parker. 2013. A comparative study of different classifiers for detecting depression from spontaneous speech. In *Acoustics, Speech and Signal Processing (ICASSP), 2013 IEEE International Conference on*. IEEE, pages 8022–8026.

Murray Alpert, Enrique R Pouget, and Raul R Silva. 2001. Reflections of depression in acoustic measures of the patients speech. *Journal of Affective Disorders* 66(1):59–69. https://doi.org/10.1016/S0165-0327(00)00335-9.

Tim Althoff, Kevin Clark, and Jure Leskovec. 2016. Large-scale analysis of counseling conversations: An application of natural language processing to mental health. *arXiv preprint arXiv:1605.04462* .

APA. 2013. *Diagnostic and statistical manual of mental disorders (DSM-5®)*. American Psychiatric Pub.

Aaron T Beck. 1967. *Depression: Clinical, experimental, and theoretical aspects*. University of Pennsylvania Press.

Aaron T Beck, C Ward, M Mendelson, et al. 1961. Beck depression inventory (bdi). *Arch Gen Psychiatry* 4(6):561–571.

James T Becker, François Boiler, Oscar L Lopez, Judith Saxton, and Karen L McGonigle. 1994. The natural history of alzheimer's disease: description of study cohort and accuracy of diagnosis. *Archives of Neurology* 51(6):585–594.

Chris Brew. 2016. Classifying reachout posts with a radial basis function svm. *red* 14(23):27.

Rafael A. Calvo, David N. Milne, M. Sazzad Hussain, and Helen Christensen. 2017. Natural language processing in mental health applications using non-clinical texts. *Natural Language Engineering* page 137. https://doi.org/10.1017/S1351324916000383.

Michael Cannizzaro, Brian Harel, Nicole Reilly, Phillip Chappell, and Peter J Snyder. 2004. Voice acoustical measurement of the severity of major depression. *Brain and cognition* 56(1):30–35.

Munmun De Choudhury, Michael Gamon, Scott Counts, and Eric Horvitz. 2013. Predicting depression via social media. In *ICWSM*.

Jeffrey F Cohn, Tomas Simon Kruez, Iain Matthews, Ying Yang, Minh Hoai Nguyen, Margara Tejera Padilla, Feng Zhou, and Fernando De La Torre. 2009. Detecting depression from facial actions and vocal prosody. In *Affective Computing and Intelligent Interaction and Workshops, 2009. ACII 2009. 3rd International Conference on*. IEEE, pages 1–7.

Glen Coppersmith, Mark Dredze, Craig Harman, Kristy Hollingshead, and Margaret Mitchell. 2015. Clpsych 2015 shared task: Depression and ptsd on twitter. In *Proceedings of the 2nd Workshop on Computational Linguistics and Clinical Psychology: From Linguistic Signal to Clinical Reality*. pages 31–39.

Nicholas Cummins, Julien Epps, Michael Breakspear, and Roland Goecke. 2011. An investigation of depressed speech detection: Features and normalization. In *Interspeech*. pages 2997–3000.

Nicholas Cummins, Julien Epps, Vidhyasaharan Sethu, and Jarek Krajewski. 2014. Variability compensation in small data: Oversampled extraction of i-vectors for the classification of depressed speech. In *Acoustics, Speech and Signal Processing (ICASSP), 2014 IEEE International Conference on*. IEEE, pages 970–974.

Nicholas Cummins, Jyoti Joshi, Abhinav Dhall, Vidhyasaharan Sethu, Roland Goecke, and Julien Epps. 2013. Diagnosis of depression by behavioural signals: a multimodal approach. In *3rd ACM international workshop on Audio/visual emotion challenge Proc.*. ACM, pages 11–20.

Nicholas Cummins, Stefan Scherer, Jarek Krajewski, Sebastian Schnieder, Julien Epps, and Thomas F Quatieri. 2015a. A review of depression and suicide risk assessment using speech analysis. *Speech Communication* 71:10–49.

Nicholas Cummins, Vidhyasaharan Sethu, Julien Epps, Sebastian Schnieder, and Jarek Krajewski. 2015b. Analysis of acoustic space variability in speech affected by depression. *Speech Communication* 75:27–49.

Munmun De Choudhury, Scott Counts, Eric J Horvitz, and Aaron Hoff. 2014. Characterizing and predicting postpartum depression from shared facebook data. In *Proceedings of the 17th ACM conference on Computer supported cooperative work & social computing*. ACM, pages 626–638.

Emil Durkheim. 1951. Suicide (g. simpson, trans.).

Paul Ekman, Wallace V Friesen, and Joseph C Hager. 1978. Facial action coding system (facs). *A technique for the measurement of facial action. Consulting, Palo Alto* 22.

Kathleen C Fraser, Frank Rudzicz, and Graeme Hirst. 2016. Detecting late-life depression in alzheimers disease through analysis of speech and language. *Proceedings of the Third Workshop on Computational Lingusitics and Clinical Psychology* .

Jeffrey M Girard, Jeffrey F Cohn, Mohammad H Mahoor, S Mohammad Mavadati, Zakia Hammal, and Dean P Rosenwald. 2014. Nonverbal social withdrawal in depression: Evidence from manual and automatic analyses. *Image and vision computing* 32(10):641–647.

Jonathan Gratch, Ron Artstein, Gale M Lucas, Giota Stratou, Stefan Scherer, Angela Nazarian, Rachel Wood, Jill Boberg, David DeVault, Stacy Marsella, et al. 2014. The distress analysis interview corpus of human and computer interviews. In *LREC*. pages 3123–3128.

William M Grove, David H Zald, Boyd S Lebow, Beth E Snitz, and Chad Nelson. 2000. Clinical versus mechanical prediction: a meta-analysis. *Psychological assessment* 12(1):19.

Max Hamilton. 1960. A rating scale for depression. *Journal of neurology, neurosurgery, and psychiatry* 23(1):56.

Florian Hönig, Anton Batliner, Elmar Nöth, Sebastian Schnieder, and Jarek Krajewski. 2014. Automatic modelling of depressed speech: relevant features and relevance of gender. In *INTERSPEECH*. pages 1248–1252.

Jyoti Joshi, Roland Goecke, Gordon Parker, and Michael Breakspear. 2013. Can body expressions contribute to automatic depression analysis? In *Automatic Face and Gesture Recognition (FG), 2013 10th IEEE International Conference and Workshops on*. IEEE, pages 1–7.

Sunghwan Mac Kim, Yufei Wang, Stephen Wan, and Cécile Paris. 2016. Data61-csiro systems at the clpsych 2016 shared task. In *CLPsych@HLT-NAACL*.

Kurt Kroenke, Robert L Spitzer, and Janet BW Williams. 2001. The phq-9. *Journal of general internal medicine* 16(9):606–613.

Kurt Kroenke, Tara W Strine, Robert L Spitzer, Janet BW Williams, Joyce T Berry, and Ali H Mokdad. 2009. The phq-8 as a measure of current depression in the general population. *Journal of affective disorders* 114(1):163–173.

Henry A. Lieberman and Albert R. Meyer. 2014. Visualizations for mental health topic models. In *Massachusetts Institute of Technology Master's Thesis*.

Lu-Shih Alex Low, Namunu C Maddage, Margaret Lech, Lisa B Sheeber, and Nicholas B Allen. 2011. Detection of clinical depression in adolescents speech during family interactions. *IEEE Transactions on Biomedical Engineering* 58(3):574–586.

Shervin Malmasi, Marcos Zampieri, and Mark Dras. 2016. Predicting post severity in mental health forums. *order* 2:8.

David N Milne, Glen Pink, Ben Hachey, and Rafael A Calvo. 2016. Clpsych 2016 shared task: Triaging content in online peer-support forums. In *Proceedings of the Third Workshop on Computational Lingusitics and Clinical Psychology*. pages 118–127.

Stuart A Montgomery and MARIE Asberg. 1979. A new depression scale designed to be sensitive to change. *The British journal of psychiatry* 134(4):382–389.

Elliot Moore, Mark Clements, John W Peifer, Lydia Weisser, et al. 2008. Critical analysis of the impact of glottal features in the classification of clinical depression in speech. *Biomedical Engineering, IEEE Transactions on* 55(1):96–107.

Michelle Renee Morales and Rivka Levitan. 2016a. Mitigating confounding factors in depression detection using an unsupervised clustering approach. In *Computing and Mental Health Workshop*.

Michelle Renee Morales and Rivka Levitan. 2016b. Speech vs. text: A comparative analysis of features for depression detection systems. In *Spoken Language Technology Workshop (SLT), 2016 IEEE*. IEEE, pages 136–143.

Megan A Moreno, Lauren A Jelenchick, Katie G Egan, Elizabeth Cox, Henry Young, Kerry E Gannon, and Tara Becker. 2011. Feeling bad on facebook: depression disclosures by college students on a social networking site. *Depression and anxiety* 28 6:447–55.

James C. Mundt, Adam P. Vogel, Douglas E. Feltner, and William R. Lenderking. 2012. Vocal Acoustic Biomarkers of Depression Severity and Treatment Response. *Biological Psychiatry* 72(7):580–587. https://doi.org/10.1016/j.biopsych.2012.03.015.

Thin Nguyen, Dinh Phung, Bo Dao, Svetha Venkatesh, and Michael Berk. 2014. Affective and content analysis of online depression communities. *IEEE Transactions on Affective Computing* 5(3):217–226.

James W Pennebaker. 1997. Writing about emotional experiences as a therapeutic process. *Psychological science* 8(3):162–166.

James W Pennebaker, Roger J Booth, and Martha E Francis. 2007. Linguistic inquiry and word count: Liwc [computer software]. *Austin, TX: liwc. net* .

Chris Poulin, Brian Shiner, Paul Thompson, Linas Vepstas, Yinong Young-Xu, Benjamin Goertzel, Bradley Watts, Laura Flashman, and Thomas McAllister. 2014. Predicting the risk of suicide by analyzing the text of clinical notes. *PloS one* 9(1):e85733.

Sameer Pradhan, Noemie Elhadad, Wendy Chapman, Suresh Manandhar, and Guergana Savova. 2014. Semeval-2014 task 7: Analysis of clinical text. In *Proceedings of the 8th International Workshop on Semantic Evaluation (SemEval 2014)*. volume 199, pages 54–62.

Tom Pyszczynski and Jeff Greenberg. 1987. Self-regulatory perseveration and the depressive self-focusing style: a self-awareness theory of reactive depression. *Psychological bulletin* 102(1):122.

Andrew G. Reece and Christopher M. Danforth. 2016. Instagram photos reveal predictive markers of depression. *CoRR* abs/1608.03282.

Philip Resnik, William Armstrong, Leonardo Claudino, Thang Nguyen, Viet-An Nguyen, and Jordan Boyd-Graber. 2015. Beyond lda: exploring supervised topic modeling for depression-related language in twitter. *NAACL HLT 2015* page 99.

Stephanie Rude, Eva-Maria Gortner, and James Pennebaker. 2004. Language use of depressed and depression-vulnerable college students. *Cognition & Emotion* 18(8):1121–1133.

A John Rush, Madhukar H Trivedi, Hicham M Ibrahim, Thomas J Carmody, Bruce Arnow, Daniel N Klein, John C Markowitz, Philip T Ninan, Susan Kornstein, Rachel Manber, et al. 2003. The 16-item quick inventory of depressive symptomatology (qids), clinician rating (qids-c), and self-report (qids-sr): a psychometric evaluation in patients with chronic major depression. *Biological psychiatry* 54(5):573–583.

Stefan Scherer, Giota Stratou, Jonathan Gratch, and Louis-Philippe Morency. 2013a. Investigating voice quality as a speaker-independent indicator of depression and ptsd. In *Interspeech*. pages 847–851.

Stefan Scherer, Giota Stratou, Gale Lucas, Marwa Mahmoud, Jill Boberg, Jonathan Gratch, Louis-Philippe Morency, et al. 2014. Automatic audiovisual behavior descriptors for psychological disorder analysis. *Image and Vision Computing* 32(10):648–658.

Stefan Scherer, Giota Stratou, Marwa Mahmoud, Jill Boberg, Jonathan Gratch, Albert Rizzo, and Louis-Philippe Morency. 2013b. Automatic behavior descriptors for psychological disorder analysis. In *Automatic Face and Gesture Recognition (FG), 2013 10th IEEE International Conference and Workshops on*. IEEE, pages 1–8.

H Andrew Schwartz, Johannes Eichstaedt, Margaret L Kern, Gregory Park, Maarten Sap, David Stillwell, Michal Kosinski, and Lyle Ungar. 2014. Towards assessing changes in degree of depression through facebook. In *Proceedings of the Workshop on Computational Linguistics and Clinical Psychology: From Linguistic Signal to Clinical Reality*. pages 118–125.

H. H Stassen, S Kuny, and D Hell. 1998. The speech analysis approach to determining onset of improvement under antidepressants. *European Neuropsychopharmacology* 8(4):303–310. https://doi.org/10.1016/S0924-977X(97)00090-4.

Shannon Wiltsey Stirman and James W Pennebaker. 2001. Word use in the poetry of suicidal and non-suicidal poets. *Psychosomatic Medicine* 63(4):517–522.

Victoria Stodden and Sheila Miguez. 2013. Best practices for computational science: Software infrastructure and environments for reproducible and extensible research. *SSRN* .

Douglas E Sturim, Pedro A Torres-Carrasquillo, Thomas F Quatieri, Nicolas Malyska, and Alan McCree. 2011. Automatic detection of depression in speech using gaussian mixture modeling with factor analysis. In *Interspeech*. pages 2981–2984.

Andrea Carolina Trevino, Thomas Francis Quatieri, and Nicolas Malyska. 2011. Phonologically-based biomarkers for major depressive disorder. *EURASIP Journal on Advances in Signal Processing* 2011(1):1–18.

Michel Valstar, Jonathan Gratch, Bjorn Schuller, Fabien Ringeval, Dennis Lalanne, Mercedes Torres Torres, Stefan Scherer, Giota Stratou, Roddy Cowie, and Maja Pantic. 2016. Avec 2016: Depression, mood, and emotion recognition workshop and challenge. In *Proceedings of the 6th International Workshop on Audio/Visual Emotion Challenge*. ACM, pages 3–10.

Michel Valstar, Björn Schuller, Kirsty Smith, Timur Almaev, Florian Eyben, Jarek Krajewski, Roddy Cowie, and Maja Pantic. 2014. Avec 2014: 3d dimensional affect and depression recognition challenge. In *4th Audio/Visual Emotion Challenge Proc.*. ACM, pages 3–10.

Michel Valstar, Björn Schuller, Kirsty Smith, Florian Eyben, Bihan Jiang, Sanjay Bilakhia, Sebastian Schnieder, Roddy Cowie, and Maja Pantic. 2013. Avec 2013: the continuous audio/visual emotion and depression recognition challenge. In *3rd ACM international workshop on Audio/visual emotion challenge Proc.*. ACM, pages 3–10.

V. Venek, S. Scherer, L.-P. Morency, A. Rizzo, and J. P. Pestian. 2016. Adolescent suicidal risk assessment in clinician-patient interaction. *IEEE Transactions on Affective Computing* https://doi.org/10.1109/TAFFC.2016.2518665.

Xinyu Wang, Chunhong Zhang, Yang Ji, Li Sun, Leijia Wu, and Zhana Bao. 2013. A depression detection model based on sentiment analysis in micro-blog social network. In *Trends and Applications in Knowledge Discovery and Data Mining*, Springer, pages 201–213.

James R Williamson, Elizabeth Godoy, Miriam Cha, Adrianne Schwarzentruber, Pooya Khorrami, Youngjune Gwon, Hsiang-Tsung Kung, Charlie Dagli, and Thomas F Quatieri. 2016. Detecting depression using vocal, facial and semantic communication cues. In *Proceedings of the 6th International Workshop on Audio/Visual Emotion Challenge*. ACM, pages 11–18.

James R Williamson, Thomas F Quatieri, Brian S Helfer, Gregory Ciccarelli, and Daryush D Mehta. 2014a. Vocal and facial biomarkers of depression based on motor incoordination and timing. In *4th Audio/Visual Emotion Challenge Proc.*. ACM, pages 65–72.

Le Yang, Dongmei Jiang, Lang He, Ercheng Pei, Meshia Cédric Oveneke, and Hichem Sahli. 2016. Decision tree based depression classification from audio video and language information. In *Proceedings of the 6th International Workshop on Audio/Visual Emotion Challenge*. ACM, pages 89–96.

Jörg Zinken, Katarzyna Zinken, J Clare Wilson, Lisa Butler, and Timothy Skinner. 2010. Analysis of syntax and word use to predict successful participation in guided self-help for anxiety and depression. *Psychiatry research* 179(2):181–186.

In your wildest dreams: the language and psychological features of dreams

Kate G. Niederhoffer
Circadia Labs
kate@circadialabs.com

Jonathan Schler
Circadia Labs
schlerj@cs.biu.ac.il

Patrick Crutchley
Qntfy
patrick@qntfy.com

Kate Loveys
Qntfy
kate@qntfy.com

Glen Coppersmith
Qntfy
glen@qntfy.com

Abstract

In this paper, we provide the first quantified exploration of the structure of the language of dreams, their linguistic style and emotional content. We present a collection of digital dream logs as a viable corpus for the growing study of mental health through the lens of language, complementary to the work done examining more traditional social media. This paper is largely exploratory in nature to lay the groundwork for subsequent research in mental health, rather than optimizing a particular text classification task.

1 Introduction

Despite a prominent role in the origin of psychology (Freud, 2013; Jung, 2002), scientific research about the meaning and value of dreams has waned in the 21st century. Cartwright (2008), for one, has argued that dreams lost their prominence in the latter half of the 20th century as psychology attempted to become a more empirical science focused on observable behavior and mental activity and less reliant on memory. In the last decade, the distinctive brain patterns of dreaming have become more identifiable (Siclari et al., 2017) and research has amassed on the impact of dreams on waking life with links to mood (Cartwright, 2013), relationship health (Selterman et al., 2012) and decision-making (Morewedge and Norton, 2009). While scientists debate the purpose of dreams (Barrett, 2007; Cartwright et al., 2006), dreams continue to be a universal and time intensive experience across humanity.

Until recently, dreams remained an offline phenomena, qualitatively separate from other forms of social interaction via social media. Online platforms such as Facebook and Twitter are fertile grounds for research in social science (Wilson et al., 2012; boyd and Ellison, 2007) and more recently, in mental health via computational approaches in text analysis (Pennebaker et al., 2015; De Choudhury et al., 2013; Coppersmith et al., 2014) and network structure (Christakis and Fowler, 2014). However, dreams have remained as private, albeit important conversational currency (Wax, 2004). When dreams are studied, they are gathered from sleep labs, psychotherapeutic and inpatient settings, personal dream journals and occasionally classroom settings where "most recent dreams" and "most vivid dreams" are collected (Domhoff, 2000). The recent development of a social network dedicated to dreams offers scientists unprecedented access to the language of dreams at scale, collected with consistent methodology. Understanding the structure of this large corpus of dreams gives us access to previously unobservable mental activity and enables future research to identify abnormal patterns in themes, emotional tone, and styles associated with mental health diagnoses and therapeutic outcomes.

We begin with a brief overview of the impetus for this work and a discussion of related work in the intersection of dreams and text analysis. We then provide details on the corpus of dreams and discuss our results organized around three research questions. The paper concludes with implications for subsequent research on dreams, both to better understand nuances in the medium, and for mental health purposes.

1.1 Previous research on dream content and text analysis

Dreams are challenging to understand. Dreams are a diverse medium that vary from being perceptual or cognitive, from involving simple settings to complicated narratives, which may be similar or dissimilar to waking life (Siclari et al.,

Proceedings of the Fourth Workshop on Computational Linguistics and Clinical Psychology, pages 13–25,
Vancouver, Canada, August 3, 2017. © 2017 Association for Computational Linguistics

2017). Analyzing them is similarly complex; researchers have put extensive effort into the development of systems to score their global content, specific themes, psychological intensity, and theoretical underpinnings (Schredl, 2010). Different researchers, research goals, collection vehicles and analytic techniques present issues in replication, reliability and the validity of standardized methods for the content analysis of dreams. The Hall-Van de Castle coding system is the most comprehensive protocol for content analysis of dreams, with eight main categories and over 300 sub scales in the dream manual (Hall and Castle, 1966). Categories include: Physical surroundings (e.g. indoor, outdoor), Characters (e.g. persons, animals), Social interactions (e.g. friendly vs. aggressive), Activities (e.g. communication, thinking), Achievement outcomes (e.g. success, failure), Environmental press (e.g. fortune, misfortune), Emotions (e.g. anger, happiness), Descriptive elements (e.g. size, age, color), and Theoretical scales (e.g. castration anxiety, regression).

A handful of studies have used automated text analysis to explore dreams, specifically to discern differences from waking narratives and identify the relationship between dream language and personality (Hawkins and Boyd, in press), for automated sentiment detection (Nadeau et al., 2006) and to distinguish linguistic features from personal narratives (Hendrickx et al., 2016). To our knowledge, no study has examined as large a sample of dreams from a naturalistic setting (neurotypical research participants, online social context) across methodologies for psychological purposes (i.e. non classification/ non hypothesis driven).

Hawkins and Boyd (in press) analyze dreams across three samples of recent dream reports, two undergraduate and one sample from Amazon's Mechanical Turk[1]. Using Linguistic Inquiry and Word Count (Pennebaker et al., 2007), they find a distinctive pattern for recent dreams that differs from the base rate norms for waking narratives, specifically characterized by more function words, common words, pronouns, personal pronouns, first person pronouns, past tense verbs, and more use of words describing leisure activities; less use of present tense and future tense verbs, causation words, second person pronouns, numbers, swear words, and assent words. They did not find consistent relationships between dream language features and personality. Hawkins & Boyd's research paves the way for understanding how and why a dream narrative differs from a waking narrative and what these differences mean from a psychological perspective. For example, what does it mean for a dream to have more function words than a waking narrative? What is the relationship between the content of dreams and the more "invisible" word differences (pronouns, prepositions, articles)?

Nadeau et al. (2006) also used LIWC on dreams to gauge the efficacy of automated sentiment analysis to bypass human judges or dreamer estimates of emotion. Comparing the performance of LIWC, the General Inquirer, a weighted lexicon (HM) and standard bag of words approach, they find machine learning outperforms human judgments - and specifically demonstrate that LIWC and the GI have the best features for sentiment classification. While a step in a promising direction, Nadeau et al.'s sample was small (100 dreams from 29 individuals) and sentiment was classified on a limited negative scale (4-class, from neutral to highly negative) omitting nuance in the purported emotional content of dreams, c.f. Cartwright (2013).

Hendrickx et al. (2016) looked at the distinguishing features from dreams as compared to personal narratives (diary entries from Reddit and personal stories from Prosebox) via text classification, topic modeling and text coherence. The authors find dreams can be classified with near perfect precision based on the presence of uncertainty markers (somebody, remember, somewhere, recall) and descriptions of scenes (setting, riding, building, swimming, table, room), with lower discourse coherence. Personal narrative markers (non-dream) include time (2014, today, tonight, yesterday, day, months) and conversational expressions (please, :), ?, thanks). Hendrickx et al. also applied LDA topic modeling to explore the main themes in dreams as compared to personal narratives validating the classification results. Dream topics span everyday activities, setting descriptions, and uncertainty expressions. The Hendrickx et al. research is notable in its exploration of male vs. female topic distributions within dreams in addition to comparisons across corpus type (dream vs. personal narrative) though does not explore the relationship between topic

---

[1]Mechanical Turk users do short human intelligence tasks for small payments. For more see http://www.mturk.com.

and emotion and excludes the analysis of function words, which we believe is a critical piece in understanding the psychological value of dreams and dreamers, given previous findings (Chung and Pennebaker, 2007).

1.2 Relevant research on mental health and text analysis

Computational text analysis allows for assessment of larger samples and proactive identification of mental illness. Language in social media can indicate the likelihood a user self-reports a particular mental disorder (Coppersmith et al., 2015), or has received a mental health diagnosis (De Choudhury et al., 2013). The language of online dreams has yet to be analyzed relative to mental health conditions, however prior laboratory research suggests that dream content may differ between clinical conditions. We refer the reader to Skancke et al.'s comprehensive review of dream content grouped by clinical disorder (Skancke et al., 2014). In brief, patterns in emotional tone, themes, and actor focus have been associated with diagnoses of mood and anxiety disorders, schizophrenia, personality, and eating disorders. Though, it remains unclear whether dream content can distinguish between clinical disorders.

Nightmares are especially relevant to mental health, featuring as a diagnostic symptom for post-traumatic stress disorder (Campbell and Germain, 2016), and a common correlate with schizophrenia (Okorome Mume, 2009), depression and anxiety (Swart et al., 2013), and personality disorders (Schredl et al., 2012). Nightmare frequency and intensity have been positively correlated with incidence of suicidal thoughts and behaviors (Bernert et al., 2005), suggesting nightmares could be a near-term risk factor to assess during crisis. In sum, analysis of dream topics and emotional tone may provide some insight to the mental health of the dreamer.

2 Data

Dreams were collected from DreamsCloud, a social network for sharing dreams. DreamsCloud is available to the public; those who register for the site are informed that their data can be used for research purposes. DreamsCloud is moderated by professional dream reflectors who comment on dreams, in addition to the broader community of registered users who can also "like" and comment on dreams.

DreamsCloud has the largest available digital collection of dreams with over 119k dreams from 73k users and an overall community of over 300k registered users. Visitors to the site come from 234 countries (according to Google Analytics) and have shared dreams in 8 languages. DreamsCloud differs from online dream banks in that dreams are voluntarily shared for social purposes rather than collections from research studies.

A random sample of 10k English dreams over 100 words from September 1, 2013 through December 31, 2016 was used in this study. Data cleansing removed 322 dreams due to incorrectly classified language (Spanish), lyrics or news content copied from the Internet by the user, and duplicated data. The remaining sample included 9,678 dreams. No additional data about the gender, age, name, or ethnicity of the participants are included in our study. Only the original dream texts are analyzed. While DreamsCloud has comments and conversations around many of these dreams, we put off analysis of commentary for subsequent research and focus directly on the first-person accounts of dreams. The average length of dreams in the sample is 208 words (SD = 116.7). Data is organized by an encrypted alphanumeric Dreamer ID and a unique, encrypted alphanumeric Dream ID for each dream logged.

2.1 Ethical considerations

While community members agree to Terms of Service that explicitly state their content is owned by the company and will be used for research purposes, the nature of the content is very intimate. Because of the unknowns about the science behind why we dream, what our dreams mean, how dreams are related to life events, there is less of a stigma about sharing otherwise private or bizarre information. The site refers to dream-sharing as an "anonymous-as-you-want" activity. Although the analyses in this paper are structural and aggregate in nature, deeper analysis of this data could raise privacy concerns as well as questions about appropriate intervention. Our hope is that additional research in this area will shed light on the relationship between dreaming and waking life to help address these questions.

3 Results

Three approaches are used to examine the dream narratives: content analysis using an LDA topic model (Blei et al., 2003), analysis of linguistic style via function words using LIWC (Pennebaker et al., 2015), and categorization of emotions using an emotion classification model (Coppersmith et al., 2016).

3.1 The topical structure of dreams

Topic models are statistical models which discover topics in a corpus. Topic modeling is especially useful in large data, where it is too cumbersome to extract the topics manually. Due to the large volume of dreams in our corpus and the lack of prior knowledge about their subjects, we follow other content-based studies in employing topic modeling to understand the content of the dreams (Kireyev et al., 2009; Yin et al., 2011; Chae et al., 2012; Mitchell et al., 2015; Hendrickx et al., 2016). We analyzed the topical structure of the dream corpus using a popular topic modeling algorithm, latent Dirichlet allocation (LDA) (Blei et al., 2003). LDA is an algorithm for the automated discovery of topics. LDA treats documents as a mixture of topics, and topics as a mixture of words. Each topic discovered by LDA is represented by a probability distribution which conveys the affinity for a given word to that particular topic.

We used the LDA implementation available in the Mallet package (McCallum, 2002). We converted the text to lower case and, because the topic analysis is focused on content of dream narratives, excluded all function words and punctuation marks. (Function and style will be considered in the following section.) No reduction in inflection (i.e. stemming, lemmatization) was performed to satisfy the goals of exploring the nuance of dream narratives as a medium and subsequently make inferences about the psychological orientation of the authors (see section 3.2). Further, in order to make more valid comparisons to the existing literature based on human coding, it is important to understand how distributions of singular vs. plural nouns and present vs. past tense verbs, for example are distributed topically. We selected 25 topics for LDA to infer and used 2000 iterations of Gibbs sampling to fit the model. The number of topics was informed by maximizing the computed information gain of the resulting feature sets, while maintaining a reasonable training time.

LDA provides insightful information about the topics in the corpus. However, interpreting the 'aboutness' of a topic based on a list of words requires human judgment based on term frequency, exclusivity, meaning, and subjective inference. Interestingly, we found 23 of 25 topics to be interpretable based on semantic meaning and 2 (Topics 17 and 22) which appeared more syntactically related. Most heavily weighted topic words are quoted in results tables, and the full 25-topic distribution with manual labeling is included in Appendix A. Note that the topic number is randomly assigned by LDA and does not indicate anything meaningful like rank, weight, or importance.

Although we utilize a 25-topic solution as compared to Hendrickx et al.'s 50-topic solution, we see some consistency in the topics identified as characteristic of dream narratives. Specifically, we see similar support for the continuity hypothesis of dreams - that dreams are a continuation of waking life activities - in topics such as Topic 19 about School, Topic 12 about food and eating, and Topic 15 about driving and cars. Similar to their research, we also see clustering of present tense verbs in Topic 0, a water topic (11), and home settings topic (5). We see an almost exact replication of their "dreaming in general," in our Topic 18. Comprehensive comparisons in distributions or characteristic words are not possible with the data their published research makes available.

In inspecting the topical distribution and noting the support for the continuity hypothesis, what also stands out is the lack of support for the 'dreams-as-psychotic-state' hypothesis. Beginning with Freud and Jung, researchers have drawn similarities between dreaming and psychosis. These similarities range from phenomenological to neurobiological, qualitatively manifested as a loosening of associations, incongruity and bizarreness of personal experience, and distortion of time and space parameters (Scarone et al., 2008). Reviewing the content of our 25-topic solution, we see no reason to interpret the clustering of words within any given topic as incongruous nor do we detect support for the content to be evaluated as "bizarre" (Hobson et al., 1987). The topics instead appear closely aligned with reality, reflective or overt (actions) and covert (thoughts) behaviors and demonstrate semantic congruity within topic. However, an automated approach to coding as subjective a construct as bizarreness demands inspection beyond content words alone.

LDA is an effective means to understand the distribution of content words in a given corpus. Importantly, it was developed for the purpose of dimensionality reduction - document summarization and information retrieval (Blei et al., 2003). Some of the assumptions that enable the algorithms behind topic models, such as the exclusion of words that have no content relevance (e.g. function words), leave room for additional methods to explore the psychological meaning of a given document, the author's mindset, and emotions.

3.2 The linguistic style of dreams

Recent research on language from a psychological perspective demonstrates that function word use reflects and is a reliable marker of personality and a range of social and psychological processes, cognitive thinking styles and psychological states (Pennebaker, 2011). Pennebaker proposes that function words are the infrastructure for thought and perspective: they connect (e.g. conjunctions, auxiliary verbs), shape (e.g. pronouns) and organize (e.g. articles, prepositions) content. Content is important in dreams, and often metaphorical (Lakoff, 1993). The style in which we remember and share our dreams can give important clues to how we make sense of our dreams, and in turn, ourselves. Said another way, our goals in this paper are not just to explore the stuff that dreams are made of but the style of dreams as a reflection of the dreamers' psychological states. With multiple lenses on the data, we can obtain an enhanced picture of the psychological value of the corpus.

LIWC categorizes the words in a given text into approximately 80 variables. Variables represent the proportion of words in a given document (i.e. dream) that correspond to a lexicon composed of different categories of words, including function words (pronouns, prepositions), affect words (positive emotion, anxiety), and content words (money, religion, leisure activities). We reduced the window of interest in LIWC categories to function words, affect, and cognitive processes, as justified by what remains from the LDA analysis (e.g. functions words) and comparisons to results from the empirical literature described thus far (Hawkins and Boyd, in press; Nadeau et al., 2006). Table 1 shows the means and SDs for all LIWC categories within the Linguistic Processes dictionaries with Cognitive, Social and Affective Processes added. Unweighted means from the aggregated sample of expressive writing in Pennebaker et al. (2015) are provided for context.

As compared to the base rates from expressive writing (Pennebaker et al., 2015), a dream narrative comes across as a first person (1st person pronouns) account of a past event (past tense) with particular attention to people (family, friends, women, and men), objects (articles), locations (prepositions) and what is seen, heard, and felt (perceptual processes) more than known or understood (cognitive processes).

Low cognitive processes (M = 9.29; SD = 3.48) would suggest dreamers are not on a search for meaning in sharing their dreams, however it is unclear if this is a case of displaced cognitive processing due to the more dominant perceptual experience of dreams. Previous research indicates that narrative coherence has an inverse relationship with cognitive processing words (Klein and Boals, 2010; Boals et al., 2011). Boals et al. (2011) show that cognitive process words are related to sense making as a process which occurs prior to the development of a narrative (sense making as an outcome). This might suggest that dreamers do not tend to be caught up in why they had a given dream as much as explaining what happened. In other words, dreams are shared as complete stories. A dream narrative's low proportion of emotion words (Mean Affect = 3.42, SD= 1.90) are unexpected given recent research on the emotion regulatory function of dreams and call for additional investigation, which we address below. One possibility is the sensitivity of a lexicon-based instrument to the way in which emotions are expressed in dream narratives. In general, our findings are consistent with Hawkins and Boyd (in press), despite differences in the collection vehicle (recall: Hawkins and Boyd use the 'most recent dream' and 'most vivid dream' paradigm) and previous version of LIWC (2007 vs. 2015).

3.3 How is language style related to the content of dreams?

To explore the relationship between dream topic and language style, we focus on function words only: pronouns, prepositions, articles, auxiliary verbs, and negations. In particular, we use an index composed of the proportions of these classes of words called the Categorical Dynamic Index (CDI; Pennebaker et al. 2014) that measures the

	Dreams (n=9,678)		Expressive Writing (n=6,179)	
	Mean	SD	Mean	SD
Word Count	208.85	116.61	408.94	248.23
Words per sentence	30.34	40.49	18.42	14.89
Words < 6 letters	11.66	3.41	13.62	4.12
Dictionary words	91.87	4.06	91.93	5.03
Total Function Words	60.04	4.32	58.27	6.26
Total Pronouns	19.72	4.31	18.03	5.36
Personal Pronoun	14.87	4.17	12.74	4.28
1st person sing.	9.54	3.36	8.66	4.25
1st person plur.	1.24	1.54	0.81	1.22
2nd person	0.27	0.65	0.68	2.14
3rd person sing.	3.06	2.71	2.01	2.95
3rd person plur.	0.77	1.05	0.57	0.82
Impersonal Pronoun	4.82	2.13	5.28	2.36
Articles	6.99	2.62	5.7	2.56
Prepositions	13.99	2.67	14.27	2.82
Auxiliary verbs	8.08	2.38	9.25	3.06
Adverbs	5.03	2	6.02	2.3
Conjunctions	8.52	2.62	7.46	2.06
Negations	1.4	1	1.69	1.25
Cognitive Processes	9.29	3.48	12.52	5.11
Social Processes	11.18	5.07	8.69	5.46
Affective Processes	3.42	1.9	4.77	2.59
Positive emotion	1.64	1.4	2.57	1.63
Negative emotion	1.75	1.37	2.12	1.74

Table 1: Linguistic Processes Categories in LIWC2015

extent to which thinking is Categorical (high prepositions, articles) versus Dynamic (pronouns, auxiliary verbs).

The CDI is a simple unit-weighted computation which adds the proportions of articles and prepositions and subtracts personal pronouns, impersonal pronouns, auxiliary verbs, conjunctions, adverbs and negations. It has been shown to be a reliable marker of cognitive style which we use to understand differences in the experience of various topics in dreams. Being categorical versus dynamic are different ways of sense-making. One of the goals of our research is to understand how people use "the dream" as a medium on the path to self insight and social connection. In the most basic sense, do people share dreams about certain topics as a narrative personal experiences indicating changes over time? Do certain topics lend themselves to a more distant style- stories of what hap-

pened to whom with precise descriptions of events and goals?

The top five Categorical dream topics and top five Dynamic topics are depicted in Table 2. Topics that are the most categorical are primarily marked by physical environments: trees, sky, house, beach, road. Dynamic dream narratives are characterized by intimate relationships (baby, mom, boyfriend, sister) and experiences (remember, time). The CDI acts a shortcut to identify those dreams that are experienced as a narrative, potentially offering cues to the role of the dreamer as the main character, a distinguishing factor in dreams of healthy controls as compared to psychiatric patient samples (Skancke et al., 2014). Additionally, this shortcut points to a style of dream that would be difficult to discern with a topical lens only; that is, interpersonal situations with multiple characters and complex relationships. Interestingly, Cartwright et al. (1984) find that complex dreams containing multiple characters and shifts of scenes were one marker of depression remission in their five month longitudinal REM tracking study. Appendix B includes two samples of dreams with high and low CDI scores.

	LDA Topic	Words Characterizing Topic	Correlation with CDI (Pearson's r)
Categorical	13	walking tree trees small forest	0.25
	8	see sky plave flying building	0.21
	5	room door house floor stairs	0.2
	11	water pool beach boat swimming	0.17
	15	car driving road bus drive truck	0.11
Dynamic	21	baby hospital boy pregnant girl	-0.12
	4	mom dad house brother sister	-0.13
	18	remember know time think	-0.16
	17	guy phone told boyfriend	-0.22
	9	friend guy boyfriend friends	-0.34

Table 2: Top and Bottom Five dream Topics on CDI continuum

One of the goals of this paper is to investigate how emotions are revealed in dreams, which emotions, and how they vary with the topics that emerge. One prominent hypothesis in dream research posits that the function of dreams is to help regulate negative emotion by "intervening" between waking emotional concerns and post sleep mood (Cartwright, 2008). Much of the literature points to a central role for emotions in dreams, yet there are inconsistencies in the frequencies of the emotional array detected and their valance. The inconsistencies are dependent on a similar variety of reasons to those cited above which make standardized dream content analysis challenging, with the added challenge that make emotions difficult to detect and discern in the broader computer science literature (Sikka et al., 2014; Schredl and Doll, 1998). For example, Merritt et al. (1994) tested a small student population (n=20) and found that there are an average of 3.6 emotions per dream with 95% of dreams having at least one emotion, with fear being the most pervasive. This is directionally consistent with Hall and Castle (1966) who find negative emotions to be more prominent, however the frequencies vary. Sikka et al. (2014) find consistent differences in the external judgments of emotions in dreams as compared to self ratings. The predicted labels of each dream narrative should not be taken as a definitive representation of the overall emotion of that narrative (a difficult task for even human annotators to accomplish consistently; see Purver and Battersby 2012). Instead, these results should be viewed as an additional feature of each narrative, able to be evaluated automatically and quickly to gain insight and explore broader trends.

In our exploration of language style with a lexicon-based approach, LIWC detected a low proportion of affect (Mean Affect = 3.42, SD= 1.90). To assess the emotional content of dreams in an unsupervised manner (i.e., without annotating each narrative manually), we turn to a model for classifying emotional content from text. (We briefly summarize here, but for complete details, see Coppersmith et al. 2016.) A series of character language models (one for each of anger, fear, joy, sadness, surprise, and no emotion) are trained on a large corpus of Twitter data with an included emotional hashtag, e.g., "#anger". Tweets containing indications of sarcasm were removed. Tweets were labeled by the emotional hashtag contained, and then that hashtag was removed for training the model, thus learning what words might contribute to something being tagged "#anger". A two-step semi-supervised process is used to produce the no-emotion model, since most tweets with emotional content are not labeled with #[emotion]. (We also scored each narrative using the Mohammad and Turney 2013 NRC Emotional Lexicon and opted for the character language models for greater vocabulary coverage and possible explicit "no emotion" label.)

We apply each of the emotion character language models (CLM) to each of the dream narratives, producing a probability that each narrative's content results from each emotion's CLM. We then label that narrative with the maximum-probability emotion. Concretely, we expect dreams to have a mixture of emotions, and this technique is likely to surface the dominant emotion in the dream (as measured by the number of words used that indicate that emotion). Percent breakdown of predicted emotion labels were as follows: *sadness*, 31.6%; *fear*, 21.0%; *surprise*, 19.9%; *joy*, 18.7%; *anger*, 8.7%; *no emotion*, 0.0%. Only two narratives out of almost 10,000 were labeled *no-emotion*, and only 6 had the *no-emotion* label above 10% of the estimated emotional content within a dream; see caveats of this approach below.

To continue to deepen our understanding of the psychological value of the corpus and gain insight on the relationship between dream content and emotion, we correlate each emotion's CLM probability with each of the 25 LDA topics. Table 3 shows the most positively-correlated topic and most negatively-correlated topic for each emotion. Consistent with previous research (Merritt et al., 1994; Hall and Castle, 1966), we demonstrate emotions present in all dreams, with more negative than positive emotion: 61.3% negative emotions (sadness, fear, anger), and sadness as the dominant emotion. Drawbacks of this approach of relying on self-stated emotional content tags are outlined in Coppersmith et al. (2016). In short, even given the two-step semi-supervised method of obtaining the most emotionally neutral tweets possible to use as *no-emotion* exemplars, it is likely that some nontrivial percentage of the tweets contain significant emotional content. In addition, even in a single tweet, emotional content is often mixed, and the training method employed allows for only one label that may not be sufficiently descriptive. Perhaps the largest caveat of these results comes from the mismatch between the Twitter data the model was trained on and the dream data it is applied to here. The featurization and parameters of the model are optimized for Twitter messages that are constrained to 140 characters, while the dream narratives are 1,047 characters on average (SD 716). Content varies as well; the dream narratives, at least in theory, have a consistent purpose and theme: recounting the content of a dream. Content of tweets is incredibly varied, from a segment of a story, meant to be read in the context of additional tweets; to a single hyperlink, perhaps with a few words of commentary; to a single emoji repeated 140 times. Future research directions include training a semi-supervised emotion classifier that includes the dream narratives to generalize better across domains.

	Topic number	Correlation with topic (Spearman ρ)	Words characterizing topic
Anger	16	0.187	people kill man trying guy gun shot killed
	9	-0.08	friend guy boyfriend friends love girl
Fear	18	0.17	remember know time think felt life feeling
	19	-0.139	school class teacher high game friend friends
Joy	0	0.151	see says look know comes walk run looks
	9	-0.13	friend guy boyfriend friends love girl
Sadness	9	0.237	friend guy boyfriend friends love girl
	0	-0.101	see says look know comes walk run looks

Table 3: Most positively and negatively-correlated topics for each emotion

4 Conclusion

Our paper presents three types of analyses on an innovative corpus. First we explored the content of dreams with LDA topic modeling. The results demonstrate topics easily interpreted by a human including everyday activity, dreaming itself, and themes common in the dream literature (teeth, animals, flying). These results are consistent with the limited amount of existing research in this area. Our second lens on the data using LIWC portrays dreams, in general, as first person accounts of past events with disproportionate social references and abstract descriptions of settings. Dreams tend to focus on perceptual processes more than cognitive processes. However, there are qualitative distinctions in the content of dreams such that certain topics are experienced as dynamic and others, more categorical. Lastly, we further explored the emotional content in dreams with an unsupervised approach. Our results indicate that emotion is present in dreams and is disproportionately negative, with the most common emotion being sadness. With a sensitive tool, emotion can help disambiguate content in dreams that would otherwise be lumped together, for example dreams about friends, romance, and love which show a complex configuration of emotion.

One major question that underlies this paper is whether we are investigating how we dream or how we story and share our dreams. In future research, we hope to compare dream data to other corpora to better understand how this way of knowing a person, through their dreams, is related to other forms of self expression. Identifying a reasonable comparative dataset for dreams collected from a social network is challenging. This data set is unique in its length (e.g. 140 character Tweets vs. 210 word dreams), content (intimate and quotidian content), and purpose (these dreams are shared for social connection and interaction) making most social media, which would otherwise present the appropriate scale and date range, a poor fit.

Interpreting topics in dreams is extra challenging because there is no ground truth. Language style and emotional classification enhance our understanding of topics and the mindset of a given dreamer, but it is as of yet unclear whether there are individual differences in the way dreams are experienced, or whether dreams are 'victims' of our memories and are yet another corpus to explore the same individual differences we might see in conscious thought. Continued research on dreams over time, dreamers across media and a variety of facets within dream data as compared to different outcome measures (personality, etc.)

will help address this concern.

Another limitation in our research is lack of information about potential skew in the data. For example, there may be biases in who shares dreams and why; who knows about and has access to the social network. We also did not have access to ground truth of user mental health information, so we did not analyze dream content relative to clinical disorders. At this time, site behavior is unreliable at the level of dream reporting to tell us whether there is any systematic bias in who provides dreams. Future studies will certainly explore demographic variables including age, sex, race, socioeconomic status, education level, in addition to variables related to belief in dreams, dream frequency and other psychological attributes which would make people more or less likely to share their dreams. Additionally, future research could investigate associations between mental disorder diagnoses and the content of dreams. This is a preliminary investigation into a vast data set with many additional variables to explore.

Much like this field has used social media data as a lens to study the conscious waking perceptions, emotions, and thought processes of individuals with mental health conditions, we see this as a complementary set of quantifiable signals related to the person's unconscious processes. While more traditional social media data is a convolution of the person's internal state and the world they inhabit, we see this dream data as a convolution of their dreaming self, as recalled and recorded by their waking self. Considered in context of the Fluid Vulnerability Theory, dream content could serve as one of many dynamic, near-term risk factors for detecting transitions into psychological crisis (Rudd, 2006). Given the richness of social media data for uncovering unknown signals related to mental health, we strongly suspect this data may hold similar and complementary power.

In sum, our paper offers preliminary evidence that the language of dreams can be an insightful contribution to human-centric big data, as a means for an enhanced understanding of human behavior and cognition alongside standard psychological means and modern neuroimaging. Paired with large scale analysis of social media language, Internet behavior, and wearable sensor information that predict mental health, the language of dreams could serve as an additional data source from which to evaluate mental health by digital life traces.

References

Deirdre Barrett. 2007. An evolutionary theory of dreams and problem-solving. In *The New Science of Dreaming: Content, Recall, and Personality Correlates*, Praeger Publishers, volume 2, pages 133–154.

Rebecca A. Bernert, Thomas E. Joiner, Kelly C. Cukrowicz, Norman B. Schmidt, and Barry Krakow. 2005. Suicidality and sleep disturbances. *Sleep* 28(9):1135–1141.

David M. Blei, Andrew Y. Ng, and Michael I. Jordan. 2003. Latent Dirichlet allocation. *Journal of Machine Learning Research* 3:993–1022.

Adriel Boals, Jonathan B. Banks, Lisa M. Hathaway, and Darnell Schuettler. 2011. Coping with Stressful Events: Use of Cognitive Words in Stressful Narratives and the Meaning-Making Process. *Journal of Social and Clinical Psychology* 30(4):378–403. https://doi.org/10.1521/jscp.2011.30.4.378.

danah m. boyd and Nicole B. Ellison. 2007. Social network sites: Definition, history, and scholarship. *Journal of Computer-Mediated Communication* 13(1):210–230. https://doi.org/10.1111/j.1083-6101.2007.00393.x.

Rebecca L. Campbell and Anne Germain. 2016. Nightmares and Posttraumatic Stress Disorder (PTSD). *Current Sleep Medicine Reports* 2(2):74–80. https://doi.org/10.1007/s40675-016-0037-0.

R. Cartwright. 2013. History of the Study of Dreams. In Clete A. Kushida, editor, *Encyclopedia of Sleep*, Academic Press, Waltham, pages 124–128. DOI: 10.1016/B978-0-12-378610-4.00028-0.

Rosalind Cartwright. 2008. The Contribution of the Psychology of Sleep and Dreaming to Understanding Sleep-Disordered Patients. *Sleep Medicine Clinics* 3(2):157–166. https://doi.org/10.1016/j.jsmc.2008.01.002.

Rosalind Cartwright, Mehmet Y. Agargun, Jennifer Kirkby, and Julie Kabat Friedman. 2006. Relation of dreams to waking concerns. *Psychiatry Research* 141(3):261–270. https://doi.org/10.1016/j.psychres.2005.05.013.

Rosalind D Cartwright, Stephen Lloyd, Sara Knight, and Irene Trenholme. 1984. Broken dreams: A study of the effects of divorce and depression on dream content. *Psychiatry* 47(3):251–259.

J. Chae, D. Thom, H. Bosch, Y. Jang, R. Maciejewski, D. S. Ebert, and T. Ertl. 2012. Spatiotemporal social media analytics for abnormal event detection and examination using seasonal-trend decomposition. In *2012 IEEE Conference on Visual Analytics Science and Technology (VAST)*. pages 143–152. https://doi.org/10.1109/VAST.2012.6400557.

Nicholas A. Christakis and James H. Fowler. 2014. Friendship and natural selection. *Proceedings of the National Academy of Sciences* 111(Supplement 3):10796–10801. https://doi.org/10.1073/pnas.1400825111.

Cindy Chung and James Pennebaker. 2007. The psychological functions of function words. *Social Communication* .

Glen Coppersmith, Mark Dredze, and Craig Harman. 2014. Quantifying mental health signals in Twitter. In *Proceedings of the ACL Workshop on Computational Linguistics and Clinical Psychology.*

Glen Coppersmith, Mark Dredze, Craig Harman, and Kristy Hollingshead. 2015. From ADHD to SAD: Analyzing the language of mental health on Twitter through self-reported diagnoses. In *Proceedings of the Workshop on Computational Linguistics and Clinical Psychology: From Linguistic Signal to Clinical Reality*. North American Chapter of the Association for Computational Linguistics, Denver, Colorado, USA.

Glen Coppersmith, Kim Ngo, Ryan Leary, and Tony Wood. 2016. Exploratory data analysis of social media prior to a suicide attempt. In *Proceedings of the Workshop on Computational Linguistics and Clinical Psychology: From Linguistic Signal to Clinical Reality*. North American Chapter of the Association for Computational Linguistics, San Diego, California, USA.

Munmun De Choudhury, Scott Counts, and Eric Horvitz. 2013. Social media as a measurement tool of depression in populations. In *Proceedings of the 5th ACM International Conference on Web Science.*

G. William Domhoff. 2000. Methods and measures for the study of dream content. In Meir H. Kryger, Thomas Roth, and William C. Dement, editors, *Principles and Practice of Sleep Medicine*, W. B. Saunders, Philadelphia.

Sigmund Freud. 2013. *The Interpretation Of Dreams*. Read Books Ltd. Google-Books-ID: U0t8CgAAQBAJ.

Calvin Springer Hall and Robert L. Van de Castle. 1966. *The content analysis of dreams*. Appleton-Century-Crofts.

R. C. II Hawkins and Ryan L. Boyd. in press. Such stuff as dreams are made on: Dream language, {LIWC} norms, and personality correlates. *Dreaming* .

Iris Hendrickx, Louis Onrust, Florian Kunneman, Ali Hürriyetoğlu, Antal van den Bosch, and Wessel Stoop. 2016. Unraveling reported dreams with text analytics. *arXiv:1612.03659 [cs]* ArXiv: 1612.03659. http://arxiv.org/abs/1612.03659.

J Allan Hobson, Steven A Hoffman, Rita Helfand, and Delia Kostner. 1987. Dream bizarreness and the activation-synthesis hypothesis. *Human neurobiology* .

Carl Gustav Jung. 2002. *Dreams*. Routledge. Google-Books-ID: SWvdQyo_ZX0C.

Kirill Kireyev, Leysia Palen, and Kenneth M. Anderson. 2009. Applications of topics models to analysis of disaster-related twitter data. In *NIPS Workshop on Applications for Topic Models: Text and Beyond*. volume 1.

Kitty Klein and Adriel Boals. 2010. Coherence and Narrative Structure in Personal Accounts of Stressful Experiences. *Journal of Social and Clinical Psychology* 29(3):256–280. https://doi.org/10.1521/jscp.2010.29.3.256.

George Lakoff. 1993. How metaphor structures dreams: The theory of conceptual metaphor applied to dream analysis. *Dreaming* 3(2):77–98. https://doi.org/10.1037/h0094373.

Andrew Kachites McCallum. 2002. MALLET: A machine learning for language toolkit. http://mallet.cs.umass.edu. [Online; accessed 2015-03-02].

Jane M. Merritt, Robert Stickgold, Edward Pace-Schott, Julie Williams, and J. Allan Hobson. 1994. Emotion Profiles in the Dreams of Men and Women. *Consciousness and Cognition* 3(1):46–60. https://doi.org/10.1006/ccog.1994.1004.

Margaret Mitchell, Kristy Hollingshead, and Glen Coppersmith. 2015. Quantifying the language of schizophrenia in social media. In *Proceedings of the Workshop on Computational Linguistics and Clinical Psychology: From Linguistic Signal to Clinical Reality*. North American Chapter of the Association for Computational Linguistics, Denver, Colorado, USA.

Saif M. Mohammad and Peter D. Turney. 2013. Crowdsourcing a word-emotion association lexicon 29(3):436–465.

Carey K. Morewedge and Michael I. Norton. 2009. When dreaming is believing: the (motivated) interpretation of dreams. *Journal of Personality and Social Psychology* 96(2):249–264. https://doi.org/10.1037/a0013264.

David Nadeau, Catherine Sabourin, Joseph De Koninck, Stan Matwin, and Peter D. Turney. 2006. Automatic dream sentiment analysis. In *Proceedings of the workshop on computational aesthetics at the twenty-first national conference on artificial intelligence (AAAI-06)*. Boston, USA.

Celestine Okorome Mume. 2009. Nightmare in schizophrenic and depressed patients. *The European Journal of Psychiatry* 23(3):177–183.

James W. Pennebaker. 2011. The secret life of pronouns. *New Scientist* 211(2828):42–45.

James W. Pennebaker, Ryan L. Boyd, Kayla Jordan, and Kate Blackburn. 2015. The development and psychometric properties of LIWC2015. Technical report. https://repositories.lib.utexas.edu/handle/2152/31333.

James W. Pennebaker, Cindy K. Chung, Joey Frazee, Gary M. Lavergne, and David I. Beaver. 2014. When Small Words Foretell Academic Success: The Case of College Admissions Essays. *PLOS ONE* 9(12):e115844. https://doi.org/10.1371/journal.pone.0115844.

James W. Pennebaker, Cindy K. Chung, Molly Ireland, Amy Gonzales, and Roger J. Booth. 2007. *The development and psychometric properties of LIWC2007*. LIWC.net, Austin, TX.

Matthew Purver and Stuart Battersby. 2012. Experimenting with Distant Supervision for Emotion Classification. In *Proceedings of the 13th Conference of the European Chapter of the Association for Computational Linguistics*. Association for Computational Linguistics, Stroudsburg, PA, USA, EACL '12, pages 482–491. http://dl.acm.org/citation.cfm?id=2380816.2380875.

M David Rudd. 2006. Fluid vulnerability theory: A cognitive approach to understanding the process of acute and chronic suicide risk. .

Silvio Scarone, Maria Laura Manzone, Orsola Gambini, Ilde Kantzas, Ivan Limosani, Armando D'agostino, and J Allan Hobson. 2008. The dream as a model for psychosis: an experimental approach using bizarreness as a cognitive marker. *Schizophrenia Bulletin* 34(3):515–522.

Michael Schredl. 2010. Dream content analysis: Basic principles. *International Journal of Dream Research* 3(1):65–73. https://doi.org/10.11588/ijodr.2010.1.474.

Michael Schredl and Evelyn Doll. 1998. Emotions in Diary Dreams. *Consciousness and Cognition* 7(4):634–646. https://doi.org/10.1006/ccog.1998.0356.

Michael Schredl, Franc Paul, Iris Reinhard, Ulrich Walter Ebner-Priemer, Christian Schmahl, and Martin Bohus. 2012. Sleep and dreaming in patients with borderline personality disorder: A polysomnographic study. *Psychiatry Research* 200(23):430–436. https://doi.org/10.1016/j.psychres.2012.04.036.

Dylan Selterman, Deirdre Barrett, and Patrick McNamara. 2012. Attachment, sleep and dreams. In *Encyclopedia of Sleep and Dreams*, Greenwood Publishers, Santa Barbara, CA.

Francesca Siclari, Benjamin Baird, Lampros Perogamvros, Giulio Bernardi, Joshua J. LaRocque, Brady Riedner, Melanie Boly, Bradley R. Postle, and Giulio Tononi. 2017. The neural correlates of dreaming. *Nature Neuroscience* advance online publication. https://doi.org/10.1038/nn.4545.

Pilleriin Sikka, Katja Valli, Tiina Virta, and Antti Revonsuo. 2014. I know how you felt last night, or do i? self-and external ratings of emotions in rem sleep dreams. *Consciousness and cognition* 25:51–66.

Joacim Skancke, Ingrid Holsen, and Michael Schredl. 2014. Continuity between waking life and dreams of psychiatric patients: A review and discussion of the implications for dream research. *International Journal of Dream Research* 7(1):39–53. http://journals.ub.uni-heidelberg.de/index.php/IJoDR/article/view/12184.

Marijke L. Swart, Annette M. van Schagen, Jaap Lancee, and Jan van den Bout. 2013. Prevalence of Nightmare Disorder in Psychiatric Outpatients. *Psychotherapy and Psychosomatics* 82(4):267–268. https://doi.org/10.1159/000343590.

Murray L. Wax. 2004. Dream sharing as social practice. *Dreaming* 14(2-3):83–93. https://doi.org/10.1037/1053-0797.14.2-3.83.

Robert E. Wilson, Samuel D. Gosling, and Lindsay T. Graham. 2012. A Review of Facebook Research in the Social Sciences. *Perspectives on Psychological Science* 7(3):203–220. https://doi.org/10.1177/1745691612442904.

Zhijun Yin, Liangliang Cao, Jiawei Han, Chengxiang Zhai, and Thomas Huang. 2011. Geographical Topic Discovery and Comparison. In *Proceedings of the 20th International Conference on World Wide Web*. ACM, New York, NY, USA, WWW '11, pages 247–256. https://doi.org/10.1145/1963405.1963443.

Appendix A: Full list of LDA topics

Topic	Label	Top words
0	Active first person dreams	see says look know comes walk run looks find wake
1	Sex dreams, some explicit	girl guy sex room bathroom wanted girls shower naked talking
2	Animal dreams	dog house cat snake dogs trying black big came bear
3	Metadreaming	room bed woke sleep night wake asleep time felt see
4	Family presence	mom dad house brother sister told came saw home family
5	Strange homes and settings	room door house floor stairs old open window building doors
6	About family members	house family husband mother old son sister home daughter father
7	Friendship	friend friends party people wedding church best seemed told wanted
8	Flying	see sky plane flying building ground people fire city air fly high huge storm
9	Young love	friend guy boyfriend friends love girl told talking felt life real know
10	Teeth, limbs, body parts	felt face eyes body hand head see looked blood feel
11	Water	water pool beach boat swimming ocean river ship people lake
12	Food and eating	food table sitting people eating eat kitchen restaurant left bathroom
13	Picturesque landscapes	walking tree trees small area forest place beautiful hill little
14	Performance	work people thought asked show working wanted office told music
15	Driving and Cars	car driving road bus drive truck train seat drove home street
16	Violence	people kill man trying guy gun shot killed group dead knife die
17	Friends and Exes	guy phone told boyfriend remember call girl friend asked know
18	Dream sense-making	remember know time think felt life feeling thing real people feel knew
19	School dreams	school class teacher high game friend friends old girl walking time
20	Colorful dreams	white hair black man looked wearing blue dark see red woman light
21	Pregnancy and baby	baby hospital boy pregnant girl know child told little woke
22	Cinematic, sophisticated dreams	woman name life person place words world read help found
23	Shopping and money	store find people money place shop found work left mall
24	Chase dreams	ran saw looked came running house told woke tried door

Appendix B: Sample dreams by CDI

Categorical	This dream appears to me as if it were movie. A crowd of people are running away from a horde of zombies. The crowd of people run up a skyscraper. The zombies are running and still chasing them. At the top of the building, the people are stranded and can hear the dead catching up to them on the stairs. One man in a brown overcoat pulls a leather tome out of his coat and flips through it. "THE PROPHECY IS COMING TRUE!" He yells. The clouds part above them and an angel made entirely out of tiny swords floats down. The people all marvel for a moment. Then the angel disintegrates into a cloud of blades and flies at the zombie horde, decimating them. As this happens, Japanese rock music starts playing. The scene cuts to a montage of zombie people and cows getting disintegrated as credits roll past the "screen" in front of my eyes. I wake up.
Dynamic	So I was going to this thing and my crush was there. It was this hill and it was snowing. So I ran and hugged my crush when I saw him because we're bestfriends. So then I saw one of my old friends. He told me he liked me like 3 years ago. So I hugged him too because I haven't seen him forever. So then I got tired so we sat down at this table and the guy who told me he liked me (this was in real life when he told me) but in my dream he sat next to me and bought me a drink and we kinda just smiled at each other for a while. And that's it.

A Corpus Analysis of Social Connections and Social Isolation in Adolescents Suffering from Depressive Disorders

Jia-Wen Guo[1] Danielle L Mowery[2] Djin Lai[1] Katherine Sward[1] Mike Conway[2]

[1]College of Nursing
University of Utah
[2] Department of Biomedical Informatics
University of Utah

Abstract

Social connection and social isolation are associated with depressive symptoms, particularly in adolescents and young adults, but how these concepts are documented in clinical notes is unknown. This pilot study aimed to identify the topics relevant to social connection and isolation by analyzing 145 clinical notes from in-patients with depression diagnosis. We found that providers, including physicians, nurses, social workers, and psychologists, document descriptions of both social connection and social isolation.

1 Introduction

Social connection and social isolation are associated with health problems, including mental health issues (Matthews et al., 2015; Williams & Galliher, 2006). The Institute of Medicine (IOM) recommends healthcare providers collect social relationship information from individuals using NHANES III Social Connection and Isolation Questions (IOM, 2015). For example, this survey inquiries about how many times per week an individual speaks on the telephone with family, friends, or neighbors, gets together with friends or others, attends church or religious services, or attends meetings of the clubs or organizations. While these questions focus on the *quantity* of the social interactions, the survey fails to assess the *quality* of social relationship and interaction.

The electronic health record (EHR) can be a rich source of clinical information. However, it is not clear whether the EHR contains adequate documentation to support a detailed assessment of social connection and social isolation. In this study, our goals are to understand how social connection and social isolation are documented in the clinical notes for patients diagnosed with major depressive disorder: (1) which providers more frequently document social connection and social isolation information? (2) what types of clinical notes most likely contain descriptions of social connection and social isolation? and (3) what types of social connection and social isolation are documented in clinical notes?

2 Method

In this Institutional Review Board (IRB)- approved pilot study, we selected a cohort of adolescent patients ages 12-25 (mean=17.14, standard deviation=3.61) admitted to a major healthcare system between 2013-2016 with at least one visit coded with International Classification of Disease, version 9 (ICD-9) billing codes for major depressive disorder; resulting in 181,880 in-patient clinical notes. From this set, we originally planned to randomly sample 100 notes based on the distribution of notes generated by provider type: social worker (33.5%), therapist (28.8%), physician (22.3), psychologist (12.0%), intern (1.8%), pharmacist (0.5%), dietitian (0.4%), nurse (0.1%), and other providers (0.6%). It resulted that there was only one note individually represented to five provider types (i.e., intern, pharmacist, dietitian, nurse, and other providers). We, therefore, randomly selected additional 9 notes to supplement the sample of notes for those five provider types. Totally, 145 notes were used in this pilot study.

2.1 Definitions

Social connection (SC) is *the belonging and interpersonal closeness between an individual and other people or society, including friends, family, and others* (Haslam, Cruwys, Haslam, & Jetten, 2015; Milner et al., 2015; van Bel, Smolders, IJsselsteijn, & de Kort, 2009). High quality social

Proceedings of the Fourth Workshop on Computational Linguistics and Clinical Psychology, pages 26–31,
Vancouver, Canada, August 3, 2017. © 2017 Association for Computational Linguistics

connections or networks are associated with increased positive health behaviors (Cohen & Janicki-Deverts, 2009; Walton & Cohen, 2011), improved academic outcome (Walton & Cohen, 2011), and reduced depressive symptoms (Williams & Galliher, 2006).

Social isolation (SI) is *a lack of contact and engagement between oneself and society* (Cacioppo & Cacioppo, 2014; Nicholson, 2012; Zavaleta, Samuel, & Mills, 2014). There are two types of social isolation: objective isolation, such as absence or limited number of meaningful social interactions; and subjective isolation where an individual reports feeling socially isolated or loneliness (Cacioppo & Cacioppo, 2014; Zavaleta et al., 2014). Social isolation has been associated with depression (Matthews et al., 2015; Tiwari & Ruhela, 2012).

2.2 Corpus Annotation

We developed an initial codebook based on the NHANES III Questions for social connections. For social isolation, we . Other codes Then,

Two annotators who are registered nurses with clinical experienced, including taking care of depressive patients, reviewed ten notes and developed a coding schema. Then, each individually coded another ten notes, and inter-annotator agreement (IAA) was calculated. The IAA was high for both SC (observed agreement: 0.974; Cohen's kappa: 0.80) and SI (observed agreement: 0.997, Cohen's kappa: 0.90); hence, both annotators continued independently annotating mentions of SC and SI from the remaining 135 notes. The annotation outcome was reviewed together and any discrepancy discussed. To be explicit about the codes for SC and SI, we used the concepts from NHANES III as subtypes of SC. We identified subtypes of SI from review of the clinical notes and based on the literature. Qualitative data analysis software, NVivo (version 11), was used for this corpus analysis.

2.3 Corpus Analysis

For the corpus analysis, we (1) described the subtypes of SC and SI, (2) determined the distribution of SC and SI mentions by provider type, and (3) determined the distribution of subtypes of SC and SI across clinical notes.

3 Results

Among 145 clinical notes, 34.5% (n=50) contain either SC or SI mentions; 7% (n=10) of notes contain both SC and SI mentions. 32.4% (n=47) of notes contain only SC mentions; in contrast to, 9.0% (n=10) with only SI mentions.

3.1 Subtypes of SC and SI

We report the distribution of SC and SI subtypes based on the number of clinical notes and the number of mentions (**Table 1**).

	# of notes n (%)	# of mentions n(%)
Social Connections	(N=47)	(N=241)
Family or relatives	43 (91.5)	136 (56.8)
School activity	16 (34.0)	48 (19.9)
Friend	15 (31.9)	36 (14.9)
Employment	6 (12.8)	8 (3.3)
Marital status	2 (4.3)	7 (2.9)
Social-cultural	2 (4.3)	3 (1.2)
Spiritual activity	2 (4.3)	2 (0.8)
Social Isolation	(N=13)	(N=22)
Being restricted from contact with others	6 (46.2)	7 (31.8)
Being asked to leave others or groups	3 (23.1)	3 (13.6)
Distancing self from desired relationships	3 (23.1)	3 (13.6)
Isolation	2 (15.4)	3 (13.3)
Not being understood	1 (7.7)	2 (9.1)
Lack of meaningful social institutions	1 (7.7)	2 (9.1)
Feeling loneliness	1 (7.7)	1 (4.5)
Lack of meaningful social relationship	1 (7.7)	1 (4.5)

Table 1. Distribution of SC and SI mentions

Seven SC subtypes were observed: *family or relatives, school activity, friend, marital status, social-cultural, spiritual activities, and employment.* They included activities or experiences with others: engaging in spiritual, academic, cultural, or work activities and committing to a personal relationship status. For example, *"patient stated her parents and family are her biggest support."*

Eight SI subtypes were observed: *restriction from contact with others, being asked to leave others or groups, distancing self from desired relationships, isolation, not being understood, lack of meaningful social institutions, feeling loneliness,* and *lack of meaningful social relationship.* These subtypes can be divided into objective isolation (i.e., *restriction from contact with others, being asked to leave others or groups, distancing self from desired relationships,* and *isolation*) and subjective isolation (i.e., *not being understood, lack of meaningful social institutions, feeling loneliness,* and *lack of meaningful social relationship*) based on whether the mention related to self-expression. For example, "*patient mentioned that Mom doesn't understand symptoms of depression and thinks I am lazy.*"

The most frequent subtypes of SC were: *family or relatives, school activity,* and *friend.* The most frequent subtypes of SI were: *restriction from contact with others, being asked to leave others or groups, distancing self from desired relationships,* and *isolation* (**Table 1**).

3.2 Provider Types

In **Table 2**, we report the distribution of notes containing one or more mentions of SC and SI by provider type. The highest frequencies of SC and SI mentions were written by physicians and social workers.

Provider Type	n (%) SC (N=47)	n (%) SI (N=13)
Physician	15 (31.9)	4 (30.8)
Social Worker	14 (29.8)	2 (15.4)
Psychologist	7 (14.9)	2 (15.4)
Nurse	5 (10.6)	3 (23.1)
Therapist	2 (4.3)	2 (15.4)
Others	2 (4.3)	-
Intern	1 (2.1)	-
Dietitian	1 (2.1)	-
Pharmacist	-	-

Note. Others: e.g., Health Care Assistant.

Table 2. Distribution of SC and SI notes by healthcare provider

3.3 Clinical Note Types

Among 145 notes, more than 20 different note types were observed. The majority of notes were:

behavioral health group notes (n=41, 28.3%), unspecified due to lack of the note title (n=28, 19.3%), psychiatric attending daily progress notes (n=17, 11.7%), psychology progress notes (n=12, 8.3.7%), nutrition reassessments (n=9, 6.2%), and progress notes (n=9, 6.2%). Some note types are written by multiple providers. For example, social workers, psychologists, or therapists can document behavioral health group notes. Similarly, a provider could be the author of multiple note types. For example, a social worker can document behavioral health group notes, behavior health social work notes, or discharge notes. The detailed distribution of each SC or SI subtype by note types is presented in **Table 3**.

SC Subtypes	n A	n B	n C	n D	n E	n F
Family or relatives	31	30	24	16	6	30
School activity	23	1	4	3	10	7
Friend	16	5	1	5	5	4
Marital status	6	0	0	0	0	1
Employment	2	0	0	0	2	4
Social-cultural	0	0	0	3	0	0
Spiritual activity	0	1	0	1	0	0
SI Subtypes	**A**	**B**	**C**	**D**	**E**	**F**
Being restricted from contact with others	1	3	1	0	1	1
Being asked to leave others or groups	1	0	0	0	1	1
Distancing self from desired relationships	0	0	0	0	1	2
Isolation	2	0	0	0	1	0
Lack of meaningful social group	2	0	0	0	0	0
Lack of meaningful social relationship	0	0	0	0	0	1
Loneliness	0	0	0	0	1	0
Not being understood	0	0	2	0	0	0

Note. A: Psychiatric attending admit note, B: Psychology progress note, C: Psychiatric attending daily progress note, D: Behavior health social work, E: Behavior health clinical intake assessments, F: Other notes

Table 3. Distribution of note type by SC and SI subtypes.

More than 80% of SC mentions were observed in psychiatric attending admit notes (n=78, 32.4%), psychology progress notes (n=37, 15.4%), psychiatric attending daily progress notes (n=29, 12.0%), behavior health social work notes (n=28, 11.6%), and behavior health clinical intake assessments (n=23, 9.5%). More than 80% of SI mention were identified from psychiatric attending admit notes (n=6, 27.3%), behavior health clinical intake assessments (n=5, 22.7%), psychology progress notes (n=3, 13.6%), psychiatric attending daily progress notes (n=3, 13.6%), and behavioral health group notes (n=2, 9.1%).

4   Discussion

We conducted a corpus analysis to characterize the documentation of SC and SI mentions in clinical notes from patients diagnosed as depression. About a third of notes contain only mentions of SC; in contrast to 9% of notes with only mentions of SI. There are two possible explanations. First, the subtypes of SC were named or grouped by social entity because SC has the meaning of *belonging* to certain social groups (Haslam et al., 2015). This may be easier to identify from the notes while the subtypes of SI were described specific situations which may require more interpretation or judgment form the annotators. Second, we did not double annotate the mentions but some SC mentions with negative meanings could possibly be interpreted as SI. For example, the SC mention, *"Patient's mom states that my son has had difficulty his entire life making friends"*, implying that mom has been paying attention about her son's friendship (a form of SC); however, this mention could be also annotated as *Lack of meaningful social relationship* of SI. Therefore, we plan to update the annotation protocol for the double annotation mention when it is needed.

Mentions of SC often include interactions and relationships between the patient and other individuals, the most frequent of which describe *family or relatives*. In this context, most SC mentions describe receiving support from a parent or sibling or perhaps missing loved ones who live at a distance. *School activities* are one of the most annotated mentions; this could be because most of the patients were school age. *School activities* mentions include attending school (middle school through college) and living away from home (dorms). *Friends* are also often reported as a source of connection including descriptions of spending leisure time with a close other or having a roommate at home.

However, patients also report SC difficulties such as making friends, desiring a relationship, experiencing jealousy when not receiving attention of others, and ending close relationships. *Marital status* mentions were consistently reporting single status; however, this is not surprising given the age of our study population. *Spiritual activity* was not always a source of connection. For example, one patient reports not identifying with family religious values. More informative descriptions of SC include loving to learn at school and reporting high grades in classes, but also include patient's accounts of dealing with school stresses (bullying) and being expelled from school. Patients also report *social-culture* as a reason for a lack of connection including descriptions of ethnicity, language barriers, and moving cities.

Although not as frequent as SC, SI mentions were observed. Common themes of SI mentions include general struggles with *isolation* as well as particular types of isolation including verbal isolation, e.g., *being asked to leave others or groups* (*"getting kicked out of the house or dorms"*), physical isolation e.g., *restricting from contact with others* i.e., avoiding others, being placed in time out, having phone privileges revoked, and *distancing self from desired relationships* i.e., voluntarily removing oneself from the group, asking others to leave, and refusing to talk with others. Patients report a *lack of meaningful social group* e.g., unable to find meaningful work and a *lack of meaningful social relationships* e.g., difficulty establishing relationships outside of family. Implications and reasons for SI include feeling *loneliness* and *not feeling understood* by family e.g., *"doesn't understand their illness or listen to them"*.

The notes containing the highest frequencies of SC and SI mentions were written by physicians, social workers, psychologist, and nurses. This suggests that future efforts could be focused on specific providers' notes.

5   Limitations and Future Work

This pilot work has limitations. We only annotated 145 clinical notes and new information about SC and SI may emerge with continued annotation efforts on a larger sample. Therefore, we plan to continue the annotation work until there is no new information identified. The patients were adolescents or young adults with depression; therefore, the findings may not generalize to other patient populations or clinical problems.

6 Conclusion

This study is the first study to explore SC and SI from EHR clinical notes and a precursor to more computational work for extracting SC and SI information from the notes. We found that SC and SI information documented in the notes and can be reliably identified with human review suggesting the content may be amenable to more automated methods (natural language processing). We are actively developing a linguistic model to support SC and SI information extraction and qualification of the relationship of SC and SI information as this relates to a patient's mental health status and outcomes of depression treatment.

References

Cacioppo, J. T., & Cacioppo, S. (2014). Social relationships and health: The toxic effects of perceived scial iolation. *Social and personality psychology compass, 8*(2), 58-72. doi:10.1111/spc3.12087

Cohen, S., & Janicki-Deverts, D. (2009). Can we improve our physical health by altering our social networks? *Perspectives on Psychological Science, 4*(4), 375-378. doi:10.1111/j.1745-6924.2009.01141.x

Haslam, C., Cruwys, T., Haslam, S. A., & Jetten, J. (2015). Social connectedness and health. In N. A. Pachana (Ed.), *Encyclopedia of Geropsychology* (pp. 1-10). Singapore: Springer Singapore.

Institute of Medicine [IOM], Committee on the Recommended Social and Behavioral Domains and Measures for Electronic Health Records, & Board on Population Health and Public Health Practice. (2015). *Capturing Social and Behavioral Domains and Measures in Electronic Health Records: Phase 2*. Washington, DC: National Academies Press.

Matthews, T., Danese, A., Wertz, J., Ambler, A., Kelly, M., Diver, A., . . . Arseneault, L. (2015). Social Isolation and Mental Health at Primary and Secondary School Entry: A Longitudinal Cohort Study. *Journal of the American Academy of Child & Adolescent Psychiatry, 54*(3), 225-232. doi:http://doi.org/10.1016/j.jaac.2014.12.008

Milner, A., Page, A., Morrell, S., Hobbs, C., Carter, G., Dudley, M., . . . Taylor, R. (2015). Social connections and suicidal behaviour in young Australian adults: Evidence from a case–control study of persons aged 18–34 years in NSW, Australia. *SSM - Population Health, 1*, 1-7. doi:http://doi.org/10.1016/j.ssmph.2015.09.001

Nicholson, N. R. (2012). A Review of Social Isolation: An Important but Underassessed Condition in Older Adults. *The Journal of Primary Prevention, 33*(2), 137-152. doi:10.1007/s10935-012-0271-2

Tiwari, P., & Ruhela, S. (2012). *Social isolation and depression among adolescent: A comparative perspective*. Paper presented at the 2nd International Conference on Social Science and Humanity, Singapore.

van Bel, D. T., Smolders, K., IJsselsteijn, W. A., & de Kort, Y. (2009). Social connectedness: Concept and measurement. *Intelligent Environments, 2*, 67-74.

Walton, G. M., & Cohen, G. L. (2011). A brief social-belonging intervention improves academic and health outcomes of minority students. *Science, 331*(6023), 1447-1451. doi:10.1126/science.1198364

Williams, K. L., & Galliher, R. V. (2006). Predicting depression and self–esteem from social connectedness, support, and competence. *Journal of Social and Clinical Psychology, 25*(8), 855-874. doi:10.1521/jscp.2006.25.8.855

Zavaleta, D., Samuel, K., & Mills, C. (2014). Social isolation: A conceptual and measurement proposal. *OPHI Working Papers, 67*.

Monitoring Tweets for Depression to Detect At-risk Users

Zunaira Jamil, Diana Inkpen, Prasadith Buddhitha
School of Electrical Engineering and Computer Science
University of Ottawa, Ottawa, ON, Canada, K1N 6N5
{zjami096, diana.inkpen, pkiri056}@uottawa.ca

Kenton White
Advanced Symbolics, Ottawa, ON, Canada, K1N 5S7
kenton.white@advancedsymbolics.com

Abstract

We propose an automated system that can identify at-risk users from their public social media activity, more specifically, from Twitter. The data that we collected is from the #BellLetsTalk campaign, which is a wide-reaching, multi-year program designed to break the silence around mental illness and support mental health across Canada. To achieve our goal, we trained a user-level classifier that can detect at-risk users that achieves a reasonable precision and recall. We also trained a tweet-level classifier that predicts if a tweet indicates depression. This task was much more difficult due to the imbalanced data. In the dataset that we labeled, we came across 5% depression tweets and 95% non-depression tweets. To handle this class imbalance, we used undersampling methods. The resulting classifier had high recall, but low precision. Therefore, we only use this classifier to compute the estimated percentage of depressed tweets and to add this value as a feature for the user-level classifier.

1 Introduction

According to a recent report of the World Health Organization (WHO), mental health is an integral part of health and well-being (WHO, 2004). Mental disorders can affect anyone, rich or poor, male or female, of any age or social group. The experience of mental illness is often described as difficult, especially when associated with demeaning prejudices and lack of understanding. Mental illness is also difficult to diagnose. There is no reliable laboratory test for most forms of mental illness and typically, diagnostic is based on the patient's self-reported experiences, behaviors reported by relatives, and a mental status examination. Unfortunately, mental disorder problems are increasing worldwide.

In the context of mental illness, depression is very common. In Canada, 5.3% of the population had presented a depressive episode in the past 12 months.[1] According to Canadian Mental Health Association (CMHA, 2016), 20% of Canadians belonging to different demographics have experienced mental illness during their lifetime, and around 8% of adults have gone through major depression. Mental Health Commission of Canada (MHCC, 2016) has reported on the broad implications of mental illness, where from nearly 4,000 Canadians that die each year by suicide, 90% of them were identified as having some form of a mental disorder. According to World Health Organization (WHO, 2016), suicide is a preventable health problem and to be successful in preventing suicide; therefore, it is of great importance to identify depression as a first indicator of further problems.

Apart from the severity of mental disorders and their influence on one's mental and physical health, the social stigma or discrimination in the forms of rejection, isolation, abuse and fear of embarrassment have made the individuals with mental disorders to be neglected by the community, as well as to stay away from obtaining the necessary treatments (WHO, 2016). Due to the severity mental disorders can cause to one's life and the impact it has on the entire society, organizations such as Bell Canada have initiated programs to raise funding for mental health programs as well as to create awareness within the society.[2]

The goal of this research is to exploit the mas-

---

[1] http://www.phac-aspc.gc.ca/cd-mc/mi-mm/depression-eng.php
[2] http://letstalk.bell.ca/en/

Proceedings of the Fourth Workshop on Computational Linguistics and Clinical Psychology, pages 32–40,
Vancouver, Canada, August 3, 2017. © 2017 Association for Computational Linguistics

sive data issued from Twitter and apply social media mining and sentiment analysis methods to detect users at-risk of depression. It is an open question whether a tweet-level or user-level classifier is best for detecting at-risk people. A tweet-level classifier monitors individual tweets, identifying messages that indicate risk for depression; a user-level classifier looks at the tweet history and determines if a person is at risk from their corpus of messages over a period of time. This paper describes experiments on both classifiers.

Our system can be used by authorities to find a focused group of at-risk users. It is not a platform for labeling an individual as a patient with depression, but only a platform for raising an alarm so that the relevant authorities could take necessary interventions to further analyze the predicted user to confirm his/her state of mental health. We respect the ethical boundaries relating to the use of social media data and therefore do not use any user identification information in our research.

2   Related Work

With the gradual increase in social media usage and the extensive level of self-disclosure within such platforms (Park et al., 2012), research has been conducted to identify mental disorders at an individual as well as at a society level. Researchers have used features such as behavioural characteristics, depression language, emotion and linguistic style, reduced social activity, increased negative affect, clustered social network, raised interpersonal and medical fears and increased expression in religious involvement, use of negative words, in order to determine the cues of major depressive disorder (De Choudhury et al., 2013a; Tsugawa et al., 2015). Tsugawa et al. (2015), also used syntactical features such as bag of words (BOW) and word frequencies to identify the ratio of tweet topics and managed to conclude that topic modeling also adds a positive contribution to the predictive model compared to the use of the bag-of-words model, which could also result in over-fitting.

The successful use of computational linguistics techniques in identifying the progress and level of depression of individuals in online therapy could bring greater insights to clinicians, to apply interventions effectively and efficiently. Howes et al. (2014) used 882 transcripts gathered from an online psychological therapy provider to determined

that use of linguistic features can be considered as more valuable in predicting the progress of a patient compared to sentiment and topic-based analysis. In contrary to traditional sentiment analysis approaches that use three main polarity classes (i.e., positive, negative, and neutral), Shickel et al. (2016), divided the neutral class into two classes: neither positive nor negative and both positive and negative. With the use of syntactic, lexical, and also by representing words as vectors in the vector space (word embeddings), the authors managed to achieve an overall accuracy of 78% for the four-class polarity prediction.

De Choudhury et al. (2013b) and Schwartz et al. (2014) proposed methods to identify the level of depression among social media users (SMDI: Social Media Depression Index). Schwartz et al. (2014) used a classification model trained with n-grams, linguistic behavior and Latent Dirichlet Allocation (LDA) topics as features for predicting the individuals who are susceptible to having depression. In addition to open-vocabulary analysis and lexicon-based approaches such as Linguistic Inquiry and Word Count (LIWC), Coppersmith et al. (2014a) suggested language models, primarily based on unigrams and character 5-grams to determine the existence of mental disorders.

The Computational Linguistics and Clinical Psychology (CLPsych) 2015 shared task (Coppersmith et al., 2015) used self-reported data on Twitter about Post Traumatic Stress Disorder (PTSD) and depression, collected according to the procedure introduced by Coppersmith et al. (2014b). The shared task participants were provided with a dataset of self-reported users on PTSD and depression. For each user in the dataset, nearly 3,200 most recent posts were collected using the Twitter API. Resnik et al. (2015a), whose system ranked first in the CLPsych 2015 Shared Task, created 16 systems based on features derived using supervised LDA, supervised anchors (for topic modeling), lexical TF-IDF, and a combination of all. An SVM classifier with a linear kernel obtained an average precision above 0.80 for all the three tasks (i.e., depression vs. control, PTSD vs. control and depression vs. PTSD) and a maximum precision of 0.893 for differentiating PTSD users from the control group. Preotiuc-Pietro et al. (2015) employed user metadata and textual features from the corpus provided by the CLPsych 2015 Shared Task to develop a linear classifier to predict users having either one of the mental illnesses. They have used the bag-of-words approach to aggregate word counts, topics derived from clustering methods and metadata (e.g., followers, followees, age, gender) from the users Twitter profile as the main feature categories. With the use of logistic regression and linear SVM in an ensemble of classifiers, the authors managed to obtain an average precision above 0.800 for all the three tasks and with a maximum score of 0.867 for differentiating users in the control group from the users with depression.

The use of the supervised LDA and the supervised anchor model was proven to be highly successful compared to the unsupervised clustering approaches, and even more efficient than using linguistic methods such as the use of n-grams and other lexicon based approaches (Resnik et al., 2015b). Resnik et al. (2015a) proved that such approaches can be successfully used in identifying users with depression, who have self-disclosed their mental illnesses on Twitter. In general, a clear distinction in the lexical and syntactic structure of the language used by individuals with different mental disorders, as well as between individuals within a control group, can be identified throughout the literature mentioned above, as well as from the explorative analysis conducted by Gkotsis et al. (2016). Due to the reliability of the lexical and behavioral features used in many of the models mentioned above, our proposed solution also focused on these feature categories. Even though the dataset we have used is relatively smaller than the ones used by most of the experiments mentioned above, we managed to obtain reliable results in identifying users with mental disorders.

3   Datasets

For this research, we prepared a dataset consisting of tweets from users who participated in #BellLetsTalk 2015 campaign. #BellLetsTalk is a campaign created by Bell Canada to help reduce stigma and promote awareness and understanding of mental health issues. Canadians opened up the dialogue on mental health, contributing more than 122 million tweets, texts, calls and social media shares on #BellLetsTalk Day, helping to raise more than $6.1 million for mental health initia-

tives.[3]

We collected data for the year 2015 and we limited it to Canadian users. 156,612 tweets were obtained from 25,362 users. Only data made public by users was collected for this task. To clean the dataset, we used LDA (Grün and Hornik (2011)), to obtain topics from tweets. Prominent topics included "campaign publicity", "mental health awareness", "raising donations", "facts about mental health". If a tweet contained two or more keywords from any of the mentioned topics, it was removed from the dataset. Additionally, retweets, tweets beginning with a mention (@), short tweets (less than 5 words), and URLs were removed. We then used words like "depressed", "suffer", "attempt", "suicide", "battle", "struggle", "diagnosed", in addition to first person pronouns, to identify a subset of tweets where users are talking about depression. A human annotator reviewed these tweets to verify whether the user is disclosing their own depression or talking about a friend or family member. Using this method we identified 95 users who disclosed their own depression. For these 95 users we collect all tweets from 2015 and refer to these as "self-disclosed" set. All remaining users were considered as control users. Similarly, for control users, all tweets from 2015 are collected and referred to as "control" set.

To prepare a dataset to label at tweet-level, we selected 60 users who had between 100 and 300 tweets. 30 users were selected from self-disclosed set, and 30 from control set. We asked two annotators to label 10 users with depression level 0-1, where 0 indicates no depression and 1 indicates some depression.[4] We found that most tweets fell into the "no depression" class. Since annotation is an expensive and a time-consuming task, we looked for tweets that could be removed without losing relevant tweets. Our first intuition was to remove tweets containing positive words, but this intuition proved to be false as many of the tweets labeled as depressed contained positive words. Next we looked for neutral tweets. Most neutral tweets were labeled as "no depression" and hence we decided to remove these from our dataset. The list of positive and negative words was obtained

---

[3] http://www.ctvnews.ca/health/bell-let-s-talk-breaks-records-raises-more-than-6m-for-mental-health-1.2211607

[4] Our annotators were not experts, though one of them is a student in Psychology. We would like to have the annotations verified by an expert, in the future.

from Hansen et al. (2011). The final dataset consisted of 8,753 tweets. We refer to this dataset as **60Users**.[5] The annotators were then asked to label the remaining 50 users. The Kappa value for 2-annotator agreement was found to be 0.67. If a tweet was labeled as depressed by at least one annotator, the tweet was considered as depressed.[6]

We prepared a larger dataset to be labeled at user-level. This dataset consists of 80 users from self-disclosed set and 80 control users. It included the 60 users annotated above at tweet-level. We refer to this dataset as **160Users**.[7] For fast annotation at user-level, we provided an undersampled version of the dataset to annotators. It was undersampled using our tweet-level classifier discussed in section 4. Nonetheless, for our experiments, we used all tweets from 160 users. The dataset was annotated by two annotators as "depressed" and "not-depressed" user. The conflicts were resolved by a third annotator. The following guidelines were provided for the task:

- Depressed: The user shows clear signs of depression, or shows signs that could result in depression in near future. There is enough reason for a public health member or doctor to investigate further. Additionally, users who self-disclose depression but there are no other tweets indicative of depression, are also labeled as depressed.[8]

- Not-depressed: the user does not show any signs of depression.

A third dataset is obtained from CLPsych shared task 2015 (Coppersmith et al., 2015). The dataset consists of 1,746 users. The training set consists of 327 depression users, 246 PTSD users, and, for each, an age and gender matched control user. The test set consists of 150 depression users, 150 PTSD users, but we cannot use it because the labels for the test set are not available. For our task, we use the depression and control users from the training set. We refer to this as the **CLPsych2015** dataset.

The 60Users dataset was split to contain one-third of the tweets for testing (2,971 tweets) and two-thirds for training purposes (5,782 tweets). In the case of 160Users and the CLPysch2015 datasets, we split each dataset into 70% training and 30% test set. Each model was trained on the training set using 10-fold cross validation and then tested on a held out test set.

4   Tweet-level Classifier

For the tweet-level classification, a preliminary experiment was performed on 60Users dataset using BOW as features and SVM classifier. This gave a very high accuracy because it classified all the tweets in the majority class. This was due to class imbalance. The dataset consisted of 95% not depressed tweets and 5% depressed tweets. To deal with the class imbalance, we then experimented with re-sampling methods including undersampling (randomly removing examples from the majority class) and with oversampling, in particular with adding examples for the minority class using Synthetic Minority Oversampling Technique (SMOTE) (Chawla et al., 2002). For evaluation, we will look at recall, precision, and F-measure for the class of interest (depression), instead of accuracy.

The goal of training a tweet-level classifier is to predict whether a given tweet indicated depression or not. For this, we perform two sets of experiments. The first set of experiments uses 7 features derived from tweet's text. These include polarity words, depression words, first person pronoun, and second person pronoun counts. These are referred to as **initial features**. Polarity words include counts of very negative words, negative words, positive words and very positive words. The list of polarity words was obtained from AFINN (Hansen et al., 2011). Depression related terms are obtained from Maigrot et al. (2016). The second set of experiments uses unigrams (BOW), in addition to the 7 initial features.

Each set consists of 3 experiments performed on the 8,753 tweets from the 60Users dataset.

1. Linear SVM trained on the original dataset

2. Linear SVM trained on the dataset balanced using SMOTE[9]

---

[5]The 60Users dataset annotated at tweet-level will be made available on request for further research

[6]Considering a tweet as depressed only when both annotators agreed that the tweet was depressed reduced the amount of positive training samples, but did not impact performance

[7]The 160Users dataset will be made available on request for further research.

[8]The users who self-disclose depression, but do not have other tweets indicative of depression in the dataset are marked as depressed in order to maximize the number of at-risk users predicted by the classifier.

[9]For oversampling, we use the SMOTE function from the

3. Linear SVM trained on the dataset balanced by undersampling[10]

5 User-Level Classifier

The goal of training a user-level classifier is to predict if a given user is at-risk of suffering from depression. For this, we train models on the 160Users dataset. For user-level classification, we start by making tweet-level predictions using the best model obtained from experiments described in Section 4. The initial features are generated as a requirement for the tweet-level classifier. The tweet-level predictions are then used to compute the percentage of depressed tweets for each user. Next, the text of all the tweets for each user is merged, and the initial features are summed.[11]

During data annotation of the #BellLetsTalk users, we noticed that several users disclosed depression, but their tweets, at least those included in our dataset, did not indicate depression. Although these users were labeled as depressed, we noticed that removing such users from training set helps us to improve our models. For this we compute an additional feature called IsSelfReported for each user. The percentage of depressed tweets (hereafter called %DT) along with isSelfReported is used to decide whether a user should be removed from the training set. If IsSelfReported is True AND %DT is less than 10%, only then, the user is removed from the training set.

Several sets of experiments are performed for this task. An initial baseline experiment is performed using 7 initial features. The second set of experiments uses 8 features (the initial features + %DT). The third set of experiments uses 9 features (the initial features + %DT + isSelfReported). The fourth set of experiments uses a total of 115 features. The purpose for this was to identify whether increasing the number of features has a significant impact on performance. These **additional-features** include LIWC features, sentiment features, emoticon counts, text readability (SMOG, Flesh, Kincaid), and community features such as favorite counts, replies, mentions, retweets, in addition to initial features, %DT, and IsSelfReported.

DMwR package (Torgo, 2010) with default values. This implementation is based on (Chawla et al., 2002)

[10]For undersampling we used the "downSample" function in the CARET package (Kuhn et al., 2012) with default values

[11]The data is centered and scaled during model training

Each set includes three experiments performed on 160Users dataset.

1. Linear SVM trained on the original dataset

2. Linear SVM trained on the dataset balanced using SMOTE

3. Linear SVM trained on the dataset balanced by undersampling

Unlike 60Users dataset that was highly imbalanced, 160Users dataset had a relatively smaller degree of imbalance. The 160Users dataset consisted of 43% positive class and 57% negative class samples. The reason for using re-sampling methods at user-level was to investigate if performance can be improved by training a model on a fully balanced dataset.

From these experiments, we identify the model with highest performance. The set of features, and re-sampling method identified in relation to this model are then used in further experiments. These experiments include training further models using the CLPsych2015 dataset instead of the 160Users dataset. We also merge the 160Users dataset and CLPsych2015 dataset to investigate whether using a larger training data improves the performance.

6 Experimental setup

For this research, all the development is done in R version 3.3 (R Development Core Team, 2008) using the Rstudio IDE (RStudio Team, 2015). Data preparation, feature extraction, and classification tasks are performed using a variety of R packages. All classifiers were used from R's Caret package (Kuhn et al., 2012). Classifiers were trained using 10-fold cross validation to avoid over-fitting and then tested on a held-out test set. The results presented in Section 7 are those obtained on the held-out test set.

7 Results

For both tasks, tweet-level classification and user-level classification, we report precision, recall & F-measure for the positive class (depression), as performance measures. Precision and recall are more informative than accuracy, due to the data being imbalanced. For example, baseline experiments for tweet-level classification returns an accuracy of 95% by classifying all samples as majority class, which is not a true reflection of classifier's performance.

Model	training set	features
Tweet-level		
baseline.tweet	60Users	BOW
exp1	60Users	Initial features (polarity word counts, depression word count, pronoun counts)
exp2	60Users	Initial features + BOW
User-level		
baseline.user	160Users	Initial features
exp3	160Users	Initial features + %DT
exp4	160Users	Initial features + %DT + IsSelfReported
exp4 + additional features	160Users	Initial features + %DT + isSelfReported + community features + LIWC features + NRC sentiment feat. + emoticon features + readability features
exp5	CLPsych2015	Initial features + %DT + isSelfReported
exp6	160Users + CLPsych2015	Initial features + %DT + isSelfReported

Table 1: Datasets and features used for tweet-level and user-level experiments

For measuring performance at user level, we think that recall is somewhat more important for the task, therefore we aim at achieving high recall. This can be justified by keeping in mind the problem we are attempting to solve. In the context of detecting depression, a false positive (FP) is defined as a user who is predicted to have depression but does not actually suffer from depression. A false negative (FN) is defined as a user who is actually depressed but is predicted to not have depression. A classifier detecting more false positives would result in lower precision, the cost of which is that the state would need to invest more money to help users who are not actually depressed. On the other hand, a classifier detecting more false negatives would result in lower recall, the cost of which is that users suffering from depression will not get the help they need on time, which could lead to serious consequences, like suicide. So low recall could lead to loss of human life.

At the same time, we are trying to find a balance of precision and recall. A perfect recall of 1, with a very low precision (e.g., 0.2) is also not an acceptable outcome. In such cases, we look at F-measure, which combines both precision and re-

call. In particular, we look at the precision, recall, and F-measure of the positive class, obtained on the held-out test sets.

7.1 Tweet-level Classifier

Table 7.1 shows the results obtained for the tweet-level classification experiments. Performance is reported on a held-out testset obtained from 60Users dataset. None of the classifiers performed well on the task of identifying depressed tweets. The best performing model (exp1-Undersample) is identified in bold. This is a Linear SVM classifier trained on an undersampled training set and uses 7 initial features without BOW. We obtain a precision of 0.1237 and a recall of 0.8020, with F1 of 0.2144.[12]

The poor performance of all models indicates the complexity of the task and the fact that one tweet is not sufficient to detect depression.

7.2 User-level Classifier

Table 7.2 shows results obtained for user-level classification experiments. Performance is reported on a 30% held-out test set obtained from 160Users dataset. For exp3, the results improved a lot over the baseline with initial features. This shows that the features %DT computed with the tweet-level classifier helps. The best performing model (exp5) is identified in bold. This is a Linear SVM classifier trained on a balanced dataset (CLPsych2015) and uses 9 features (Initial features + %DT + isSelfReported). We obtain a precision of 0.7083, a recall of 0.85, and F1 of 0.7727.

From exp3 and exp4 in Table 7.2, we observe that the dataset balanced using re-sampling methods provide better recall. For this reason, when we train models on the combined dataset (exp6), we continue to balance the datasets using SMOTE and undersampling. The CLPsych2015 dataset (exp 5) is perfectly balanced and therefore does not require balancing using re-sampling methods.

We note that the model trained on CLPysch2015 dataset performs better than the model trained on the 160Users dataset when using the same features. This could be due to larger training data. On the other hand, performance (in terms of recall) drops when the dataset size is increased further by combining the 160Users and CLPsych2015 datasets and

---

[12]For the tweet-level and user-level classifiers, we experimented with other SVM kernels, but the results were worse. The same for other classifiers than SVM.

ModelName	Accuracy	Precision	Recall	F1
baseline	0.9469	1.0000	0.0111	0.0219
exp1-Original	0.9337	NA	0.0000	NA
exp1-SMOTE	0.7816	0.1706	0.5939	0.2650
exp1-Undersample	**0.6102**	**0.1237**	**0.8020**	**0.2144**
exp2-Original	0.9303	0.2222	0.0203	0.0372
exp2-SMOTE	0.7711	0.1124	0.3553	0.1707
exp2-Undersample	0.6143	0.1219	0.7766	0.2107

Table 2: Performance of tweet-level classifiers on the test set

balanced using SMOTE, but remains constant when balanced using undersampling.

Upon investigation as to why undersampling performs better than SMOTE, we discovered that SMOTE oversamples minority class instances, but does not fully balance the training data, whereas undersampling balances the training data. Hence, models trained on a balanced training set result in better performance.

It is interesting to see that models trained on 160Users (exp3 and exp4) perform better on CLPsych2015 dataset, while the model trained on CLPsych2015 dataset (exp5) performs better on the 160Users dataset.

The results for exp4+additionalFeatures are not reported because they are not significantly different from exp4 (though further investigations will need to be done in future work).

In terms of comparing the tweet-level classification task and the user-level classification task, we conclude that user-level models perform much better even with a small number of features.

7.3 Comparison to Related Work

Resnik et al. (2015a) and Preotiuc-Pietro et al. (2015) reported good performance on the dataset made available through the CLPsych2015 shared task, as mentioned in Section 2. We ran our top-performing user-level classifiers on the training set of CLPsych2015 shared task data. Results are provided in Table 7.3. We report only the SMOTE versions of the classifiers since they obtained better results. The feature %DT helps a lot on this dataset (according to exp3). We note that exp5 that gave the highest performance on the 160Users dataset performs consistently well on the CLPsych users, even though performance is slightly lower in comparison.

These results are not comparable with those reported by (Resnik et al., 2015a) and (Preotiuc-Pietro et al., 2015), for two reasons. First, in comparison to Resnik et al. (2015a) and Preotiuc-Pietro et al. (2015), who report performance on a different test set. We report performance on the 30% of the training users provided to us, that we kept aside for testing, because of the unavailability of the labels for the test users from the shared task. Second, the shared task uses precision at a certain recall level as the main performance measure, while we report standard precision and recall, and we selected our model to have a high recall.

8   Conclusion and Future Work

In conclusion, we proposed models for tweet-level classification and used them to compute the percentage of depressed tweets for each user. We also proposed models for user-level classification. We experimented with many features, including the percentage of depressed tweets, which was shown to help improve the performance of the user-level classifier. We annotated our own dataset from the #BellLetsTalk campaign, but we also experimented with the existing dataset from CLPsych2015.

In future work, we plan to study depression among groups of users based on their age, gender, locations and other demographic attributes. We also plan to look into identifying other kinds of mental disorders, and detecting suicidal ideation.

Acknowledgments

We appreciate the helpful comments of the anonymous reviewers. We thank the annotators (Bryan Paget and Sameen Salim) for their time and expertise. We thank the organizers of CLPsych 2015 for providing us access to their datasets. This research is funded by Natural Sciences and Engineering Research Council of Canada (NSERC).

Experiment	Accuracy	Precision	Recall	F1
baseline	0.617	1.0000	0.1000	0.1818
exp3-Original	0.6383	1.0000	0.1500	0.2608
exp3-SMOTE	0.6809	0.8571	0.3000	0.4444
exp3-Undersample	0.7021	0.7500	0.4500	0.5625
exp4-Original	0.6809	0.7778	0.3500	0.4828
exp4-SMOTE	0.766	0.7647	0.6500	0.7027
exp4-Undersample	0.766	0.7143	0.7500	0.7317
exp5-Original	**0.7872**	**0.7083**	**0.8500**	**0.7727**
exp6-SMOTE	0.7872	0.8571	0.6000	0.7059
exp6-UnderSample	0.7872	0.7083	0.8500	0.7727

Table 3: Performance of user-level classifiers on 160Users test set

Experiment	Accuracy	Precision	Recall	F1
exp3-SMOTE	0.6198	0.5966	0.7396	0.6605
exp3-Undersample	0.625	0.5984	0.7604	0.6697
exp4-SMOTE	0.5885	0.5895	0.5833	0.5864
exp4-Undersample	0.5885	0.5876	0.5938	0.5907
exp5-Original	**0.6094**	**0.5827**	**0.7708**	**0.6637**
exp6-SMOTE	0.6146	0.5902	0.7500	0.6606
exp6-UnderSample	0.6094	0.5827	0.7708	0.6637

Table 4: Performance of user-level classifiers on the CLPsych2015 test set

References

Nitesh V Chawla, Kevin W Bowyer, Lawrence O Hall, and W Philip Kegelmeyer. 2002. Smote: synthetic minority over-sampling technique. *Journal of artificial intelligence research* 16:321–357.

CMHA. 2016. Facts about mental illness. http://www.cmha.ca/media/fast-facts-about-mental-illness/#.WHbdMRsrK00.

Glen Coppersmith, Mark Dredze, and Craig Harman. 2014a. Measuring Post Traumatic Stress Disorder in Twitter. In *In Proceedings of the 7th International AAAI Conference on Weblogs and Social Media (ICWSM)..* volume 2, pages 23–45.

Glen Coppersmith, Mark Dredze, and Craig Harman. 2014b. Quantifying Mental Health Signals in Twitter. In *Proceedings of the Workshop on Computational Linguistics and Clinical Psychology: From Linguistic Signal to Clinical Reality*. pages 51–60. http://www.aclweb.org/anthology/W/W14/W14-3207.

Glen Coppersmith, Mark Dredze, Craig Harman, Hollingshead Kristy, and Margaret Mitchell. 2015. CLPsych 2015 Shared Task: Depression and PTSD on Twitter. In *Proceedings of the 2nd Workshop on Computational Linguistics and Clinical Psychology: From Linguistic Signal to Clinical Reality*. pages 31–39.

Munmun De Choudhury, Scott Counts, and Eric Horvitz. 2013a. Social media as a measurement tool of depression in populations. *WebSci '13: Proceedings of the 5th Annual ACM Web Science Conference* pages 47–56. https://doi.org/10.1145/2464464.2464480.

Munmun De Choudhury, Michael Gamon, Scott Counts, and Eric Horvitz. 2013b. Predicting Depression via Social Media. In *Proceedings of the Seventh International AAAI Conference on Weblogs and Social Media*. volume 2, pages 128–137. http://www.aaai.org/ocs/index.php/ICWSM/ICWSM13/paper/viewFile/6124/6351.

George Gkotsis, Anika Oellrich, Tim J P Hubbard, Richard J B Dobson, Maria Liakata, Sumithra Velupillai, and Rina Dutta. 2016. The language of mental health problems in social media. In *Proceedings of the 3rd Workshop on Computational Linguistics and Clinical Psychology: From Linguistic Signal to Clinical Reality*. Association for Computational Linguistics, San Diego, CA, USA, pages 63–73.

Bettina Grün and Kurt Hornik. 2011. topicmodels: An R package for fitting topic models. *Journal of Statistical Software* 40(13):1–30. https://doi.org/10.18637/jss.v040.i13.

Lars Kai Hansen, Adam Arvidsson, Finn Årup Nielsen, Elanor Colleoni, and Michael Etter. 2011. Good friends, bad news-affect and virality in twitter. *Future information technology* pages 34–43.

Christine Howes, Matthew Purver, and Rose McCabe.

2014. Linguistic Indicators of Severity and Progress in Online Text-based Therapy for Depression. In *Workshop on Computational Linguistics and Clinical Psychology*. 611733, pages 7–16.

Max Kuhn, Contributions from Jed Wing, Steve Weston, Andre Williams, Chris Keefer, and Allan Engelhardt. 2012. *caret: Classification and Regression Training*. R package version 5.15-044. http://CRAN.R-project.org/package=caret.

Cédric Maigrot, Sandra Bringay, and Jérôme Azé. 2016. Concept drift vs suicide : How one can help prevent the other? In *17th International Conference on Intelligent Text Processing and Computational Linguistics (CICLing 2016)*. Konya, Turkey.

MHCC. 2016. http://www.mentalhealthcommission.ca/ sites/default/files/mhcc_annualreport2015_en.v7-ebook_0.pdf.

Minsu Park, Chiyoung Cha, and Meeyoung Cha. 2012. Depressive Moods of Users Portrayed in Twitter. In *ACM SIGKDD Workshop on Healthcare Informatics (HI-KDD)*. pages 1–8.

Daniel Preotiuc-Pietro, Maarten Sap, H. Andrew Schwartz, and Lyle Ungar. 2015. Mental Illness Detection at the World Well-Being Project for the CLPsych 2015 Shared Task. In *Proceedings of the 2nd Workshop on Computational Linguistics and Clinical Psychology: From Linguistic Signal to Clinical Reality*. pages 40–45.

R Development Core Team. 2008. *R: A Language and Environment for Statistical Computing*. R Foundation for Statistical Computing, Vienna, Austria. ISBN 3-900051-07-0. http://www.R-project.org.

Philip Resnik, William Armstrong, Leonardo Claudino, and Thang Nguyen. 2015a. The University of Maryland CLPsych 2015 Shared Task System. In *CLPsych 2015 Shared Task System*. c, pages 54–60.

Philip Resnik, William Armstrong, Leonardo Claudino, Thang Nguyen, Viet-an Nguyen, and Jordan Boyd-graber. 2015b. Beyond LDA : Exploring Supervised Topic Modeling for Depression-Related Language in Twitter. In *Proceedings of the 2nd Workshop on Computational Linguistics and Clinical Psychology: From Linguistic Signal to Clinical Reality*. volume 1, pages 99–107.

RStudio Team. 2015. *RStudio: Integrated Development Environment for R*. RStudio, Inc., Boston, MA. http://www.rstudio.com/.

H Andrew Schwartz, Johannes Eichstaedt, Margaret L Kern, Gregory Park, Maarten Sap, David Stillwell, Michal Kosinski, and Lyle Ungar. 2014. Towards Assessing Changes in Degree of Depression through Facebook. In *Proceedings of the Workshop on Computational Linguistics and Clinical Psychology: From Linguistic Signal to Clinical Reality*. pages 118–125.

http://www.aclweb.org/anthology/W/W14/W14-3214.

Benjamin Shickel, Martin Heesacker, Sherry Benton, Ashkan Ebadi, Paul Nickerson, and Parisa Rashidi. 2016. Self-Reflective Sentiment Analysis. In *Computational Linguistics and Clinical Psychology*. Association for Computational Linguistics, San Diego, CA, USA, pages 23–32. http://www.aclweb.org/anthology/W16-0303.

L. Torgo. 2010. *Data Mining with R, learning with case studies*. Chapman and Hall/CRC. http://www.dcc.fc.up.pt/ ltorgo/DataMiningWithR.

Sho Tsugawa, Yusuke Kikuchi, Fumio Kishino, Kosuke Nakajima, Yuichi Itoh, and Hiroyuki Ohsaki. 2015. Recognizing Depression from Twitter Activity. In *Proceedings of the 33rd Annual ACM Conference on Human Factors in Computing Systems - CHI '15*. pages 3187–3196. https://doi.org/10.1145/2702123.2702280.

WHO. 2004. Promoting mental health: Concepts, emerging evidence, practice: Summary report .

WHO. 2016. Mental health: a state of well-being. http://www.who.int/features/factfiles/mental_health/en/.

Investigating Patient Attitudes Towards the use of Social Media Data to Augment Depression Diagnosis and Treatment: a Qualitative Study

Jude Mikal
Minnesota Population Center
University of Minnesota
Minneapolis, MN, USA
jpmikal@umn.edu

Samantha Hurst
Family Medicine & Public Health
University of California San Diego
La Jolla, CA, USA
shurst@ucsd.edu

Mike Conway
Biomedical Informatics
University of Utah
Salt Lake City, UT, USA
mike.conway@utah.edu

Abstract

In this paper, we use qualitative research methods to investigate the attitudes of social media users towards the (opt-in) integration of social media data with routine mental health care and diagnosis. Our investigation was based on secondary analysis of a series of five focus groups with Twitter users, including three groups consisting of participants with a self-reported history of depression, and two groups consisting of participants without a self-reported history of depression. Our results indicate that, overall, research participants were enthusiastic about the possibility of using social media (in conjunction with automated Natural Language Processing algorithms) for mood tracking under the supervision of a mental health practitioner. However, for at least some participants, there was skepticism related to how well social media represents the mental health of users, and hence its usefulness in the clinical context.

1 Introduction

The widespread use of social media — including Twitter, Facebook, and online discussion forums such as Reddit — in combination with the maturation of technologies like Natural Language Processing (NLP) and Machine Learning has led to an increasing use of social media in population health research, with applications in infectious disease surveillance (e.g. Signorini et al. (2011); Collier et al. (2008); Freifeld et al. (2008)), understanding health behaviours and risk factors (e.g.

Hanson et al. (2013); Alvaro et al. (2015); Powell et al. (2016)), and investigating public attitudes towards health topics (e.g. Myslín et al. (2013); Oscar et al. (2017); Surian et al. (2016)). In addition to its proven utility for addressing research questions in population health, social media may also have considerable potential to enhance clinical care, particularly mental health care, by providing frequent, naturalistic, behavioural data that can be used by mental health practitioners to track moods and symptoms over time, allowing mental health clinicians to triangulate diagnoses and to better understand patient progress between appointments, hence improving quality of care.

In this paper, we use qualitative research methods to investigate the attitudes of social media users to the (opt-in) integration of social media data with routine mental health care and diagnosis. Our investigation was based on the secondary analysis of a series of five focus groups with Twitter users, conducted by author JM. Three of the groups were made up of participants with a diagnosed history of depression, and two of the groups were made up of participants without a diagnosed history of depression. These focus groups concentrated on ethical issues in utilising social media for population health monitoring (as reported in Mikal et al. (2016)), but also covered several related areas, including integrating automated analysis of social media data with routine mental health care. We presented Twitter users with the idea of allowing, with consent, mental health practitioners access to their patients' social media data in order to track mood over time, and ultimately improve care quality.

Our results indicate that, overall, research par-

Proceedings of the Fourth Workshop on Computational Linguistics and Clinical Psychology, pages 41–47,
Vancouver, Canada, August 3, 2017. © 2017 Association for Computational Linguistics

ticipants were enthusiastic about the possibility of using social media (in conjunction with automated NLP algorithms) for mood tracking in the context of a therapeutic relationship with a mental health practitioner. However, for at least some participants, there was skepticism related to how well social media represents the mental health of users.

2 Background

2.1 Public Mental Health Research & Social Media

Social media has become an increasingly important resource for population level mental health research (Conway and O'Connor, 2016) with data sources including Reddit (e.g. Chen et al. (2015)), Twitter (e.g. Coppersmith et al. (2014)), and Facebook (e.g. Park et al. (2014)). Applications have included investigating new mothers' experiences of postpartum depression (De Choudhury et al., 2014), analysing language patterns associated with schizophrenia (Mitchell et al., 2015), examining the role of age and gender in tweeting about mental illness (Preoţiuc-Pietro et al., 2015), and tracking suicide risk factors (Jashinsky et al., 2014). Focussing specifically on major depressive disorder — one of the most common forms of mental illness with a lifetime prevalence of 16.2% (Kessler et al., 2003) — has been work on using computational methods for detecting changes in degree of depression based on Facebook status updates (Schwartz et al., 2014), and using unsupervised Machine Learning techniques to explore depression-related language on Twitter (Resnik et al., 2015).

2.2 Combining Electronic Health Record Data with Social Media

There is little research on public attitudes towards combining social media with Electronic Health Record (EHR) data for research and clinical care. A notable exception is Padrez et al. (2015), who — in the context of a large, urban academic medical center in the United States — sought consent from 5256 "walk in" Emergency Room (ER) patients to link their social media (Facebook and Twitter) accounts with both their ER visit report, and their longitudinal EHR. Over one third of "walk-in" ER patients consented to this data linkage, indicating that at least for some social media users in some contexts, privacy concerns are not a barrier to linking EHR and social media data in the context of

research. However, the research was not explicitly focussed on mental health, and users may feel particularly sensitive regarding the use of their mental health data for research purposes.

3 Methods

Qualitative data used in this study is derived from a series of five focus groups conducted between March and April 2015 by author JM (reported in Mikal et al. (2016)), with the principal purpose of exploring the ethical implications of using Twitter for population-level mental health monitoring. We opted for the use of focus groups to encourage the spontaneous generation of ideas through group interaction. Focus groups are considered to be an ideal method for the exploration of new ideas, and have the additional benefit that — unlike standard interviews — they emphasise interactions between participants and de-emphasise the role of the interviewer (Kitzinger, 1995). The first two focus group interviews were conducted with individuals with no diagnosed history of depression, while the subsequent three were conducted with individuals with a diagnosed history of depression In total, 26 participants were recruited (average age: 26.9; age range: 18-54; 2:1 male:female ratio — see Table 1 for participant characteristics). Focus groups were conducted face-to-face, and lasted two hours each — as is typical for focus group studies (Kitzinger, 1995). Interactions were audio-recorded and transcribed using a professional, HIPAA-compliant[1] transcription service.

Each focus group began with participants introducing themselves. Control group participants stated their name (or pseudonym), age, occupation, and general Twitter use habits. Participants with depression also provided information on their depression history they were comfortable sharing: including diagnosis, medication, and therapy.

Qualitative coding was conducted manually (i.e. without the aid of qualitative analysis software like NVivo or ATLAS.ti) by author JM, then authors JM and MC met to discuss emergent themes. We used an inductive technique to allow themes to emerge from the data itself, guided by our research foci (Boeije, 2002).

---

[1] The Health Insurance Portability and Accountability Act (HIPAA) stipulates security standards for protected health information in the United States.

Table 1: Participant characteristics

Group	Age	Sex
FG1:Control	27	M
FG1:Control	22	M
FG1:Control	26	F
FG1:Control	19	M
FG1:Control	22	F
FG2:Control	29	M
FG2:Control	21	F
FG2:Control	21	F
FG2:Control	40	F
FG2:Control	24	M
FG3:Depression	29	M
FG3:Depression	20	M
FG3:Depression	29	M
FG3:Depression	54	M
FG4:Depression	42	M
FG4:Depression	21	F
FG4:Depression	23	M
FG4:Depression	33	M
FG5:Depression	20	F
FG5:Depression	18	M
FG5:Depression	30	M
FG5:Depression	22	M
FG5:Depression	22	M
FG5:Depression	21	M
FG5:Depression	24	F
FG5:Depression	31	M

4 Results

4.1 Therapeutic Utility of Social Media Data

The possibility of using social media data under the supervision of a qualified mental health practitioner met with marked enthusiasm and approval in our focus groups. Participants reported that their mood and state of mind fluctuated over time, and that social media data could provide a more accurate assessment of their emotional state. When presented with the idea, Laurence[2], a participant from one of our depression groups, had the following exchange with James, another participant:

> **Laurence**: I think that sounds great! Especially I think one of the common questions is like, "How long have you felt this way?" "I don't know. I don't know."
>
> **James:** Right, exactly. Forever.

[2]Note that all participant names are pseudonyms

Laurence: But if you could look at Twitter and just immediately [generate] a graph that shows mood swings over time. Absolutely!

Michael — a participant in a different depression group — similarly questioned his ability to accurately summarise his general state of mind between appointments, particularly if a significant amount of time had passed since his previous visit. When presented with the idea of having his mental health practitioner access his social media data, Michael says:

> I'm all for that, because I know like when I've gone to therapists or my doctor or whatever, like I'm not the best at reporting how I've been doing. Like when I'm actually in an appointment. Especially like to go see them for the first time. Or to see them after I haven't seen them for a while. Like that would be fantastic to have something else to either support what I think, or to actually say, "Hey, you actually are going through something right now, and you should probably get some help for that." Just because I'm not reliable about accurately assessing how I'm doing.

Overall, research participants appreciated the potential use of social media data to confirm or contradict self-assessments, or to provide concrete evidence of emotional ups and downs in their day-to-day lives that they may not be able to recall when speaking with a therapist. In addition to objective mood assessment, social media data may help practitioners to pick up on cues that may be lost or ignored in peer-flagging programs:

> **Joe**: Oh, I was just going to say– this probably makes me a bad person– but whenever I get the vague like "My life is terrible" Facebook posts, I just unfollow that person.
>
> **Lori**: Seriously. They just want the attention.
>
> **Sara**: I just wish there was an eye-roll button.

As summarized above, members of a peer network may not reach out in the instance of mental distress — or may block or choose to unfollow certain members of their peer groups because of the emotional ups and downs that may signify distress. Another advantage of algorithm-based social media analysis use in conjunction with a mental health practitioner is that algorithms and mental health providers may pay attention where the attention of peers may falter.

4.2 Social Media and Self Presentation

Results indicated that most participants felt as though their moods would be evident from their social media postings. For example when asked if his mental state would be evident from the data he generated on social media, Karl reported:

> Yeah. For sure ... like my senior year, like I would just tweet just because I wanted my friends to see it, and to know that I didn't feel good, or that I was upset or mad at someone. And I definitely remember like going to Twitter to complain about people, or complain about how I felt. Or complain about like my day, or just say that I feel like shit, you know? I think it would be very obvious, actually.

When asked if the tweets would create an *accurate* assessment of his mental state, Karl states:

> I think they would probably be a little exaggerated, honestly, if I was to like look through them now, I would probably be like embarrassed at some of the shit that I said on the internet. Just like not thinking that it could go where it could go almost. But at the time, when you're just like in that fog, and like can't make yourself get out of bed, or don't want to do anything. Like just kind of having somewhere to like just send your thoughts was nice.

Interestingly, while Karl indicates that the tweets might present an exaggerated depiction of his depression, the tweets came at a time when he felt he that he was in a fog and was unable to get out of bed: likely signs of depression. This conflicting account of his "exaggerated" tweets during a time he would likely identify as having been depressed - illustrates the point made above: that social media may provide a more objective account, or at least *another* account of his feelings during

this time that may be used to assess whether he was depressed or not.

Other focus group participants reported that not only were their own moods evident from social media posting, but that they could observe the moods of their own friends. For example, one of our focus group participants, Steve, worked in student affairs at a local university and said that during certain times of year it was possible to see an overall decline in student mood,

> If you look at a student's Facebook or Twitter, especially like during finals time, you see how stressed people are. You see people aren't sleeping. They aren't eating and all they're doing is studying. And their moods are just getting worse and worse on social media.

Another participant, Dave, from the same focus group, who worked as a student life peer advisor echoed this view. Dave says that looking at the activities friends post about on Twitter may help give insight into their current state of being:

> I mean you can tell when people are in certain moods on Twitter. Like if somebody was tweeting that they're watching a lot of Netflix and sitting around a lot – where they used to be outside or walking their dog, you can see a physical progression of the change through their Twitter. The cloud just gets darker as we progress in Twitter.

Additional information on sleep patterns, eating habits, and physical activity may provide helpful insights to mental health care providers to determine not only whether individuals are suffering from depression, but also whether the depression may be exacerbated by health-related behaviours.

Nevertheless, in discussing the accuracy of information shared on social media, the participants were mostly divided. For some, what they shared with a therapist in the context of a therapy session was more likely to be guarded or censored if they are not yet comfortable with the therapist. According to John:

> [On social media], it's like you're in your natural environment. If I'm ever going to talk to [a therapist] I'm going to talk to them differently than I normally am because I'm not going to feel

comfortable with them. But that's not
going to cross my mind if I want to
tweet something or if I want to Facebook something.

Conversely, some participants stated that they
were unlikely to post about the things that were
making them the most depressed. For them, social media data focuses on current events in their
own lives and across the world. When asked if she
thought her mood would be evident from her social media behaviour, Katy responds:

> No. Because I don't post super of-
> ten and even when I do it usually does
> not really reflect my mood. It's usually
> like news or reaction to some kind of
> other thing that I've seen online or like
> a picture of my cat. Any kind of psy-
> chologist would not be able to see what
> I'm actually feeling because that's not
> something that I feel the need to express
> online. How I'm feeling goes into my
> physical diary.

According to another participant, not all social
media accounts are created equal and what a therapist might surmise using her Twitter account data
is not the same as what a therapist might surmise
from her Facebook data. Cassie summarizes as
follows,

> [When posting on Facebook], it
> doesn't matter if I'm happy or sad. You
> can't see - there she got a scholarship
> or oh she didn't get a scholarship. You
> can't see that a credit card bill was late.
> You don't see any of the things that are
> bummers. It's all just like look at what
> I ate, this is where I was. But Twitter
> might be better – because my Twitter is
> more like when I do post on Twitter it's
> a little bit more expressive because it's
> just thoughts. So it's like oh I'm really
> bummed right now.

In light of this, when evaluating social media
data for evidence of depression or mental health
dysfunction, it may be important to ask individuals
who are seeking help both *whether* their accounts
would provide any useful insight into their state of
mind, and *which* account would provide the most

accurate assessment. In addition, it may be helpful to have individuals flag certain events that may
have triggered a depression episode.

Other concerns highlighted by participants centred on how often users posted and how accurately
they portrayed themselves. Individuals' Twitter
use varied from those who were occasional tweet-
ers, to individuals who maintained upwards of ten
Twitter profiles and tweeted multiple times per
day. According to one participant, Bob, the data
generated by more active users was more likely to
provide an accurate assessment of mental distress
than social media data generated by more passive
users. Bob says:

> Your accuracy level is very much
> going to depend on the activity of the
> user. For example, [...] if your psy-
> chiatrist or your therapist had access to
> your entire process, and they could see
> that you have an increased amount of
> depression Tweets during winter, imme-
> diately they can say, okay, "Well, pos-
> sible Seasonal Depressional Disorder."
> You know, based on that access. They
> look at mine, who the hell– I'm so all
> over Twitter, nobody's going to have any
> idea, because I'm not a regular user. So
> [I] think that's definitely going to have
> to play in.

Additionally, users reported that they were careful to manage their self-presentation on Twitter.
Sara, a stay at home parent, reported that she *only*
says positive things on Twitter. According to another participant, Sara's experiences may not be
the exception. For Karen, social media is about
explicitly presenting a persona (Goffman, 1971) -
and as such, would be of little help in diagnosing
mental distress. Karen says:

> Yeah, but like at the same time, I
> feel like people are really big on mak-
> ing themselves sound more interesting
> on social networks. Ever since social
> networks became huge I feel like peo-
> ple have this image. What's said be-
> tween like me and my therapist, that's
> like the full, raw details, but on the In-
> ternet I could just be like, "Oh, I went
> to this one show," and people will think
> I'm fine. But what I'm telling my thera-
> pist is, like, the exact opposite.

5 Limitations

This study has several limitations. First, the results are qualitative in nature, and based on the secondary analysis of focus group data, hence generalisability is limited. Second, our participants were all drawn from a relatively socially conservative region of the western United States. Third, our recruitment method relied on advertising on a local community Reddit site, and therefore our sample — like Reddit — skewed young and male (Pew Research Center, 2016).

6 Conclusions

In conclusion, we have explored two broad areas that have emerged from focus group discussions with respect to using automated analysis of social media data to enhance mental health care: *therapeutic utility of social media data* and *social media & self presentation*. Note that while there were some doubts expressed concerning the ability of NLP algorithms to successfully identify mental status from social media data (i.e. a technological limitation) most of the discussion around accuracy centred on questions of self-presentation in social media. Overall, participants were enthusiastic about the idea of opt-in utilisation of social media in the context of clinician-led mental health care, but at least for some participants, there was some skepticism related to how well social media represents the mental health of users.

Acknowledgments

We would like to thank Dr Daniel O'Connor (Wellcome Trust) for valuable feedback in the early stages of this research.

Research reported in this publication was supported the National Library of Medicine (United States National Institutes of Health) under award numbers K99LM011393 and R00LM011393. The content is solely the responsibility of the authors and does not necessarily represent the official views of the National Institutes of Health. Note that the real names of participants have been replaced by pseudonyms in order to protect participant anonymity.

Ethical Approval

The research reported in this paper was approved by the University of Utah Institutional Review Board [Ethics Committee] (#00077913).

References

Nestor Alvaro, Mike Conway, Son Doan, Christoph Lofi, John Overington, and Nigel Collier. 2015. Crowdsourcing Twitter annotations to identify first-hand experiences of prescription drug use. *J Biomed Inform* 58:280–7. https://doi.org/10.1016/j.jbi.2015.11.004.

Hennie Boeije. 2002. A purposeful approch to the constant comparitive method in the analysis of qualitative interviews. *Qual Quant* 36:391–409.

Annie T Chen, Shu-Hong Zhu, and Mike Conway. 2015. What online communities can tell us about electronic cigarettes and hookah use: A study using text mining and visualization techniques. *J Med Internet Res* 17(9):e220. https://doi.org/10.2196/jmir.4517.

Nigel Collier, Son Doan, Ai Kawazoe, Reiko Matsuda-Goodwin, Mike Conway, Yoshio Tateno, Quoc-Hung Ngo, Dinh Dien, Asanee Kawtrakul, Koichi Takeuchi, Mika Shigematsu, and Kiyosu Taniguichi. 2008. BioCaster: Detecting Public Health Rumors with a Web-based Text Mining System. *Bioinformatics* 24(24):2940–2941. https://doi.org/10.1093/bioinformatics/btn534.

Mike Conway and Daniel O'Connor. 2016. Social media, big data, and mental health: Current advances and ethical implications. *Current Opinion in Psychology* 9:77–82. https://doi.org/10.1016/j.copsyc.2016.01.004.

Glen Coppersmith, Mark Dredze, and Craig Harman. 2014. Quantifying mental health signals in Twitter. In *Proceedings of the Workshop on Computational Linguistics and Clinical Psychology: From Linguistic Signal to Clinical Reality*. Association for Computational Linguistics, Baltimore, Maryland, USA, pages 51–60. http://www.aclweb.org/anthology/W/W14/W14-3207.

Munmun De Choudhury, Scott Counts, Eric Horvitz, and Aaron Hoff. 2014. Characterizing and predicting postpartum depression from shared facebook data. In *Computer Supported Cooperative Work, CSCW '14, Baltimore, MD, USA, February 15-19, 2014*. ACM, pages 626–638. http://doi.acm.org/10.1145/2531602.2531675.

Clark C Freifeld, Kenneth D Mandl, Ben Y Reis, and John S Brownstein. 2008. Healthmap: global infectious disease monitoring through automated classification and visualization of internet media reports. *J Am Med Inform Assoc* 15(2):150–7. https://doi.org/10.1197/jamia.M2544.

Erving Goffman. 1971. *The presentation of self in everyday life*. A Pelican book. Penguin, Harmondsworth.

Carl L Hanson, Scott H Burton, Christophe Giraud-Carrier, Josh H West, Michael D Barnes, and Bret

Hansen. 2013. Tweaking and tweeting: exploring Twitter for nonmedical use of a psychostimulant drug (adderall) among college students. *J Med Internet Res* 15(4):e62.

Jared Jashinsky, Scott H Burton, Carl L Hanson, Josh West, Christophe Giraud-Carrier, Michael D Barnes, and Trenton Argyle. 2014. Tracking suicide risk factors through Twitter in the US. *Crisis* 35(1):51–9.

Ronald C Kessler, Patricia Berglund, Olga Demler, Robert Jin, Doreen Koretz, Kathleen R Merikangas, A John Rush, Ellen E Walters, Philip S Wang, and National Comorbidity Survey Replication. 2003. The epidemiology of major depressive disorder: results from the national comorbidity survey replication (NCS-R). *JAMA* 289(23):3095–105. https://doi.org/10.1001/jama.289.23.3095.

Jenny Kitzinger. 1995. Qualitative research. introducing focus groups. *BMJ* 311(7000):299–302.

Jude Mikal, Samantha Hurst, and Mike Conway. 2016. Ethical issues in using Twitter for population-level depression monitoring: a qualitative study. *BMC Med Ethics* 17:22. https://doi.org/10.1186/s12910-016-0105-5.

Margaret Mitchell, Kristy Hollingshead, and Glen Coppersmith. 2015. Quantifying the language of schizophrenia in social media. In *Proceedings of the 2nd Workshop on Computational Linguistics and Clinical Psychology: From Linguistic Signal to Clinical Reality*. Association for Computational Linguistics, Denver, Colorado, pages 11–20. http://www.aclweb.org/anthology/W15-1202.

Mark Myslín, Shu-Hong Zhu, Wendy Chapman, and Mike Conway. 2013. Using Twitter to examine smoking behavior and perceptions of emerging tobacco products. *J Med Internet Res* 15(8):e174.

Nels Oscar, Pamela A Fox, Racheal Croucher, Riana Wernick, Jessica Keune, and Karen Hooker. 2017. Machine learning, sentiment analysis, and tweets: An examination of Alzheimer's disease stigma on Twitter. *J Gerontol B Psychol Sci Soc Sci* https://doi.org/10.1093/geronb/gbx014.

Kevin A Padrez, Lyle Ungar, Hansen Andrew Schwartz, Robert J Smith, Shawndra Hill, Tadas Antanavicius, Dana M Brown, Patrick Crutchley, David A Asch, and Raina M Merchant. 2015. Linking social media and medical record data: a study of adults presenting to an academic, urban emergency department. *BMJ Quality & Safety* https://doi.org/10.1136/bmjqs-2015-004489.

Gregory Park, H. Andrew Schwartz, Johannes C Eichstaedt, Margaret L Kern, Michal Kosinski, David J Stillwell, Lyle H Ungar, and Martin E P Seligman. 2014. Automatic personality assessment through social media language. *Journal of Personality and Social Psychology* 108(6):934–952.

Pew Research Center. 2016. Nearly eight-in-ten Reddit users get news on the site. http://www.webcitation.org/6pQiU7EKp.

Gregory E Powell, Harry A Seifert, Tjark Reblin, Phil J Burstein, James Blowers, J Alan Menius, Jeffery L Painter, Michele Thomas, Carrie E Pierce, Harold W Rodriguez, John S Brownstein, Clark C Freifeld, Heidi G Bell, and Nabarun Dasgupta. 2016. Social media listening for routine post-marketing safety surveillance. *Drug Saf* 39(5):443–54. https://doi.org/10.1007/s40264-015-0385-6.

Daniel Preoţiuc-Pietro, Johannes Eichstaedt, Gregory Park, Maarten Sap, Laura Smith, Victoria Tobolsky, H. Andrew Schwartz, and Lyle Ungar. 2015. The role of personality, age, and gender in tweeting about mental illness. In *Proceedings of the 2nd Workshop on Computational Linguistics and Clinical Psychology: From Linguistic Signal to Clinical Reality*. Association for Computational Linguistics, Denver, Colorado, pages 21–30. http://www.aclweb.org/anthology/W15-1203.

Philip Resnik, William Armstrong, Leonardo Claudino, Thang Nguyen, Viet-An Nguyen, and Jordan Boyd-Graber. 2015. Beyond LDA: Exploring supervised topic modeling for depression-related language in Twitter. In *Proceedings of the 2nd Workshop on Computational Linguistics and Clinical Psychology: From Linguistic Signal to Clinical Reality*. Association for Computational Linguistics, Denver, Colorado, pages 99–107. http://www.aclweb.org/anthology/W15-1212.

H. Andrew Schwartz, Johannes Eichstaedt, Margaret L. Kern, Gregory Park, Maarten Sap, David Stillwell, Michal Kosinski, and Lyle Ungar. 2014. Towards assessing changes in degree of depression through Facebook. In *Proceedings of the Workshop on Computational Linguistics and Clinical Psychology: From Linguistic Signal to Clinical Reality*. Association for Computational Linguistics, Baltimore, Maryland, USA, pages 118–125. http://www.aclweb.org/anthology/W/W14/W14-3214.

Alessio Signorini, Alberto Maria Segre, and Philip M Polgreen. 2011. The use of Twitter to track levels of disease activity and public concern in the U.S. during the influenza A H1N1 pandemic. *PLoS One* 6(5):e19467. https://doi.org/10.1371/journal.pone.0019467.

Didi Surian, Dat Quoc Nguyen, Georgina Kennedy, Mark Johnson, Enrico Coiera, and Adam G Dunn. 2016. Characterizing Twitter discussions about HPV vaccines using topic modeling and community detection. *J Med Internet Res* 18(8):e232. https://doi.org/10.2196/jmir.6045.

Natural-language Interactive Narratives in Imaginal Exposure Therapy for Obsessive-Compulsive Disorder

Melissa Roemmele, Paola Mardo, and Andrew S. Gordon
Institute for Creative Technologies, University of Southern California
roemmele@ict.usc.edu, paolamardo@gmail.com, gordon@ict.usc.edu

Abstract

Obsessive-compulsive disorder (OCD) is an anxiety-based disorder that affects around 2.5% of the population. A common treatment for OCD is exposure therapy, where the patient repeatedly confronts a feared experience, which has the long-term effect of decreasing their anxiety. Some exposures consist of reading and writing stories about an imagined anxiety-provoking scenario. In this paper, we present a technology that enables patients to interactively contribute to exposure stories by supplying natural language input (typed or spoken) that advances a scenario. This interactivity could potentially increase the patient's sense of immersion in an exposure and contribute to its success. We introduce the NLP task behind processing inputs to predict new events in the scenario, and describe our initial approach. We then illustrate the future possibility of this work with an example of an exposure scenario authored with our application.

1 Introduction

Obsessive-compulsive disorder (OCD) is a debilitating anxiety condition characterized by recurrent, intrusive, and distressing thoughts (obsessions). A person may respond to these obsessions by engaging in repetitive behaviors (compulsions) aimed at reducing their anxiety. As with other anxiety disorders, the standard approach to OCD treatment, along with medication, is cognitive-behavioral therapy (Butler et al., 2006; Clark, 2006; Rothbaum et al., 2000). Specifically, therapists use exposure therapy to challenge patients to experience their obsession without performing any

compulsions (Foa and Kozak, 1986; Lindsay et al., 1997; Rowa et al., 2007). Initially, the exposure results in intense anxiety. But by repeating it over and over again, the anxiety decreases until eventually the patient can tolerate the feared thoughts in the absence of compulsions. Exposure therapy is used for treating many anxiety disorders, not just OCD (Abramowitz et al., 2011).

In many cases, compulsions are outwardly observable behaviors: hand washing in response to an obsession with contamination, for instance. In these cases, it is straightforward to apply exposure therapy to an action that evokes the obsessive thought: for instance, someone might touch a 'dirty' surface and try to resist the urge to wash their hands. In other cases, however, obsessions focus more on distressing imaginary scenarios that are not manifested in real life interactions. In this case, exposure therapy targets these thoughts through imaginal exposure, in which the patient is mentally immersed in the worst-case scenario they fear (Abramowitz, 1996; Foa et al., 1980). An example is Harm OCD (OCDLA, 2016a), where the patient has unwanted thoughts about causing injury to other people. An exposure for this might involve the patient imagining themselves actually following through with hurting someone. Often compulsions associated these these types of obsessions are more internal, like trying to avoid thinking about the feared outcome, checking for evidence that it happened, or constantly reassuring oneself that it won't happen (Gillihan et al., 2012; Wochner, 2012). Imaginal exposure challenges these mental compulsions.

There are different strategies for imaginal exposure, which also depend on the patient's progress in treatment, as exposures should gradually increase in intensity (Abramowitz and Arch, 2014; Jacofsky et al., 2014; Kircanski and Peris, 2015). To initiate the process, a therapist might ask the

Proceedings of the Fourth Workshop on Computational Linguistics and Clinical Psychology, pages 48–57,
Vancouver, Canada, August 3, 2017. © 2017 Association for Computational Linguistics

patient to read or watch media related to the patient's fears (e.g. for harm obsessions, this could be biographies of serial killers). Then the therapist might prompt the patient to imagine a feared scenario and describe out loud what they are sensing and feeling (Tompkins, 2016). Another technique is for the patient and therapist to write a story that vividly portrays the scenario from the patient's perspective (Gillihan et al., 2012; Kazantzis et al., 2005; Pedrick and Hyman, 2011; OCDLA, 2016b). Figure 1 shows an example story from the OCD Center of LA website[1]. Once the story is written, the patient reads it repeatedly on their own, typically multiple times per day. In line with the purpose of any exposure, the goal is to read it until it becomes less anxiety-provoking. Therapists often recommend reading it out loud, or the patient can even record themselves reading it and play back the audio.

Our paper focuses on this story-based approach to imaginal exposure for OCD. We propose a technology that potentially facilitates this approach through interactive versions of these stories. We make use of a general application, called the Data-driven Interactive Narrative Engine (DINE), where users are presented with stories that require their participation in order to advance the narrative. Users participate by providing natural language input, which is dynamically processed by the application to simulate new events in the scenario. By eliciting this input, the user becomes an agent in the story. When used for the purpose of imaginal exposure for OCD patients, a patient's choice of actions in the story lead to outcomes targeted by their obsessions. This paper is organized as follows: Section 2 provides some further background on OCD and the story-based approach to imaginal exposure therapy. Section 3 mentions some related work on incorporating technology into exposure therapy. In Section 4, we introduce the DINE system for interactive narrative. Section 5 presents the vision for conducting imaginal exposure through DINE experiences, illustrated with an example scenario. Finally, Section 6 briefly summarizes the future possibilities of this work.

2 OCD and Imaginal Exposure Stories

It is currently estimated that around 2.5% of the population is affected by OCD (Karno et al., 1988). However, OCD is frequently misdiagnosed

I am sitting on the sofa with my sister. Suddenly, I grab the scissors from the desk, and lunge them into my sister's right eye. My father grabs me and pries the scissors out of my hand, but the damage has already been done. My sister is blinded and unable to continue with her profession. I am arrested and convicted of attempted murder and gross mutilation, which carries a sentence of fifty years in state prison. My family cuts all ties with me, and my friends desert me. After forty years, I am paroled, but don't know a soul in the world. My dream of raising a family is no longer possible. I spend the rest of my life living with the fact that I destroyed my sisters art career. When I die, my soul is sent off to eternal damnation in hell.

Figure 1: Example of an imaginal exposure story for Harm OCD

by medical professionals (Glazier et al., 2015). While clinicians can often recognize some OCD obsessions like contamination, there is less awareness about other subtypes like Harm OCD mentioned above. Harm OCD falls under the larger category of what is often referred to as *Pure Obsessional OCD* (Pure-O) (Baer, 1994; OCDLA, 2016c), where obsessive thoughts may focus on acts the patient deems violent, sexually deviant, sacrilegious, or otherwise immoral. Patients with these obsessions may be incorrectly treated as aggressive and dangerous, making it even harder for them to get the right treatment (GroundWork, 2017). Moreover, there are many myths about OCD among society at large (Lopresti and Ryback, 2016), which are perpetuated by its inaccurate portrayal in the media (Schuster, 2015; Wahl, 2000). For instance, OCD is often mistaken with a preference for cleanliness or organization. In reality, patients do not find their OCD valuable or satisfying, as the symptoms can significantly interfere with job performance, relationships, and general well-being.

OCDLA (2016b) gives some general guidelines for maximizing the therapeutic impact of personal imaginal exposure stories. To summarize, they recommend that stories 1) are written in the first-person from the patient's perspective (e.g. "I stabbed my sister", rather than "She stabbed her sister"), 2) are written in the present tense, as if the patient is experiencing the events in this mo-

---

[1]ocdla.com/imaginal-exposure-ocd-anxiety-4847

ment, 3) depict a situation that actually provokes the patient's anxiety right now, not a previous concern, 4) depict a scenario that the patient actually imagines happening, not something entirely unbelievable, 5) directly portray the feared outcomes rather just working up to or alluding to them, and 6) portray the most extreme version of the obsessive thoughts, i.e. the patient's worst fear.

There are a few reasons why imaginal exposure stories are believed to be an effective therapeutic tool (Abramowitz et al., 2011). The simplest mechanism (and one that applies to exposure therapy in general) is that repeated exposure to any situation makes it less threatening, a general phenomenon known habituation. Moreover, exposure stories address thought-action fusion (Berle and Starcevic, 2005; Shafran et al., 1996), which is often observed in OCD patients. Thought-action fusion is the notion that thinking about an action is morally equivalent to performing that action (e.g. the patient imagining stabbing their sister is just as bad as actually stabbing her). A related phenomenon is magical thinking (Einstein and Menzies, 2004), the belief that thinking about an event makes it more likely to occur. By constantly re-reading the exposure story, the patient repeatedly thinks about the event and observes that it doesn't occur in real life, thus distinguishing the thought from the action. Additionally, many patients expect that reading the story will always be unbearably distressing. After multiple re-readings the patient observes that their distress becomes more tolerable, giving them more confidence that they can withstand the anxiety. OCDLA recommends reading the story until it actually seems more boring than scary.

3   Related Work

Lind et al. (2013) summarizes the existing work on the use of computers in OCD treatment, which has enabled patients to receive treatment in the absence of face-to-face interaction with therapists. Some of this research has started to explore technology-based approaches to exposure therapy. For instance, Kirkby et al. (2000) developed an interface that depicted an avatar with contamination obsessions, where patients could manipulate the avatar to touch dirt or wash its hands. They asked patients to guide the avatar through an exposure by directing it to dirty its hands without washing them. The interface showed an 'anxiety ther-

mometer' indicating the avatar's level of anxiety, which would go down as the patient repeatedly resisted washing. Kim et al. (2008) created a virtual reality scenario that prompted patients to engage in checking compulsions before leaving the house (e.g. making sure lights, stove burners, and faucets were turned off), and then investigated patients' behavior in this interaction as an assessment tool.

Virtual reality is now a well-recognized approach to exposure therapy for treating anxiety disorders in general. Krijn et al. (2004) and Powers and Emmelkamp (2008) broadly review this research and the evidence of its treatment efficacy. Virtual reality has specifically been used to develop exposure scenarios for phobias (Parsons and Rizzo, 2008, e.g.), social anxiety (Anderson et al., 2003, e.g.), panic disorder (Botella et al., 2007, e.g.), and posttraumatic stress disorder (PTSD) (Cukor et al., 2015, e.g.). For example, a virtual reality exposure for a patient with a phobia of spiders may visually depict spiders crawling on the patient's body without the patient being able to remove them. The interactivity afforded by virtual reality may lead to a stronger sense of immersion in the scenario and thus better treatment outcomes (Krijn et al., 2004). Our paper explores a way to incorporate interactivity in exposures that are evoked through language rather than visually.

4   Data-driven Interactive Narrative Engine

The Data-driven Interactive Narrative Engine[2] (DINE) is a web-based platform for interactive fiction. Interactive fiction is the digital equivalent of a Choose Your Own Adventure book (Packard, 1982), where readers are presented with a story and prompted to make choices that change the direction of the story. In DINE, users specify their choices through natural-language input (text or voice) and the system processes the input to select the next segment of the story. The goal of the system is to predict an outcome that fits coherently with the user's intent. This narrative prediction task is an emerging area of NLP research (Mostafazadeh et al., 2016).

DINE has a simple interface both for 'playing' interactive scenarios as well as authoring them. To author a story, the writer creates a sequence of *pages*. Each page consists of a *setup* and a list of potential *outcomes*. The text in the setup

---

[2]dine.ict.usc.edu

presents the user with a scenario and elicits an initial decision for what should happen next. Figure 2 shows an example DINE page, which is further detailed in the next section. The setup of this page is the initial three paragraphs opening with "It's 9pm. I'm just now leaving my office for the day...". The text of each outcome continues the story and prompts the user to specify further actions leading to new outcomes. In Figure 2, each italicized passage after the setup is an outcome. For each outcome they define, authors can provide a list of example inputs that should trigger that outcome, where each input typically consists of a single sentence. The bolded sentences under the outcomes in Figure 2 are examples of potential user inputs. An author can also link an outcome to a new page so that when that the user sees that outcome, they are sent to another page with a whole new setup and outcome list. For instance, the outcome that appears last on the page in Figure 2 ("As I drive home...") routes to the second page shown in Figure 3. Alternatively, authors can specify that a particular outcome should end the scenario, as with the last outcome ("The police take me away...") in Figure 3. The advantage of DINE from an authoring perspective is that it requires no technical knowledge of the underlying model for matching user inputs to outcomes, so authors can focus on the writing task itself.

There is ongoing research on exploring different approaches for automatically predicting the most appropriate outcome for users' natural-language input on a given DINE page. The current work uses a straightforward unsupervised approach that measures lexical similarity between an input and an outcome. It relies on word2vec embeddings (Mikolov et al., 2013), which represent words as n-dimensional vectors of real values. The principle behind word embeddings is that words with similar meanings will have similar embedding values. Accordingly, the similarity between two words can be computed as the cosine similarity between their vectors. We use embeddings trained on the 100-billion word Google News dataset[3]. We compute the overall similarity between each word $w1$ in the user input in and each word $w2$ in an outcome out, to score the likelihood that out

should result from in:

$$Sim(in, out) = \frac{\sum_{w1 \in in} \max_{w2 \in out} sim(w1, w2)}{length(in)}$$

$$(1)$$

where sim is vector cosine similarity. We call this calculation Average Maximum Similarity, as an alternative to just computing the average similarity between all words in the input and outcome. Instead, for each word in the input we find its most similar word in the outcome and then average these maximum similarity scores across the input. The motivation behind this is that it gives high weight to keyword similarity, i.e. words that are the same or almost the same appearing in both the input and outcome.

When example inputs for an outcome are provided by the author, this same similarity measure can be applied to compute $Sim(in, ex)$ between a user input in and an example input ex. The scores for an outcome's example inputs $exins$ can be combined with the score for the outcome itself so that the overall score for out is:

$$\max_{ex \in exins} (Sim(in, ex), Sim(in, out)) \quad (2)$$

In other words, for a given user input, the score for an outcome is whichever sequence has the highest similarity to the input, either one of the example inputs or the outcome text itself. Outcomes for a given input are ranked by score so that the outcome with the highest score is the top prediction. Since outcomes can consist of several sentences, an initial evaluation showed that scoring outcomes based only on their first ten words produced the highest accuracy. The same is done for example inputs, though these are often less than ten words long.

Each time the user provides input, the system responds with the highest-scoring outcome and proceeds to a subsequent DINE page if the author has made an explicit link. However, if no link has been provided, the user is prompted for an additional input on the same DINE page. In these cases, the system will respond with the highest-scoring outcome that has not already been presented to the user. This design allows authors to create DINE pages where users can try several actions within a single narrative context, where only a few might actually advance the story context to subsequent DINE pages. In our initial evaluations of DINE outcome-prediction accuracy, we found that accuracy on gold-standard annotations

---

[3]code.google.com/archive/p/word2vec

of user input varied widely based on writing of the page setup and the order-dependance of outcomes. In the current work, we modeled our pages after previously-successful designs.

All of the narrative content presented to users of DINE are static compositions of a human author, rather than generated algorithmically. This affords several options of digital media for content presentations, including audio, video, or virtual reality scenes. In the current work, we authored the same narrative content both as text and as produced audio files, one file for each page setup and outcome, delivered over the web using the standard Web Audio API. When using produced audio files, DINE accepts voice input from users by capitalizing on the high-accuracy cloud-based speech recognition capability[4] built into recent versions of Google's Chrome web browser. All speech input is converted to text within the system, so the underlying prediction approach is exactly the same. Audio output and speech input allows for a hands-free interactive experience, creating an aural performance that can be recorded at run-time in which the users themselves are part-narrators of the story.

5   An Imaginal Exposure Story in DINE

To demonstrate how DINE can be used for imaginal exposure, we authored an example story[5], shown in Figures 2 and 3. This example focuses on a hit-and-run scenario, which is a common obsession related to Harm OCD (Seay, 2016). Each figure depicts one page of the scenario. To summarize, the first page (titled *Driving Home*) places the patient in a situation where they are driving home from work and they suddenly suspect they hit something. In the second page (*Almost Home*), the patient returns to the scene a second time where it now appears to be a crime scene. The story is written in the first person and the present tense, consistent with the recommendations described in Section 2.

The italicized text under the title of each page is the setup, which prompts the patient for an initial input. Each subsequent passage of italicized text is an outcome that is triggered by the patient's input. For each outcome we show in bold three example inputs that would have produced that outcome. In both pages, the scenario prompts the patient to specify actions that reassure themselves that nothing bad happened, since this reassurance-seeking is a common OCD compulsion. The story captures some of the accompanying features of OCD: for instance, the patient's anxiety symptoms (e.g. nausea, sweating, difficulty breathing) as well as the patient's awareness that their desire for certainty is an interference (e.g. "I should just go home"). The second page shows that in spite of the patient's attempts to be sure, however, something bad has actually happened. Eventually it is revealed that they hit and killed someone, and the story ends with the patient suffering the consequences of this mistake, just as in the Figure 1 example story.

The interaction is driven by references to potential actions that the patient could pursue. For instance, the premise of the first page says "I should get out and check", suggesting that the patient's input could act on this thought. This initiates a sequence of outcomes where each suggests another information-seeking action. Alternatively, on both pages the patient may specify to drive home instead of performing the hinted actions, but the story has the same doomed ending regardless. As such, the interaction will always terminate with the last outcome in Figure 3, despite any previous incorrectly predicted outcomes. Unlike a Choose Your Own Adventure book, there is no option to change the final trajectory of the story, because the objective is to expose the patient to their ultimate fear depicted by the ending. Thus the interactivity in this example serves not so much to allow the patient to explore different outcomes, but to enable them to initiate outcomes as if they are causing them to occur. There is some evidence from virtual reality research that this sense of immersion and control may increase the intensity of exposures and therefore increase their efficacy (Price and Anderson, 2007; Walshe et al., 2003).

As mentioned in Section 2, therapists often suggest that the patient listen to themselves reading their exposure story. The voice-based audio interaction enabled by DINE is well-suited for this purpose, allowing the recording of a patient interaction at run-time, where the patient is the part-narrator of the story. To support this use case, we produced audio clips corresponding to each setup and outcome in the hit-and-run scenario, and deployed them on the web for use with DINE's interactive audio option. Both the text and audio versions of the hit-and-run scenario are available through the site.

---

[4]cloud.google.com/speech

[5]dine.ict.usc.edu/drivinghome.html

Driving Home

It's 9pm. I'm just now leaving my office for the day. It's pitch black outside, I never get out this late. I have an uneasy feeling as I unlock my car and get inside.

Shifting into reverse, I look behind me. The lot seems completely empty. But it's really dark and I can't be sure. I feel a lump rising in my throat.

I drive out of the lot onto the street. Soon I pass my son's elementary school. I told my husband I'd be home to help with bedtime. The streetlights are far too dim. Just as I turn the radio on to try to relax, I hear a thud underneath my car. I immediately hit my brakes. What was that? A pit forms in my stomach. I should get out and check. But I really need to get home.

> **I get out of the car. // I go outside to check. // I step outside to look around.**

It's silent out here except for the distant sound of a barking dog. I take a deep breath, trying to stay calm. I know I heard something, but it's too dark to see. I search my jacket for my cell phone.

> **I turn on the phone flashlight. // I use the light on my cell phone. // I open my flashlight app.**

I shine my phone flashlight on the front of the car. The only mark I see is from where my son accidentally hit it with a baseball a few years ago. But then I notice a thin trail of liquid emerging from under the car.

> **I look under the car. // I check where it's coming from. // I bend down to examine the liquid.**

Looking under the car, I see there's something slowly dripping from its underbody. An oil leak, probably. I'll need to get that checked out tomorrow. Maybe the noise was something in the engine. But it really sounded like it came from outside the car. I can see something shadowy near the back bumper, but my flashlight doesn't reach that far.

> **I walk around to the back of the car. // I go look at the shadow. // I check the back bumper.**

But the shadow is just from the trailer hitch we mounted when we went on vacation last month. I stare out into the street. I could walk down a little further to check. But this is crazy, it's getting so late. It's time to drive home.

> **I go further down the street. // I walk over there. // I go down to check.**

I walk further back, where there's a little bit of light from the streetlamp. I turn in all directions, my teeth clenched. My heart jumps when I notice a dark lump lying against the curb on my left. I feel like I'm losing my mind. I just want to go see my family.

> **I examine the lump. // I walk to the curb to find out what it is. // I go look at it.**

My legs shaking, I touch my feet to the dark object. It's soft and covered in what feels like plastic. It's a trash bag. For goodness sake. I sigh, wondering if there was even a noise to begin with or I just hallucinated it. I take one final glance around. There's nothing out here.

> **I get back in the car. // I go home. // I decide to drive home.**

As I drive home, I reassure myself: I checked. Nothing was there. I would've seen it if I had hit something. But my mind is still spinning. I wonder if I should turn back to check one more time.

As I drive back, I hear sirens approaching. The place I stopped earlier is no longer an empty street. A dozen police cars with flashing lights are parked in the middle of the road. I see the officers all huddled together in one spot, and a wave of nausea hits me. But this obviously has nothing to do with me. The best thing to do is not worry about it and go home. I told my son I'd be there to say goodnight.

(Continued →)

Figure 2: Page 1 of an DINE interaction for a hit-and-run scenario

Almost Home

I see the neighbors coming out onto their lawn. If I could just quickly find out what happened, I wouldn't have to spend the rest of the night in doubt.

> I approach the neighbors. // I walk up to the people on the lawn. // I go talk to them.

I walk toward the growing crowd on the lawn. We're several houses down from the swarm of activity, but they're putting up a wide perimeter of yellow caution tape to keep us from getting closer. Sweat starts to drip off my forehead. When I reach the lawn, I ask the neighbors what happened. No one responds. I wonder if they heard me.

> I ask again. // I repeat my question. // I ask louder if anyone knows what happened.

One woman finally acknowledges me and says "Not sure. They won't tell us." My stomach lurches when I see an ambulance arrive. I desperately want to run away, but I know I won't be able to stop thinking about this when I get home. I can walk a bit further before reaching the caution tape. I need to figure out what this is.

> I walk closer. // I approach the caution tape. // I move towards the officers.

As I move closer, I overhear a neighbor telling another: "We didn't think much of it, but then our dog was barking like crazy. Once we heard the sirens we came outside. The officers interviewed us." I stop and turn back toward the man. My throat is closing up. I have to know what he told the police.

> I ask the man what he saw. // I ask him what he told the police. // I find out what the man knows.

The man looks at me, surprised at my intrusion in the conversation. "My wife and I woke up to a thud noise. We didn't look outside. But the way the officers were talking, it sounds like someone got hit by a car." There's a punch to my gut and I gasp. I know this is just a terrible coincidence. Nothing was there when I drove away. No one. I need to go home, this isn't my business. I'll find out tomorrow what happened.

The man is looking at me suspiciously now. He asks if I live nearby.

> I tell the man no. // I lie and say yes. // I tell him I was just driving by.

Just as I answer him, I see it. The coroner's van. I fall to the ground, unable to breathe. My vision goes blurry. I can see the black body bag being lifted into the van. I shake my head vigorously and pull at my hair, willing myself to wake up from this terrible nightmare. It doesn't work. My only escape option is to go home.

> I walk back to my car and go home. // I leave and drive home. // I go back my car.

When I pull into my driveway the officers are talking to my husband on the porch. His face is pale and contorted. My son is standing behind him in the doorway, and when he sees me he starts to cry. I go to hug him but the officers block my way.

For a moment I consider running away, but I know it's useless. I have no idea how they got here, or how they knew it was me, but it doesn't matter. I've tried my whole life to deny my reckless nature. I've always known that my own negligence and indifference would get someone killed one day. I pretended all I had to do was be careful, but I was lying to myself. For the sake of my family, I know I just need to confess so they know this is the real me, and they can move on with their lives. It's only fair to them.

> I admit that I ran someone over. // I confess. // I tell them I killed that person.

*The police take me away. I am sentenced to life in prison for hit-and-run murder. My husband tells me I will never see him or my son again. I spend each day hoping they'll change their minds, but they never come. I live the rest of my life regretting my unforgivable mistake. (**End**)*

Figure 3: Page 2 of an DINE interaction for a hit-and-run scenario

6 Conclusion

This paper explores of the use of NLP technologies in computer-based treatments of obsessive-compulsive disorder, creating interactive narratives for use in imaginal exposure therapy. This work is also applicable to other anxiety disorders, but it is particularly motivated by the story-based imaginal exposures used in OCD treatment. We present one example of an interactive imaginal exposure story as a way of demonstrating our vision. Because our initial goal is to start a discussion about the possible benefits of this type of interaction, we have not yet examined any user interactions with our example scenario. If evaluated in a clinical setting, each DINE scenario would clearly need to address the patient's specific symptoms and background. Moreover, our example showed just one design for eliciting user inputs (e.g. information seeking to alleviate fear), but therapists may envision alternative designs that better target specific objectives for exposure therapy. For example, the inputs could specify actually performing the feared actions, i.e. the patient might say "I hit the person with my car". One possibility is that DINE scenarios could be authored by therapists as a way of introducing imaginal exposure to patients, since the authoring requires no programming or technical knowledge. These interactions could orient patients toward eventually writing their own personalized exposure stories.

7 Acknowledgments

The projects or efforts depicted were or are sponsored by the U. S. Army. The content or information presented does not necessarily reflect the position or the policy of the Government, and no official endorsement should be inferred.

References

Jonathan S. Abramowitz. 1996. Variants of exposure and response prevention in the treatment of obsessive-compulsive disorder: A meta-analysis. *Behavior Therapy* 27(4):583 – 600.

Jonathan S. Abramowitz and Joanna J. Arch. 2014. Strategies for improving long-term outcomes in cognitive behavioral therapy for obsessive-compulsive disorder: Insights from learning theory. *Cognitive and Behavioral Practice* 21(1):20–31.

Jonathan S. Abramowitz, Brett J. Deacon, and Stephen P. H. Whiteside. 2011. *Exposure therapy for anxiety: Principles and practice.*. Guilford Press, New York, NY, US.

Page Anderson, Barbara O. Rothbaum, and Larry F. Hodges. 2003. Virtual reality exposure in the treatment of social anxiety. *Cognitive and Behavioral Practice* 10(3):240 – 247.

Lee Baer. 1994. Factor analysis of symptom subtypes of obsessive compulsive disorder and their relation to personality and tic disorders. *Journal of Clinical Psychiatry* 55:Suppl 18–23.

David Berle and Vladan Starcevic. 2005. Thought–action fusion: Review of the literature and future directions. *Clinical Psychology Review* 25(3):263–284.

C. Botella, A. García-Palacios, H. Villa, R. M. Baños, S. Quero, M. Alcañiz, and G. Riva. 2007. Virtual reality exposure in the treatment of panic disorder and agoraphobia: A controlled study. *Clinical Psychology & Psychotherapy* 14(3):164–175.

Andrew C. Butler, Jason E. Chapman, Evan M. Forman, and Aaron T. Beck. 2006. The empirical status of cognitive-behavioral therapy: A review of meta-analyses. *Clinical Psychology Review* 26(1):17 – 31.

David A. Clark. 2006. *Cognitive-behavioral therapy for OCD*. The Guilford Press.

Judith Cukor, Maryrose Gerardi, Stephanie Alley, Christopher Reist, Michael Roy, Barbara O. Rothbaum, JoAnn Difede, and Albert Rizzo. 2015. *Virtual Reality Exposure Therapy for Combat-Related PTSD*, Springer International Publishing.

Danielle A. Einstein and Ross G. Menzies. 2004. The presence of magical thinking in obsessive compulsive disorder. *Behaviour Research and Therapy* 42(5):539 – 549.

Edna B. Foa and Michael J. Kozak. 1986. Emotional processing of fear: Exposure to corrective information. *Psychological Bulletin* 99(1):20–35.

Edna B. Foa, Gail Steketee, Ralph M. Turner, and Steven C. Fischer. 1980. Effects of imaginal exposure to feared disasters in obsessive-compulsive checkers. *Behaviour Research and Therapy* 18(5):449 – 455.

Seth J. Gillihan, Monnica T. Williams, Emily Malcoun, Elna Yadin, and Edna B. Foa. 2012. Common pitfalls in exposure and response prevention (EX/RP) for OCD. *Journal of Obsessive-Compulsive and Related Disorders* 1(4):251 – 257.

Kimberly Glazier, Matt Swing, and Lata K. McGinn. 2015. Half of obsessive-compulsive disorder cases misdiagnosed: vignette-based survey of primary care physicians. *Journal of Clinical Psychiatry* 76(6):e761–7.

GroundWork. 2017. The Center for Anxiety and OCD - GroundWork Counseling: OCD - misunderstood and misdiagnosed. https://www.groundworkcounseling.com/ocd/ocd-misunderstood-and-misdiagnosed-orlando-ocd-therapist-raises-awareness-ocdweek/.

Matthew D. Jacofsky, Melanie T. Santos, Sony Khemlani-Patel, and Fugen Neziroglu. 2014. Exposure and response prevention (ERP) therapy for obsessive-compulsive and related disorders. https://www.mentalhelp.net/articles/exposure-and-response-prevention-erp-therapy-for-obsessive-compulsive-and-related-disorders/.

Marvin Karno, Jacqueline M. Golding, Susan B. Sorenson, and M. Audrey Burnam. 1988. The epidemiology of obsessive-compulsive disorder in five us communities. *Archives of General Psychiatry* 45(12):1094–1099.

Nikolaos Kazantzis, Frank P. Deane, Kevin R Ronan, and Luciano L'Abate. 2005. *Using homework assignments in cognitive behavior therapy*. Routledge.

Kwanguk Kim, Chan-Hyung Kim, Kyung Ryeol Cha, Junyoung Park, Kiwan Han, Yun Ki Kim, Jae-Jin Kim, In Young Kim, and Sun I. Kim. 2008. Anxiety provocation and measurement using virtual reality in patients with obsessive-compulsive disorder. *CyberPsychology & Behavior* 11(6):637–641.

Katharina Kircanski and Tara S. Peris. 2015. Exposure and Response Prevention Process Predicts Treatment Outcome in Youth with OCD. *Journal of Abnormal Child Psychology* 43(3):543–552.

K.C. Kirkby, G.E. Berrios, B.A. Daniels, R.G. Menzies, A. Clark, and A. Romano. 2000. Process-outcome analysis in computer-aided treatment of obsessive-compulsive disorder. *Comprehensive Psychiatry* 41(4):259 – 265.

M. Krijn, P. M. G. Emmelkamp, R. P. Olafsson, and R. Biemond. 2004. Virtual reality exposure therapy of anxiety disorders: A review. *Clinical Psychology Review* 24(3):259 – 281.

Christian Lind, Mark J. Boschen, and Shirley Morrissey. 2013. Technological advances in psychotherapy: Implications for the assessment and treatment of obsessive compulsive disorder. *Journal of Anxiety Disorders* 27(1):47 – 55.

M. Lindsay, R. Crino, and G. Andrews. 1997. Controlled trial of exposure and response prevention in obsessive-compulsive disorder. *The British Journal of Psychiatry* 171(2):135–139.

Courtney Lopresti and Ralph Ryback. 2016. 4 myths about OCD. https://www.psychologytoday.com/blog/the-truisms-wellness/201605/4-myths-about-ocd.

Tomas Mikolov, Ilya Sutskever, Kai Chen, Greg Corrado, and Jeffrey Dean. 2013. Distributed representations of words and phrases and their compositionality. In *Proceedings of the 26th International Conference on Neural Information Processing Systems*. Curran Associates Inc., USA, NIPS'13, pages 3111–3119.

Nasrin Mostafazadeh, Nathanael Chambers, Xiaodong He, Devi Parikh, Dhruv Batra, Lucy Vanderwende, Pushmeet Kohli, and James Allen. 2016. A corpus and cloze evaluation for deeper understanding of commonsense stories. In *Proceedings of NAACL-HLT*. pages 839–849.

OCDLA. 2016a. OCD Center of LA: Harm OCD: Symptoms and treatment. http://ocdla.com/harm-ocd-1-1982.

OCDLA. 2016b. OCD Center of LA: Imaginal exposure for OCD and anxiety. http://ocdla.com/imaginal-exposure-ocd-anxiety-4847.

OCDLA. 2016c. Ocd center of la: Pure Obsessional OCD (Pure O) symptoms and treatment. http://ocdla.com/obsessionalocd.

Edward Packard. 1982. *Cave of Time (Choose Your Own Adventure #1)*. Bantam.

Thomas D. Parsons and Albert A. Rizzo. 2008. Affective outcomes of virtual reality exposure therapy for anxiety and specific phobias: A meta-analysis. *Journal of Behavior Therapy and Experimental Psychiatry* 39(3):250 – 261.

Cherlene Pedrick and Bruce M. Hyman. 2011. *Obsessive-Compulsive Disorder*. Twenty-First Century Books.

Mark B. Powers and Paul M.G. Emmelkamp. 2008. Virtual reality exposure therapy for anxiety disorders: A meta-analysis. *Journal of Anxiety Disorders* 22(3):561 – 569.

Matthew Price and Page Anderson. 2007. The role of presence in virtual reality exposure therapy. *Journal of Anxiety Disorders* 21(5):742–751.

Barbara Olasov Rothbaum, Elizabeth A. Meadows, Patricia Resick, and David W. Foy. 2000. Cognitive-behavioral therapy. In E. B. Foa, T. M. Keane, and M. J. Friedman, editors, *Effective treatments for PTSD: Practice guidelines from the International Society for Traumatic Stress Studies*, Guilford Press, New York, NY, US, pages 320–325.

Karen Rowa, Martin M. Antony, and Richard P. Swinson. 2007. *Exposure and Response Prevention.*. American Psychological Association, Washington, DC, US.

Sarah Schuster. 2015. 5 times the internet got OCD wrong and why it matters. https://themighty.com/2015/08/how-the-internet-misunderstood-obsessive-compulsive-disorder/.

Steve Seay. 2016. Hit-and-run OCD vs. other driving fears. http://www.steveseay.com/hit-and-run-ocd-vs-other-driving-fears/.

Roz Shafran, Dana S. Thordarson, and S. Rachman. 1996. Thought-action fusion in obsessive compulsive disorder. *Journal of Anxiety Disorders* 10(5):379 – 391.

Michael A. Tompkins. 2016. San Francisco Bay Area Center for Cognitive Therapy: Nuts and bolts of imaginal exposure. https://sfbacct.com/from-ocd-to-anxiety/nuts-and-bolts-of-imaginal-exposure/.

Otto F. Wahl. 2000. Obsessive-compulsive disorder in popular magazines. *Community Mental Health* 36(3):307–312.

David G. Walshe, Elizabeth J. Lewis, Sun I. Kim, Kathleen O'Sullivan, and Brenda K. Wiederhold. 2003. Exploring the use of computer games and virtual reality in exposure therapy for fear of driving following a motor vehicle accident. *CyberPsychology & Behavior* 6(3):329–334.

Stacey K. Wochner. 2012. Pure Obsessional OCD - symptoms and treatment. *Social Work Today* 12(4):22.

Detecting anxiety on Reddit

Judy Hanwen Shen
University of Toronto
Toronto, Canada
judyhanwen.shen@mail.utoronto.ca

Frank Rudzicz
Toronto Rehabilitation Institute-UHN
University of Toronto
Toronto, Canada
frank@spoclab.com

Abstract

Previous investigations into detecting mental illnesses through social media have predominately focused on detecting depression through Twitter corpora (De Choudhury et al., 2013; Resnik et al., 2015; Pedersen, 2015). In this paper, we study anxiety disorders through personal narratives collected through the popular social media website, Reddit. We build a substantial data set of typical and anxiety-related posts, and we apply N-gram language modeling, vector embeddings, topic analysis, and emotional norms to generate features that accurately classify posts related to binary levels of anxiety. We achieve an accuracy of 91% with vector-space word embeddings, and an accuracy of 98% when combined with lexicon-based features.

1 Introduction

Anxiety disorders include a family of conditions characterized by excessive fear, emotional responses to real or perceived threats, and worry in anticipation of future threats. Common forms of anxiety include generalized anxiety, social anxiety, health anxiety, and panic attacks (American Psychiatric Association, 2013). The World Health Organization estimates the 12-month prevalence of anxiety disorders to be 26.4% in the United States (Demyttenaere et al., 2004). In adolescents aged 13-18, anxiety disorders are the most common condition with a lifetime prevalence of 31.9% for all anxiety disorders and 8.9% for severe anxiety disorders (Merikangas et al., 2010).

Anxiety disorders are primarily diagnosed by physicians or psychologists, but 77% of counties in the United States have a severe shortage of psychiatrists and non-prescribing mental health providers such as psychiatric nurses, social workers, licensed professionals, counselors, and marriage and family therapists (Thomas et al., 2009). Given the high prevalence of these disorders, and the shortage of relevant mental health professionals, there is an urgent need for mental health detection tools that are scalable to large populations, and that can be made widely accessible. In particular, the high prevalence of anxiety disorders in adolescents motivates building these screening tools on emerging social media and communication platforms.

2 Background

Social media has become an increasingly popular data source for detecting mental illnesses through text. For example, De Choudhury et al. (2013) built a corpus of more than 2 million Twitter posts, including a 'depression' class with tweets from 476 highly active users self-identified as clinically diagnosed with depression. To identify depression, they used feature vectors that included engagement with the Twitter platform, the social graph of user Twitter activity, emotional and linguistic style using Linguistic Inquiry and Word Count (LIWC) (Pennebaker et al., 2015) and a depression lexicon including antidepressant names. De Choudhury et al. (2013) used a mix of text features and metadata features and achieved 70% accuracy in predicting depression in tweets. Another major data set of tweets labelled for depression was generated by Coppersmith et al. (2015), and contained 3 million tweets from about 2000 Twitter users, including 600 self-identified clinically depressed users. From this data set, Nadeem (2016) achieved 86% accuracy with a naïve Bayes unigram classifier. Resnik et al. (2015) used the same data set with latent Dirichlet allocation

Proceedings of the Fourth Workshop on Computational Linguistics and Clinical Psychology, pages 58–65,
Vancouver, Canada, August 3, 2017. © 2017 Association for Computational Linguistics

(LDA) and supervised LDA techniques to predict the likelihood of target classes based on topics. Their supervised LDA techniques included the associated labels of documents as priors for topic modeling. This approach modified an unsupervised learning method and achieved a precision of 0.648 at a recall of 0.5. Preotiuc-Pietro et al. (2015) also participated in the shared task and applied a range methods including: LDA, word vector embeddings, GloVe vector embeddings, and unigrams in order to generate word clusters and then feature vectors based on said word clusters. The same data set has also been used to identify patients with post-traumatic stress disorder (PTSD) in social media in the Coppersmith shared task (Coppersmith et al., 2015). Using this data set, Pedersen (2015) used lexical decision lists with N-grams (N between 1 and 6) and achieved a classification accuracy of 74.2% in classifying tweets from people with PTSD.

While Twitter data are available in large volumes, tweets are limited in length and can restrict the potential for contextual processing. By contrast, LiveJournal is a platform for people to discuss common interests, and has also been studied to identify community posts by people with depression. Nguyen et al. (2014) found that affective word features from the Affective Norms for English Words (ANEW) and mood tags posted by users gave lower coverage than LIWC features and LDA Topic modeling. Using LIWC and LDA as features for classification, they achieved 93% accuracy.

Psychopathology researchers have investigated social anxiety in the context of social media. For example, Fernandez et al. (2012) studied profile information and usage patterns of Facebook users. They concluded that social anxiety was significantly negatively correlated with the number of Facebook friends and positively correlated with the number of completed sections of a Facebook profile.

Similar to LiveJournal and Facebook, Reddit offers relatively rich bodies of text from users in the context of self-assembled communities. Reddit is a social website for news aggregation, content rating, and discussion. Reddit allows posts up to 40,000 characters per comment, compared to the 140-character limit of Twitter. Each month, 234 million unique users contribute 75.15 million posts and 725.85 comments to the site [1]. The website contains more than 1 million subpages, called subreddits, each focusing on its own topic, many of which involve sharing personal stories and experiences in order to seek or give advice. The subreddits concerning depression and anxiety both involve over 100,000 community members [2]. De Choudhury and De (2014) studied mental health disclosure on Reddit and concluded that users share their experiences and challenges with mental illnesses as well as the impacts of their illnesses on their work, lives, and relationships. They also found that users use the platform not only for self-expression, but also for seeking diagnosis and treatment information for their conditions. Kumar et al. (2015) studied the r/SuicideWatch community on Reddit after celebrity suicides and found increased posting activity and increased suicidal ideation in post content, by using linguistic measures, N-gram comparison, and topic modeling.

Previous success in detecting depression on social media, combined with the previous qualitative research in anxiety on social media, suggest that there is potential for detecting anxiety and anxious behavior on social media. In this paper, we make the first attempt to detect anxiety-related posts from Reddit using various linguistic features. Specifically, we investigate the effectiveness of vector-space representations and LDA features, compared to LIWC and N-gram models, in distinguishing anxiety-related texts from more typical texts.

3 Data Collection

The extensive Reddit API allows direct access to posts by subreddit. For this experiment, we collected 22,808 posts on Reddit over 3 months. These posts include 9971 anxiety-related posts ('Anxiety') and 12,837 general posts ('Control'). The Anxiety posts are predominantly collected from r/anxiety; three other anxiety-related subreddits, including r/panicparty, r/healthanxiety, and r/socialanxiety, are also mined for posts for the Anxiety class. Since the anxiety-related posts are overwhelmingly from a first-person point-of-view, we also collected posts for the Control class from a variety of different subreddits

---

[1] about.reddit.com (2017)

[2] reddit.com/r/depression, reddit.com/r/anxiety (2017)

anxiety subreddits	control subreddits	
r/anxiety	r/askscience	r/relationships
r/healthanxiety	r/writingprompts	r/teaching
r/socialanxiety	r/writing	r/parenting
r/panicparty	r/atheism	r/christianity
	r/showerthoughts	r/jokes
	r/lifeprotips	r/writing
	r/personalfinance	r/talesfromretail
	r/theoryofreddit	r/talesfromtechsupport
	r/randomkindness	r/talesfromcallcenters
	r/books	r/fitness
	r/askdocs	r/frugal
	r/legaladvice	r/youshouldknow
	r/nostupidquestions	

Table 1: Subreddits used for data collection.

that involve first-person narratives. Using a diverse mix of subreddits also minimizes the impact of subject-specific words from any given community. Table 1 lists the subreddits included in each category of data. In the Anxiety collection, the average length of posts was 171.83 words (869.14 characters). In the Control posts group, the average length was 164.82 words (846.28 characters). These counts reflect the number of processed tokens, with URLs, HTML tags and punctuation removed. We apply further preprocessing by removing stop words and lemmatizing word tokens.

4 Feature Generation

4.1 Vector space embeddings: Word2Vec and Doc2Vec

Mikolov et al. (2013) introduced an efficient estimation of words in vector space for both skip-gram and continuous bag-of-words (CBOW) models. With all training examples, we constructed a CBOW model with a window size of 5 words between current and predicted words in the sentence, and use the mean of the context word vectors. For training, we make 5 iterations over the corpus and use negative down sampling to draw 5 noise words to speed up training. We empirically select an embedding dimension of 300. With the CBOW model, we constructed feature vectors by taking the mean of all tokens in each training example. Intuitively, this corresponds to finding the center of the cluster of words in the vector space belonging to the target label category.

Predictive models can be further strengthened by incorporating paragraph context. Le and Mikolov (2014) introduced a distributed memory model with paragraph vectors (PV-DM). Each paragraph vector was mapped to a unique vector in addition to each word being mapped to a

unique vector. In the present work, during training of the feature-generation model, in addition to word vector updates, paragraph vectors are inferred with each new training example using gradient descent. The paragraph vectors are used in addition to the word vectors to build the post's feature vector. Fixed length contexts are computed using a sliding window over the paragraph. The contexts produce paragraph information which act as a memory component to provide history when predicting the next word. We construct a PV-DM model with a window size of 10 and again empirically select an embedding dimension of 300 for all training example, and use negative down sampling to draw 5 noise words. To increase model representation capacity, we iterate over the corpus 10 times. We use the average of the paragraph and word vectors for classification. After generating the PV-DM model, we infer the feature vector using the model by averaging the paragraph vector with the vector representations with the other words in the sentence for each training example.

4.2 LDA topic modeling

Topic	Topic Words	IG
Ctrl. T1	like, want, know, go, said	0.1764
Anxi. T4	try, drive, look, car, walk	0.0850
Anxi. T2	drink, smoke, alcohol, weed, draw	0.0792
Ctrl. T2	pay, money, will, can, account	0.0699
Ctrl. T8	year, will, time, work, school	0.0691
Anxi. T3	school, class, year, college	0.0654
Anxi. T8	game, help, eat, food, play	0.0654
Anxi. T5	work, job, get, call, time	0.0654
Anxi. T0	people, feel, social, think	0.0654
Ctrl. T1	doctor, pain, medic, feel, feel	0.0654

Table 2: Topics from the LDA model with the highest information gain (IG) in bits.

Latent Dirichlet allocation (LDA) is a Bayesian generative technique that models bodies of text as a mixture of underlying latent topics where each topic is characterized by a distribution over individual words (Blei et al., 2003). First, we use the training set to generate two LDA models for the Control and Anxiety classes, respectively. After training the LDA model, we generate the latent unlabelled topics for each class. Table 2 shows the 10 topics, across both groups, with the highest information gain.

Here, each training example is represented by a 20-dimensional array of likelihoods generated by the top 10 topics for each of the Anxiety and Control LDA models.

4.3 LIWC features

Attributes	IG
Anxiety	0.3939
Negative	0.2260
Dictionary words	0.1815
Affect	0.1396
First person sing	0.1373
Emotional tone	0.1158
Authentic	0.1112
Clout	0.0988
Analytic	0.0783
Feel	0.0766

Table 3: Features from LIWC 2015 with highest information gain (IG) in bits.

We use LIWC 2015 (Pennebaker et al., 2015) to extract lexico-syntactic features as a baseline measure, and the default LIWC dictionary with 95 categories to generate the feature vectors. Table 3 shows the top 10 features from the 94 features of LIWC 2015 with the highest information gain in our data.

4.4 N-gram language models

Another standard method used to extract features from text is to calculate the probability of a document within a language model. In our experiments, we use four different corpora to calculate probabilities of unigrams and bigrams. We build the first two models using the Anxiety and Control training examples, respectively. We build the third model using 100,000 unlabelled tweets from the Sentiment140 dataset (Go et al., 2009) and use the NLTK Brown corpus (Bird, 2006) for the fourth model. To generate feature vectors, we calculate the log-probability of each input sentence as unigrams and as bigrams. For each Reddit post, the associated feature subvector contains a unigram

and bigram probability, with Laplace smoothing for each model, i.e., 8 dimensions in total.

4.5 Learning embeddings and topics

The type of model from which we extract features can be built using any corpus. Here, we compare using in-domain training examples with using another corpus for building the word vector (with word2vec), document vector (with doc2vec), and topic (LDA) models. Here, we choose Twitter as a suitable candidate, since it constitutes a similar social media platform, and since previous literature used Twitter data. To compare, 100,000 tweets from Sentiment140 (Go et al., 2009) were used to build word2vec, doc2vec and LDA topic models. These models were further used to generate training and test feature vectors. Table 4 summarizes the different accuracies of using our Reddit training set compared to using Twitter data to build the feature generation models. Higher accuracies were achieved when the models were trained with Reddit examples rather than with the 100,000 tweets for word2vec and LDA features. However, the Twitter-trained document vector model generated more effective feature vectors than the equivalent model from Reddit data. This result is likely due to the larger number of training examples used to build the Twitter doc2vec model. While word vectors are shared between documents, document vectors are always unique in each new document (Le and Mikolov, 2014). Compared to our Reddit corpus, this Twitter corpus includes a higher number of training documents but each document is shorter in length. Thus using the Twitter corpus in training vector representations may increase the complexity of the doc2vec model more than the word2vec model. To achieve higher accuracy while maintaining consistency, we hereafter use training examples to build models for feature vector generation.

	SVM		NN	
	Reddit	Twitter	Reddit	Twitter
word2vec	0.906	0.813	0.900	0.786
doc2vec	0.772	0.803	0.797	0.823
LDA	0.868	0.748	0.846	0.721

Table 4: Accuracies from feature vectors generated by models trained with Reddit data vs Twitter data.

5 Results

Several quantitative results are discussed, below.

5.1 Frequency

To compare differences in lexicon, we use the entire labelled data set of 22,808 Reddit posts. We compute the frequencies of all unigrams over both the Anxiety and Control sets. The top 200 unigrams for each category are sorted, and the unigrams which appear in both lists are removed, in order to find differentiating subsets. We use the same process for finding the most frequent bigrams. Table 5 summarizes the top 15 most frequent unigrams and top 10 most frequent bigrams, for each group.

Category	most frequent n-grams
Anxiety unigrams	*anxiety, myself, anyone, social, panic, friends, feeling, having, anxious, else, talk, bad, thought, better, felt*
Control unigrams	*our, call, us, edit, old, tell, phone, use, give, same, customer, post, money, let, reddit*
Anxiety bigrams	*(my anxiety), (social anxiety), (my life), (anxiety and), (anxiety i), (anyone else), (talk to), (panic attacks), (panic attack), (where i)*
Control bigrams	*(we are), (from the), (we have), (she was), (he was), (thank you), (that the), (and he), (and she), (what is)*

Table 5: Frequent N-grams ($N=1$, 2) in each class.

The Anxiety unigrams and bigrams explicitly mention anxiety and anxiety-related conditions such as social anxiety and panic attacks. Among the most frequent Anxiety unigrams are words related to feelings (e.g., *feeling, thought, felt, bad*). In contrast, unigrams and bigrams in Control data contain vocabulary general to Reddit (e.g., *edit, post, Reddit*). Control group data from `r/talesfromcallcenters`, `r/talesfromtechsupport` and `r/talesfromretail` contain unique customer- and phone-related words (e.g., *call, phone, customer*) that are not frequently present in the Anxiety group data. The Control set also frequently contains more third-person and first-person plural pronouns compared than the Anxiety set. The most frequent unigrams and bigrams of the Anxiety set include more first-person singular pronouns, however.

5.2 Collocations

Studying collocations captures how groups of words are combined to produce meaning beyond the sum of individual component words. While N-gram frequencies in the previous section reveal how often words appear, identifying collocations can reveal important topics mentioned within a corpus. To find the collocations in both the Control and Anxiety posts, we again analyze the entire data set. Using the NLTK collocation library, we filter collocations by empirically selecting a minimum frequency of 100 for bigrams and 75 for trigrams. We then extract the 30 most collocated N-grams ranked by pointwise mutual information (Manning et al., 1999) from each of the Anxiety and Control sets. We also remove collocations that appear in both the Anxiety and Control collocation lists. Table 6 summarizes the top 10 most collocated bigrams and trigrams for both groups.

Category	most collocated N-grams
Anxiety bigrams	*(self esteem), (side effects), (mental illness), (heart rate), (x post), (mental health), (physical symptoms), (social media), (panic attack), (hey guys)*
Control bigrams	*(blah blah), (front page), (difference between), (tech support), (credit card), (cannot afford), (weeks ago), (customer service), (minutes later), (last night)*
Anxiety trigrams	*(does anyone else), (thanks for reading), (no matter how), (wondering if anyone), (having panic attacks), (stop thinking about), (in high school), (get rid of), (has anyone else), (wanted to share)*
Control trigrams	*(thanks in advance), (the difference between), (the front page), (my best friend), (take care of), (at this point), (a call center), (as far as), (a few days), (a few minutes)*

Table 6: Highly collocated N-grams ($N=2$, 3).

Both bigram and trigram collocations in the Control group show timestamps (e.g., *last might, weeks ago, minutes later, a few days, a few minutes*). Members of the Anxiety community share self-esteem issues, side effects of drugs, how their lives interact with social media, and the physical symptoms of their experiences. Trigram collocations in the Anxiety set are predominantly phrases to ask for advice and find people with the common experiences (e.g., *does anyone else, wonder-*

ing if anyone, has anyone else, wanted to share). There are also collocations that indicate age information (e.g., *in high school*), and users' struggles with anxiety disorders (e.g., *no matter how, stop thinking about, get rid of*).

5.3 Classification

Table 7 summarizes the 10-fold cross-validated accuracy and precision rates of using various types of feature, across logistic regression (LR), a linear kernel support vector machine (SVM), and a neural network (NN) for binary classification. The LR and SVM classifiers were implemented with SciKit-Learn (Pedregosa et al., 2011). We built a custom 2-layer neural network with 256 hidden units per layer and sigmoid activations. During optimization, we empirically used a batch size of 500 and a learning rate of 0.01 for 200 iterations.

Overall, all features are useful in classifying anxiety-related posts on Reddit. For single-source features, we achieve the best results, of 91% accuracy, through word-vector embeddings (word2vec), and through N-gram probabilities. The performance of word2vec is slightly better than the word-vector techniques used by Preotiuc-Pietro et al. (2015) on the Coppersmith Twitter corpus (Coppersmith et al., 2015). By contrast, using N-gram probabilities achieve an overall slightly better precision (92% with NN) than word2vec (91% with SVM). The LDA topic features also perform better than previous results using LDA to detect depression on Twitter (Resnik et al., 2015). Whether topic modelling is more appropriate for long-form posts, as in our data, is the subject of future work.

Since our data did not include meta-data, we implemented content-based features from De Choudhury et al. (2013) including emotion, linguistic style (from LIWC 2007), and an anxiety lexicon. In addition, we combined LIWC and LDA features from Nguyen et al. (2014). The accuracies and precisions of these implementations, as well as the aggregate features, are summarized in Table 8.

For combined methods, our neural network classifier consistently produces the best results. We achieve the highest of accuracy of 98% by combining LIWC with N-gram probabilities and by combining word-vector embeddings (word2vec) with LIWC using this classifier. We improve classification accuracy by 7% over only

using word2vec and by 13% over the LIWC-only baseline. Also, N-grams+LIWC (99%) achieves slightly higher precision than word2vec+LIWC (98%), which is consistent with the difference in N-grams-only word2vec-only results. Combined models, specifically word2vec+N-gram probabilities, word2vec+LDA, and LIWC+ LDA (Nguyen et al., 2014), achieve comparable results with 95%, 94%, and 95% precision, respectively.

For all accuracy and precision values in Table 7 and Table 8, the associated recall was high; between 79% and 99% depending on the classifier. The neural network classifier consistently produced recall values above 90% with variances in the order of 10^{-4}. The SVM classifier produced the lowest recall (79%-90%) with larger variances in the order of 10^{-2}. This fluctuation may be due to using a linear kernel which has a lower representational power than a non-linear kernel

6 Discussion

The LIWC 2015 dictionary provides sufficient coverage of anxiety-related word usage to successfully classify Anxiety and Control Reddit posts. However, by combining LIWC features with N-gram probabilities or unsupervised feature-generation techniques (i.e., vector space embeddings and LDA Topic modeling), we can elevate the classification accuracy to 98%. Moreover, we find correlations between anxiety and specific LDA topics such as school and alcohol (and drug) consumption (see Table 2). This could be an effective method of identifying topics that people with anxiety or other mental illnesses discuss online. By counting unigram and bigram frequency, we also find lexicons relating to feelings and first-person, singular pronouns predominantly represented in the Anxiety group. Furthermore, studying frequent collocations suggests that authors of anxiety-related posts are looking to find other people sharing similar experiences with anxiety.

Due to the relatively recent popularity in the platform, little work has involved the linguistic aspects of Reddit, compared to Twitter. The lengths of posts and community organization of the website suggests considerable potential for sophisticated methods of feature extraction as well as qualitative analysis.

Despite the wide prevalence of anxiety disorders, few attempts have been made to create models capable of automatically detecting the disorder.

Feature	LR		SVM		NN	
	Accuracy	Precision	Accuracy	Precision	Accuracy	Precision
word2vec	0.87 (9.3E-5)	0.89 (3.4E-4)	**0.91 (1.0E-5)**	**0.91 (7.8E-5)**	0.90 (9.1E-5)	0.91 (2.2E-3)
doc2vec	0.78 (9.4E-5)	0.75 (3.7E-4)	0.77 (8.0E-6)	0.76 (3.0E-5)	0.80 (9.5E-5)	0.78 (2.3E-4)
LDA	0.80 (9.8E-5)	0.80 (1.6E-3)	0.87 (1.4E-4)	0.87 (2.8E-4)	0.85 (1.6E-4)	0.85 (7.5E-4)
LIWC	0.85 (4.2E-4)	0.85 (2.1E-3)	0.71 (1.1E-2)	0.81 (1.5E-2)	0.82 (1.0E-2)	0.85 (4.9E-3)
N-grams	0.90 (8.8E-5)	0.89 (4.1E-4)	0.85 (6.9E-3)	0.86 (9.4E-3)	**0.91 (2.2E-4)**	**0.92 (1.4E-3)**

Table 7: Accuracies, precisions (and variances) for single-source features.

Feature	LR		SVM		NN	
	Accuracy	Precision	Accuracy	Precision	Accuracy	Precision
word2vec + LIWC	0.89 (7.9E-4)	0.90 (7.3E-4)	0.84 (2.8E-3)	0.88 (1.2E-2)	**0.98 (2.3E-6)**	**0.98 (1.7E-5)**
doc2vec + LIWC	0.84 (9.3E-4)	0.88 (1.4E-3)	0.80 (3.7E-3)	0.87 (1.1E-2)	0.92 (2.4E-5)	0.93 (1.3E-4)
word2vec + LDA	0.87 (3.0E-4)	0.89 (5.5E-4)	0.91 (2.1E-5)	0.91 (1.6E-4)	0.92 (1.8E-5)	0.94 (8.8E-5)
doc2vec + LDA	0.82 (5.4E-4)	0.85 (6.9E-4)	0.82 (2.8E-3)	0.83 (2.7E-4)	0.84 (8.2E-5)	0.86 (8.7E-5)
word2vec + N-grams	0.90 (2.5E-5)	0.88 (2.1E-4)	0.89 (1.5E-3)	0.91 (2.2E-3)	0.91 (2.4E-4)	0.94 (7.2E-4)
doc2vec + N-grams	0.90 (3.5E-4)	0.90 (8.0E-4)	0.74 (3.4E-3)	0.90 (1.7E-2)	0.92 (7.5E-5)	0.93 (8.6E-4)
LDA + N-grams	0.90 (1.3E-4)	0.88 (9.6E-4)	0.88 (2.9E-3)	0.89 (8.3E-3)	0.90 (1.3E-3)	0.93 (1.1E-3)
LIWC + N-gram	0.92 (6.2E-5)	0.91 (2.6E-4)	0.98 (2.4E-4)	0.91 (2.9E-4)	**0.98 (2.0E-5)**	**0.99 (1.1E-5)**
Nguyen et al.	0.81 (6.0E-3)	0.86 (4.2E-3)	0.81 (3.4E-3)	0.79 (7.0E-3)	0.93 (1.2E-4)	0.94 (7.4E-4)
De Choudhury et al.	0.64 (8.7E-4)	0.67 (4.8E-3)	0.62 (4.7E-3)	0.60 (5.1E-3)	0.85 (1.4E-3)	0.88 (6.3E-3)

Table 8: Accuracies, precisions (and variances) for aggregate features.

Further work should also include larger data sets in combination with explicitly associated diagnostic criteria, assessments, or health records, to emphasize validity.

References

American Psychiatric Association. 2013. *Diagnostic and Statistical Manual of Mental Disorders, Fifth Edition: DSM-5®*. American Psychiatric Association.

Steven Bird. 2006. Nltk: the natural language toolkit. In *Proceedings of the COLING/ACL on Interactive presentation sessions*. Association for Computational Linguistics, pages 69–72.

David M Blei, Andrew Y Ng, and Michael I Jordan. 2003. Latent Dirichlet allocation. *Journal of Machine Learning Research* 3(Jan):993–1022.

Glen Coppersmith, Mark Dredze, Craig Harman, Kristy Hollingshead, and Margaret Mitchell. 2015. CLPsych 2015 shared task: Depression and PTSD on Twitter. In *Proceedings of ACL*. pages 31–39.

Munmun De Choudhury and Sushovan De. 2014. Mental health discourse on Reddit: Self-disclosure, social support, and anonymity. In *Proceedings of ICWSM*. pages 71–80.

Munmun De Choudhury, Michael Gamon, Scott Counts, and Eric Horvitz. 2013. Predicting depression via social media. In *Proceedings of ICWSM*. page 2.

Koen Demyttenaere, Ronny Bruffaerts, Jose Posada-Villa, Isabelle Gasquet, Viviane Kovess, Jean Pierre Lepine, et al. 2004. Prevalence, severity, and unmet need for treatment of mental disorders in the World Health Organization World Mental Health surveys. *Jama* 291(21):2581–2590.

Katya C Fernandez, Cheri A Levinson, and Thomas L Rodebaugh. 2012. Profiling: Predicting social anxiety from Facebook profiles. *Social Psychological and Personality Science* 3(6):706–713.

Alec Go, Richa Bhayani, and Lei Huang. 2009. Twitter sentiment classification using distant supervision. *CS224N Project Report, Stanford* 1(12).

Mrinal Kumar, Mark Dredze, Glen Coppersmith, and Munmun De Choudhury. 2015. Detecting changes in suicide content manifested in social media following celebrity suicides. In *Proceedings of ACM*. ACM, pages 85–94.

Quoc V Le and Tomas Mikolov. 2014. Distributed representations of sentences and documents. In *Proceedings of ICML*. volume 14, pages 1188–1196.

Christopher D Manning, Hinrich Schütze, et al. 1999. *Foundations of statistical natural language processing*, volume 999. MIT Press.

Kathleen Ries Merikangas, Jian-ping He, Marcy Burstein, Sonja A Swanson, Shelli Avenevoli, Li-hong Cui, et al. 2010. Lifetime prevalence of mental disorders in us adolescents: results from the National Comorbidity Survey Replication–Adolescent Supplement (NCS-A). *Journal of the American Academy of Child & Adolescent Psychiatry* 49(10):980–989.

Tomas Mikolov, Kai Chen, Greg Corrado, and Jeffrey Dean. 2013. Efficient estimation of word representations in vector space. *arXiv preprint arXiv:1301.3781* .

Moin Nadeem. 2016. Identifying depression on Twitter. *CoRR* abs/1607.07384. http://arxiv.org/abs/1607.07384.

Thin Nguyen, Dinh Phung, Bo Dao, Svetha Venkatesh, and Michael Berk. 2014. Affective and content analysis of online depression communities. *IEEE Transactions on Affective Computing* 5(3):217–226.

Ted Pedersen. 2015. Screening Twitter users for depression and PTSD with lexical decision lists. In *Proceedings of ACL*. pages 46–53.

Fabian Pedregosa, Gael Varoquaux, Alexander Gramfort, Vincent Michel, Bertrand Thirion, Olivier Grisel, et al. 2011. Scikit-learn: Machine learning in Python. *Journal of Machine Learning Research* 12:2825–2830.

James W Pennebaker, Ryan L Boyd, Kayla Jordan, and Kate Blackburn. 2015. The development and psychometric properties of LIWC2015. Technical report, University of Texas at Austin, Austin, Texas.

Daniel Preotiuc-Pietro, Maarten Sap, H Andrew Schwartz, and LH Ungar. 2015. Mental illness detection at the world well-being project for the clpsych 2015 shared task. *Proceedings of NAACL HLT 2015* page 40.

Philip Resnik, William Armstrong, Leonardo Claudino, Thang Nguyen, Viet-An Nguyen, and Jordan Boyd-Graber. 2015. Beyond LDA: exploring supervised topic modeling for depression-related language in Twitter. In *Proceedings of ACL*. pages 99–107.

Kathleen C Thomas, Alan R Ellis, Thomas R Konrad, Charles E Holzer, and Joseph P Morrissey. 2009. County-level estimates of mental health professional shortage in the United States. *Psychiatric Services* 60(10):1323–1328.

Detecting and Explaining Crisis

Rohan Kshirsagar
Columbia University
rmk2161@columbia.edu

Robert Morris
Koko
rob@itskoko.com

Samuel R. Bowman
Center for Data Science
and Department of Linguistics
New York University
bowman@nyu.edu

Abstract

Individuals on social media may reveal themselves to be in various states of crisis (e.g. suicide, self-harm, abuse, or eating disorders). Detecting crisis from social media text automatically and accurately can have profound consequences.

However, detecting a general state of crisis without explaining why has limited applications. An explanation in this context is a coherent, concise subset of the text that rationalizes the crisis detection. We explore several methods to detect and explain crisis using a combination of neural and non-neural techniques. We evaluate these techniques on a unique data set obtained from Koko, an anonymous emotional support network available through various messaging applications. We annotate a small subset of the samples labeled with crisis with corresponding explanations. Our best technique significantly outperforms the baseline for detection and explanation.

1 Introduction

Approximately one person dies by suicide every 40 seconds (WHO, 2016). It accounts for approximately 1.5 % of all deaths, and is the second leading cause of death among young adults (WHO, 2016). There are indications that for each adult who dies of suicide there may have been more than 20 others attempting suicide (WHO, 2016). Closely tied to suicide are self-harm, eating disorders, and physical abuse. 13 to 23% of adolescents engage in self-injury at some point (Jacobson and Gould, 2007). In the United States, about 7 million females and 1 million males suffer from eating disorders annually (Simon, 2013) and an aver-age of 20 people are physically abused by intimate partners every minute (NCADV, 2015). Self-harm victims are more likely to die by suicide by an order of magnitude (Anthony Bateman, 2014). Additionally, eating disorders and physical abuse increase the risk of suicide (Simon, 2013; NCADV, 2015).

We identify all of these phenomena (suicide, self-harm, eating disorders, physical abuse), with the term crisis. Someone who is in crisis is likely in need of some form of immediate support, be it intervention, therapy, or emergency. Roughly a third of people who think about suicide make a plan; 72% of those who report making a suicide plan actually make an attempt (Kessler et al., 1999).

Accurate, automatic detection of someone in crisis in social media, messaging applications, and voice assistants has profound consequences. A crisis classifier can enable positive outcomes by enabling human outreach at earlier stages, and rescues at later stages.

In many ways, however, it can still fall short of a human detector, by way of lacking an explanation or rationale of why classifier detected crisis. The factors that explain why someone is in crisis can range from suicidal ideation to eating disorders, from self-harm to sexual abuse.

In crisis situations, triage can improve if the detection system can explain why the person is crisis. Someone who is about to die by suicide via overdose should receive a different response than someone who is considering anorexia

due to self-image issues. Population level surveillance, diagnostics, and statistics are much improved due to factor based explanation. Finally, in human-in-the-loop crisis systems, the human responder can better sift through information if the factors of crisis were visually highlighted through automated means (Dinakar et al., 2014).

Proceedings of the Fourth Workshop on Computational Linguistics and Clinical Psychology, pages 66–73,
Vancouver, Canada, August 3, 2017. © 2017 Association for Computational Linguistics

With the rise of complex neural models in classification tasks, we've seen gains in accuracy at the cost of transparency and interpretability (Kuhn and Johnson, 2013). In this work, we present models that we validate both for their raw accuracy and for the quality of their explanations. Validating a model's explanations, in addition to its detection performance, can improve interpretability in the model. In summation, automatically generating explanations for crisis detection scales and pays off in many ways.

While we evaluate our models' explanations against human reference explanations, it is not practical to collect enough explanations to train these models on such data. Collecting an explanation requires an annotator to write free text or to highlight text for every case of crisis, sometimes more than once for a post (e.g. for a sexual abuse victim considering suicide), while merely identifying crisis is a simple binary decision task that can be performed much more quickly and cheaply.

In this paper, we explore the problem of generating explanations for crisis without explicit supervision using modern representation learning techniques. We demonstrate our success comparing our proposed models with a variety of explanatory methods and models on a rationale-labeled test set. We evaluate the generated explanations through ROUGE metrics against human-produced references. In addition, we show detection performance that outperforms prior methods.

2   Related Work

Detecting Crisis   Wood et al. (2016) identify 125 Twitter users who publicly state their suicide attempt online on a specific date and have tweets preceding the suicide attempt. They artificially balance these tweets using data from random users who are assumed to be neurotypical, acknowledging that this data will be contaminated with users who also ideate and attempt suicide. They train simple, linear classifiers that show promise in detecting these suicidal users and discuss the difficulties of realizing this technology, highlighting privacy and intervention concerns. In our work, we attempt detection and explanation on phenomena that includes but is not limited to suicide on a dataset that is significantly larger and not artificially balanced. However, we do not incorporate the record of suicide attempt as signal when labeling.

Gkotsis et al. (2016) operate on a filtered subset of mental health records to determine whether a mention of suicide is affirmed or negated. They do classification on mental health records, which are filtered by the `suicid*` keyword. The goal of their work was the development of improved information retrieval systems for clinicians and researchers, with a specific focus on suicide risk assessment. Thus, the domain is constrained. Their work also differs from ours significantly in its technical execution. Rather than use neural network classifiers, they use probabilistic context free grammars to execute negation detection. This task is quite different than ours, both in dataset and approach, and is most likely not applicable to open-domain social media text. They also do not aim to or need to provide explainable detections, as mentions of suicide are clearly present in all of their data and negation detection is sufficient 'rationale' for affirming or negating that mention.

Tong et al. (2014) annotate Twitter data for suicide-risk with the level of distress as the label and achieve high inter-annotator agreement. They use a combination of specialized keyword search and LIWC sadness scores (Pennebaker et al., 2001) to filter 2.5 million tweets down to 2000 in order to make the annotation task tractable. Our source dataset, which we introduce in the next section, has a significantly higher base rate of crisis; thus, no filtering is necessary. They train SVM classifiers on bag of n-grams to detect distress on different subsets of annotations, but do not explore neural classifiers, nor unsupervised explanations of detections.

Lehrman et al. (2012) and O'Dea et al. (2015) also detect distress on small datasets using simple classifiers. Lehrman et al. (2012) annotate 200 samples for distress level and discretize counts related to bag of word, part of speech, sentence complexity and sentiment word features to train a variety of multiclass classifiers. O'Dea et al. (2015) annotated nearly 2000 tweets for different levels of suicidality and used word counts as features, filtered by document frequency. In our work, we compare neural techniques against linear models trained on word frequency counts both for detection and explanation as a baseline. Due to the relatively large amount of data in our training set, we do not use any custom features for the baseline.

Mowery et al. (2016) detect depression in Twitter data in two stages: 1) detecting evidence of depression at all and 2) classify the specific depressive symptom if depression was detected. This is a kind of explanation in that it directly detects one of three symptoms of depression (fatigue, disturbed sleep, depressed mood). However, their data is explicitly annotated for these sub-factors, whereas our data is not. 1,656 tweets in their dataset were annotated with specific depressive symptoms.

Interpretable Neural Networks In the past few years, neural attention mechanisms over words (Bahdanau et al., 2014) have led to improvements in performance and interpretability in a range of tasks, such as translation (Bahdanau) and natural language inference (Rocktäschel et al., 2015). These models induce a soft alignment between two sequences with the primary aim of using it to remove an information bottleneck, but this alignment can be also be used quite effectively to visualize which inputs drive model behavior.

Lei et al. (2016) present a more direct method for training interpretable text classifiers. Their model is also trained end-to-end, but instead of inducing a soft weighting, it extracts a set of short subspans of each input text that are meant to serve as sufficient evidence for the final model decision. In another work with similar goals, Ribeiro et al. (2016) introduce a model agnostic framework for intepretability, LIME, that learns an interpretable model over a given sample input that is locally faithful to the original trained model.

3 Methods

Our training set consists of N examples $\{X^i, Y^i\}_{i=1}^N$ where the input X^i is a sequence of tokens $w_1, w_2, ..., w_T$, and the output Y^i is a binary indicator of crisis.

3.1 Word Embeddings

Each token in the input is mapped to an embedding. We use reference GloVe embeddings trained on Twitter data (Pennington et al., 2014). We used the 200 dimensional embeddings for all our experiments, so each word w_t is mapped to $x_t \in \mathbb{R}^{200}$. We denote the full embedded sequence as $x_{1:T}$.

3.2 Recurrent Neural Networks

A recurrent neural network (RNN) extends on a traditional neural network to recursively encode a sequence of vectors, $x_{1:T}$, into a sequence of hidden states. The hidden state of the RNN at $t - 1$ is fed back into the RNN for the next time step.

$$h_t = f(x_t, h_{t-1}; \Theta)$$

This allows the network to construct a representation incrementally as it reads the input sequence. In particular, we encode the sequence using a gated recurrent unit (GRU; Cho et al., 2014) RNN. The GRU employs an update gate z_t and reset gate r_t that are used to compute the next hidden state h_t

$$h_t = (1 - z_t)h_{t-1} + z_t\tilde{h}_t$$
$$z_t = \sigma(W_z\mathbf{x}_t + U_z\mathbf{h}_{t-1})$$
$$\tilde{h}_t = tanh(W\mathbf{x}_t + U(\mathbf{r}_t \odot \mathbf{h}_{t-1}))$$
$$r_t = \sigma(W_r\mathbf{x}_t + U_r\mathbf{h}_{t-1})$$

We use a bidirectional RNN (running one model in each direction) and concatenate the hidden states of each model for each word to obtain a contextual word representation h_t^{bi}.

3.3 Attention over Words

With attention, a scoring function scores the relevance of each contextual word representation h_t^{bi}. We employ the unconditional attention mechanism used to do document classification employed by Yang et al. (2016).

$$u_t = tanh(W_w h_t^{bi} + b_w)$$
$$\alpha_t = \frac{\exp u_t}{\sum_t \exp u_t}$$
$$d = \sum_t \alpha_t h_t$$

The attention mechanism serves two purposes. d acts as a contextual document representation which can be fed into a downstream model component for detection. In addition, the score vector $u_{1:N}$, can be utilized to seed our explanation, which will be expanded on in a following section. Optionally for detection, we encode the document by using the last hidden state of a single forward GRU, without the reverse GRU and attention mechanism. Both encoding schemes are evaluated in our experiments.

3.4 Training Objective

The final document encoding of each sample, d, is fed into a sigmoid layer with one node to detect the probability of crisis. We minimize the logistic loss objective during training.

$$l(y, p) = -ylog(p) - (1 - y)log(1 - p)$$

where y is the true value and p is the output of the logistic output layer.

3.5 Seeding the Explanations

Our next goal is to generate explanations given the inputs and outputs for our trained model. We do this by building a subset of words which 'seed' the explanation generation function. The explanation generation function is fixed while testing across all seeding techniques, thus allowing extensibility by modularizing the seed function using a relevant model. The seed function is meant to give a set of tokens from the input that most influenced the prediction, thus sewing the initial stitches of the explanation. For the task of detecting crisis, descriptive content words, such as adjectives, nouns, and verbs, are desirable compared to stop words or punctuation.

We test three techniques of seeding words for a given input: (1) Using the magnitudes of activated coefficients in a logistic regression model. This acts as our baseline. (2) Using the distribution of attention from our neural model. (3) Using LIME, which can generate words that led to a prediction for any model. Each seed function is passed in the number of seed words to return, k. This allows us to maintain similar output behavior for all three techniques; it also allows us to extend the seed functions to more complex models. We will now detail how seeding works for each of these mechanisms.

1. **Logistic Coefficients:** Logistic regression is a linear model that learns a vector of weights for a fixed set of features to detect in binary classification. As a baseline, we train a logistic regression model on unigrams to learn a vector of weights for each word in the vocabulary. For our seed function, we find the k most highly-weighted activated features according to the model. A feature is activated if the word occurs in the given input.

2. **Neural Attention:** In this setting, we select seeds by sorting the words by their attention weights u. In order to get human interpretable scores for attention, we introduced

a configurable dial to control how attention was distributed over the input by introducing an L2 penalty on the output of the attention.

3. **LIME:** The LIME API contains a `num_features` parameter in the `explain_instance` function. Each explanation will then result in learning an interpretable model, which can be used to then seed the explanation. The LIME API is applied to both models, the baseline logistic and the neural model.

3.6 Explanation Generation Algorithm

We use a novel algorithm for producing explanations that depends on seeds from a separately-developed seeding module. The algorithm acts on the input text and the k explanation seeds. It works as follows. First, the sentence of importance is identified by taking the sentence with the most seeds. The identified sentence is then parsed with a dependency parser (Honnibal and Johnson, 2015), and traversed from the root to find the highest seed in the sentence. If the highest seed token is not a verb and not the head of the entire sentence, we then traverse to the seed's head node. Subsequently, the subtree phrase of the highest seed is used for the explanation. Since the parse is projective, the subtree is necessarily a contiguous sequence of tokens.

4 Experiments

4.1 Training Data

Koko has an anonymous peer-to-peer therapy network based on an clinical trial at MIT (Morris et al., 2015), which is made available through chatbots on a variety of social media platforms including Facebook, Kik, and Tumblr. They provided us with our training data through a research partnership. The posts on the platform generally come from users who are experiencing negative thoughts and need some form of emotional support. Each post is on average 3.1 sentences long with a standard deviation of 1.7 sentences. The training set is roughly 106,000 binary labeled posts (crisis or not).

Their data was annotated for crisis by crowd-workers. During annotation, annotations were given clear instructions on what consists of crisis, examples, and common mistakes and helpful tips. These instructions were revised over multiple iter-

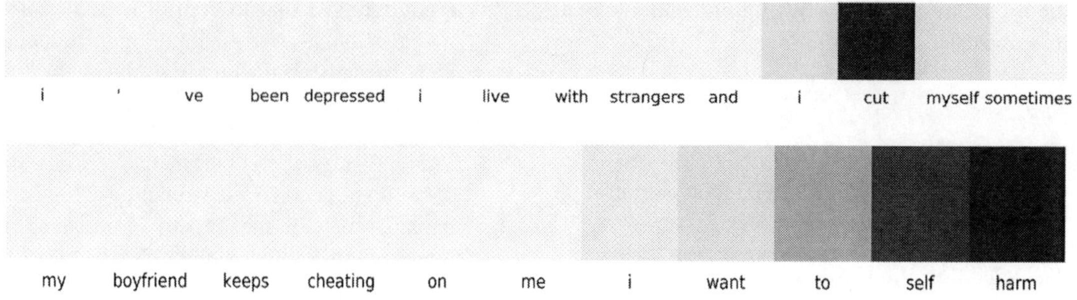

Figure 1: Visualizing Attention for crisis.

ations of small batches of data to improve inter-annotator agreement. Using a minimum of three labelers per sample, they achieve over 95% inter-annotator agreement.

Because the platform is a support network, the rates of depression and other mental disorders are high: the annotation task identified roughly 20% of the training data as crisis. This is in contrast to previous work using Twitter data, where multiple layers of filtering are required to get a reasonable sample of distress (Tong et al., 2014). Our dataset requires no filtering and estimates the natural distribution of the platform.

4.2 Explanation data

We have select a set of 1242 labeled posts as our test set. Of these, 200 are labeled crisis. We annotate the 200 crisis samples with their corresponding explanations. An explanation is a phrase or clause in the post that most strongly identifies the rationale behind the crisis label. When selecting the explanation, we aim for them to be accurate, coherent, and concise.

4.3 Model Configuration and Training

We tokenize the data using Spacy (Honnibal and Johnson, 2015). We do not fine-tune the pretrained GloVe embeddings, but rather learn a simple embedding transformation matrix that intervenes between the embeddings and the RNNs. We use 200 dimensional embeddings and 100 dimensional forward and backward GRUs (yielding 200 dimensional contextual representations). We apply an L2 penalty on the attention output using $\lambda = .0001$. We pad each input to 150 words. We train using RMSprop with a learning rate of .001 and a batch size of 256. We add dropout with a drop rate of 0.1 in the final layer before detecting to reduce overfitting. We determined the dropout rate, batch size, and input length empirically through random hyperparameter search and determined λ for the attention penalty using human evaluation. We use the best model from 20 epochs of training selected using a validation sample of 10% of the source data (excluding the test data).

5 Results and Discussion

5.1 Detection Evaluation

The neural models significantly outperform the logistic model in detection accuracy (Table 1), with the best neural model achieving a .80 F1 on the crisis detections, compared to .66 for the logistic model. The neural attention model achieves a .76 F1 score, which is still significantly better than the linear baseline. The best model does not have an attention penultimate layer, bur rather a single feedforward GRU layer.

5.2 Attention Visualization

We first validate that the attention mechanism yields distributions that meet our expectations. This is done by visualizing the attention using a heat map, with each normalized attention weight aligned with the corresponding token in the input. Initially, we found that the attention distribution had a very low entropy, placing the bulk of the probability in a single token of the input. We penalized low entropy outputs using an L2 penalty, controlled by a λ parameter. We did not further tune it to boost explanation evaluation scores, though we expect this could improve performance. Figure 1 demonstrates the attention output for two crisis samples. For the first sample, we see that

	Precision	Recall	F1
logistic	**0.87**	0.53	0.66
rnn+attention	0.85	0.69	0.76
best rnn	0.82	**0.77**	**.80**

Table 1: Crisis Detection Performance on Test Data

attention is focused around the final clause, and is not concentrated entirely on one word. As one would expect, "i cut myself" fetches the highest weight in the attention distribution. The second visualization shows singular attention on the word 'suicide', thus placing markedly less importance on the rest of the input. This differentiation between background information and crisis signal provides a reassuring signal that the model is using reasonable features.

5.3 Qualitative Explanation Results

Interestingly, all of the techniques resulted in several high quality explanations. We surveyed about 20 samples and for each one, at least one of the seeding functions contained the correct explanation. Surprisingly, the logistic baseline performed quite well in this capacity. In Table 2, we show an example where all of the techniques got the identical result. This is likely due to the predictive power of the phrase 'kill myself'. In many cases, the generated explanation contained more text than is necessary to accurately capture the gold explanation. The second example (Table 2) shows this in the neural+attention technique. This may suggest room for improvement in the explanation generation technique. The third example shows a difficult case in which the majority of the text is background information and only the last word of the input is included in the gold explanation. We see that both neural models and logistic+LIME are successful in capturing roughly the correct explanation.

5.4 Quantitative Explanation Results

We evaluate the generated explanations using ROUGE-1 and ROUGE-2 (Lin, 2004), which measure the overlapping units (unigrams and bigrams respectively) of the generated text and reference texts. In Table 3 and 4, the average ROUGE-1 and ROUGE-2 scores for the generated explanations are listed for each model and seed strat-

Text	Im really lonely and i want someone who loves me cares for me and i love (ima guy) i want to kill myself because i cant get a girlfriend
Gold	kill myself
logistic+coef	to kill myself
logistic+LIME	to kill myself
neural+attention	to kill myself
neural+LIME	to kill myself
Text	I have to face many changes in the next few months but I'm not ready. Instead I hide in fast food and tv shows. I'm scared that my depression will come back and turn to suicidal thoughts.. Big changes ahead make me worried about suicidal thoughts overwhelming me so I hide.
Gold	suicidal thoughts
logistic+coef	Big changes ahead
logistic+LIME	I have to face many changes in the next few months but I'm not ready.
neural+attention	about suicidal thoughts overwhelming me so I hide
neural+LIME	suicidal thoughts
Text	My parents want me to be a perfect child but I have depression and anxiety. Suicide
Gold	Suicide
logistic+coef	me to be a perfect child
logistic+LIME	me to be a perfect child
neural+attention	I have depression and anxiety. Suicide
neural+LIME	I have depression and anxiety.
Text	Everyone at school is calling me a nerd,bitch,loser etc... The problem is that I'm starting to believe them and lately I've started cutting..I'm gonna go insane or lose myself
Gold	I've started cutting
logistic+coef	Everyone at school is calling me a nerd, bitch, loser etc..
logistic+LIME	cutting
neural+attention	lately I've started cutting.
neural+LIME	lately I've started cutting.

Table 2: Explanation Samples

	Precision	Recall	F1
logistic+coef	0.358	0.590	0.396
logistic+LIME	0.409	0.610	0.432
neural+attention	0.360	0.605	0.406
neural+LIME	**0.492**	**0.745**	**0.536**

Table 3: ROUGE-1 Scores

	Precision	Recall	F1
logistic+coef	0.267	0.475	0.289
logistic+LIME	0.301	0.478	0.311
neural+attention	0.286	0.485	0.309
neural+LIME	**0.397**	**0.615**	**0.413**

Table 4: ROUGE-2 Scores

egy. By a large margin, the neural classifier[1] in conjunction with the LIME seed function outperformed the rest of the models. In ROUGE-2 evaluation, it beats the next best average F1 score by a margin of 10 points and in ROUGE-1 evaluation, it beats the next best average F1 by 12 points. Since LIME directly determines which input most influences the prediction, while attention does so only indirectly, this result makes sense. However, the LIME seeding function is the slowest approach we consider, taking up to a minute to generate a explanation. The neural attention seeding is negligible in contrast to this. In Table 3, the ROUGE Metrics show similar performance for the baseline logistic model and the neural model. However, in Table 1, we see that detection output is much better for the neural models. This suggests that though the logistic regression is quite reasonable in ranking features by weights, it fails to capture subtleties and dependencies in a sequence that an RNN captures. Thus, neural+attention is a better choice between the two. The logistic+LIME outperforms the baseline by 5 points in precision for ROUGE-1 and around 3.5 points in precision for ROUGE-2. This exemplifies the efficacy of LIME, which is tuned for the individual example, rather than the model coefficients, which are tuned for the training data.

6 Conclusion

In this paper, we present and compare explanation-oriented methods for the detection of crisis in social media text. We introduce a modular approach to generating explanations and make use of neural techniques that significantly outperform our baseline. The best models presented are both effective at detection and produce explanations similar to those produced by human annotators. We find this exciting for two reasons: Within the domain of crisis identification, successes in explanation help to build the trust in trained models that is necessary to deploy them in such a sensitive context. Looking beyond this, we expect that our techniques may generalize to text classification more broadly. In the future experiments, we hope to explore human evaluation of the generated explanations as an indicator of trust in the model, to investigate compression-based approaches to explanation (Lei et al., 2016), and to consider richer architectures for text classification.

Acknowledgments

We thank the anonymous reviewers and Kareem Kouddous for their feedback. Bowman acknowledges support from a Google Faculty Research Award and gifts from Tencent Holdings and NVIDIA Corporation. We thank Koko for contributing a unique dataset for this research.

References

Philip Timms Jim Bolton Anthony Bateman. 2014. Self-harm: key facts. [Online; accessed 6-April-2017].

Dzmitry Bahdanau, Kyunghyun Cho, and Yoshua Bengio. 2014. Neural machine translation by jointly learning to align and translate. *arXiv preprint arXiv:1409.0473* .

Kyunghyun Cho, Bart Van Merriënboer, Caglar Gulcehre, Dzmitry Bahdanau, Fethi Bougares, Holger Schwenk, and Yoshua Bengio. 2014. Learning phrase representations using rnn encoder-decoder for statistical machine translation. *arXiv preprint arXiv:1406.1078* .

Karthik Dinakar, Allison JB Chaney, Henry Lieberman, and David M Blei. 2014. Real-time topic models for crisis counseling. In *Twentieth ACM Conference on Knowledge Discovery and Data Mining, Data Science for the Social Good Workshop*.

George Gkotsis, Sumithra Velupillai, Anika Oellrich, Harry Dean, Maria Liakata, and Rina Dutta. 2016. Dont let notes be misunderstood: A negation detection method for assessing risk of suicide in mental health records .

---

[1]We use the RNN with attention in this result. The forward RNN in conjunction with LIME showed nearly identical ROUGE performance.

Matthew Honnibal and Mark Johnson. 2015. An improved non-monotonic transition system for dependency parsing. In *Proceedings of the 2015 Conference on Empirical Methods in Natural Language Processing*. Association for Computational Linguistics, Lisbon, Portugal, pages 1373–1378. https://aclweb.org/anthology/D/D15/D15-1162.

Colleen M Jacobson and Madelyn Gould. 2007. The epidemiology and phenomenology of non-suicidal self-injurious behavior among adolescents: A critical review of the literature. *Archives of Suicide Research* 11(2):129–147.

Ronald C Kessler, Guilherme Borges, and Ellen E Walters. 1999. Prevalence of and risk factors for lifetime suicide attempts in the national comorbidity survey. *Archives of general psychiatry* 56(7):617–626.

Max Kuhn and Kjell Johnson. 2013. *Applied predictive modeling*, volume 26. Springer.

Michael Thaul Lehrman, Cecilia Ovesdotter Alm, and Rubén A Proano. 2012. Detecting distressed and non-distressed affect states in short forum texts. In *Proceedings of the Second Workshop on Language in Social Media*. Association for Computational Linguistics, pages 9–18.

Tao Lei, Regina Barzilay, and Tommi Jaakkola. 2016. Rationalizing neural predictions. *arXiv preprint arXiv:1606.04155* .

Chin-Yew Lin. 2004. Rouge: A package for automatic evaluation of summaries. In *Text summarization branches out: Proceedings of the ACL-04 workshop*. Barcelona, Spain, volume 8.

Robert R Morris, Stephen M Schueller, and Rosalind W Picard. 2015. Efficacy of a web-based, crowdsourced peer-to-peer cognitive reappraisal platform for depression: Randomized controlled trial. *Journal of medical Internet research* 17(3):e72.

Danielle Mowery, Albert Park, Mike Conway, and Craig Bryan. 2016. Towards automatically classifying depressive symptoms from twitter data for population health. In *Proceedings of the Workshop on Computational Modeling of Peoples Opinions, Personality, and Emotions in Social Media*. pages 182–191.

NCADV. 2015. Domestic violence national statistics. [Online; accessed 6-April-2017]. http://ncadv.org/images/Domestic Violence.pdf.

Bridianne O'Dea, Stephen Wan, Philip J Batterham, Alison L Calear, Cecile Paris, and Helen Christensen. 2015. Detecting suicidality on twitter. *Internet Interventions* 2(2):183–188.

James W Pennebaker, Martha E Francis, and Roger J Booth. 2001. Linguistic inquiry and word count: Liwc 2001. *Mahway: Lawrence Erlbaum Associates* 71(2001):2001.

Jeffrey Pennington, Richard Socher, and Christopher D. Manning. 2014. Glove: Global vectors for word representation. In *Empirical Methods in Natural Language Processing (EMNLP)*. pages 1532–1543. http://www.aclweb.org/anthology/D14-1162.

Marco Tulio Ribeiro, Sameer Singh, and Carlos Guestrin. 2016. Why should i trust you?: Explaining the predictions of any classifier. In *Proceedings of the 22nd ACM SIGKDD International Conference on Knowledge Discovery and Data Mining*. ACM, pages 1135–1144.

Tim Rocktäschel, Edward Grefenstette, Karl Moritz Hermann, Tomáš Kočiský, and Phil Blunsom. 2015. Reasoning about entailment with neural attention. *arXiv preprint arXiv:1509.06664* .

Harvey Simon. 2013. Eating disorders. [Online; accessed 6-April-2017]. http://umm.edu/health/medical/reports/articles/eating-disorders.

Christopher M Homan1 Ravdeep Johar Tong, Liu1 Megan Lytle2 Vincent Silenzio Cecilia, and O Alm. 2014. Toward macro-insights for suicide prevention: Analyzing fine-grained distress at scale. *ACL 2014* page 107.

WHO. 2016. Mental health suicide data. [Online; accessed 6-April-2017].

Anthony Wood, Jessica Shiffman, Ryan Leary, and Glen Coppersmith. 2016. Language signals preceding suicide attempts. CHI 2016 Computing and Mental Health Workshop, San Jose, CA.

Zichao Yang, Diyi Yang, Chris Dyer, Xiaodong He, Alex Smola, and Eduard Hovy. 2016. Hierarchical attention networks for document classification. In *Proceedings of NAACL-HLT*. pages 1480–1489.

A Dictionary-Based Comparison of Autobiographies by People and Murderous Monsters

Micah Iserman and **Molly Ireland**
Department of Psychological Sciences, Texas Tech University, Lubbock, Texas
{micah.iserman,molly.ireland}@ttu.edu

Abstract

People typically assume that killers are mentally ill or fundamentally different from the rest of humanity. Similarly, people often associate mental health conditions (such as schizophrenia or autism) with violence and otherness—treatable perhaps, but not empathically understandable. We take a dictionary approach to explore word use in a set of autobiographies, comparing the narratives of 2 killers (Adolf Hitler and Elliot Rodger) and 39 non-killers. Although results suggest several dimensions that differentiate these autobiographies—such as sentiment, temporal orientation, and references to death—they appear to reflect subject matter rather than psychology per se. Additionally, the Rodger text shows roughly typical developmental arcs in its use of words relating to friends, family, sex, and affect. From these data, we discuss the challenges of understanding killers and people in general.

1 Introduction

In May of 2014, seven people were killed and several others injured as part of a stabbing and spree shooting in Isla Vista, California, that ended with the attacker's suicide. The killer wrote an autobiography, which, in part, attempted to explain their[1] actions. That piece of text is what initially motivated this project.

Autobiographies are works that assimilate memories of the past, largely in such a way as to make sense of the present. Attempting to understand such works brings to bear fundamental,

opposing forces in the interpretation of any form of self-report: Pulling in one direction are considerations of reliability; these are the distorted recollections of a single, biased individual, so they should be interpreted with skepticism. Pulling in the other direction are considerations of privileged insight; these are reports of experience otherwise unobservable, so they should be valued. These forces seem to be amplified when the report under consideration is from someone who has done or plans to do horrible things. Killers are often unquestioningly regarded as mentally unwell, which further questions the reliability of their reporting. Killers are also often unquestioningly regarded as (rare and interesting) monsters, further evidenced—beyond the mere fact of their actions—by the monstrous things they say. Both of these forces in such extremes work to encourage a view of those who kill as ununderstandable[2].

As an exercise in understanding, killers might be viewed as reasonable (if perhaps biased; Davies et al., 2001) people making sense of and acting on their experience (much like a symptoms approach to understanding mental disorder, such as imagining interlocutors have no faces for a perspective on autism; Graham, 2013). Perhaps more accurately, but to the same effect, the actions of killers might be thought of as the same in kind as any other action—that is, fundamentally irrational. The accuracy of such an understanding is entirely irrelevant; there is no clear ground truth when it comes to understanding others, so breadth and flexibility of perspective make for better standards than exactitude and certainty (in a similar vein to Feyerabend, 1975). Making assumptions, taking a stand for or against, and deeming truths or falsehoods are all stopping behaviors. Such behaviors allow

---

[1] *They* is used throughout to refer to all authors, singular or plural, of any sex (cf. AHD, 2016; AP, 2017).

[2] In the Jasperian sense, which has a history of use and criticism in thought on schizophrenia (Owen and Harland, 2007).

Proceedings of the Fourth Workshop on Computational Linguistics and Clinical Psychology, pages 74–84,
Vancouver, Canada, August 3, 2017. © 2017 Association for Computational Linguistics

us to move forward and to think about other things by providing a sense of clarity at the expense of complexity.

2 Methods

Comparison Texts. Publicly available autobiographies from Project Gutenberg[3] were used as comparisons to the Rodger text. This set includes the autobiography of Adolf Hitler, which we considered to be more comparable to the Rodger text, at least in terms of radical, murderous sentiment (particularly considering each text was written prior to the actions that made these authors killers). These and the authors of the other, "non-killer" comparison autobiographies are listed in Table 1, along with total word counts. Each text was cleaned of meta information such as prefaces and chapter headings, and larger segments of inserted text such as block quotes or included correspondences. Texts were then parsed into sentences, in order to analyze them at different levels while holding the number of segments constant and retaining some logical structure (as compared with segmenting by word). Most of the presented results use a set of 100 segments per text, with 17 to 113 sentences constituting each segment, depending on the length of the text[4].

Analysis. Text analysis applied to the study of extraordinary events like murder and suicide has tended to focus mostly on classification (e.g., Pestian et al., 2010), with a mind toward prevention (e.g., Brynielsson et al., 2013). Though such work is certainly interesting and worthwhile, the goals of this project are more oriented toward understanding (in a phenomenological rather than explanatory sense). To this end, our analyses were primarily concerned with patterns over time (across segments), with a particular interest in patterns appearing in both the Rodger and Hitler texts, but not in the majority of comparison texts. This was motivated in part by the apparent contamination theme (McAdams et al., 2001) through the Rodger text, in which an idyllic childhood takes a turn toward murder.

In this brief report, we focus on Linguistic Inquiry and Word Count (LIWC; Pennebaker et al., 2015) categories, looking at mean use frequencies and trends through the course of each text. All analyses (after LIWC processing) were performed in R (R Core Team, 2017). Sentiment analysis was performed with the sentimentr package (Rinker, 2017) using a dictionary based on Hu and Liu (2004), and most figures were made with a package currently in development[5]. The collected dataset and all analyses are available on the Open Science Framework[6].

3 Results and Discussion

Anger and Death. Killers are generally thought to be angrier and more death-obsessed than the general population. Though word use does map directly onto thoughts and feelings (as recently discussed by Galasiński, 2017), certain relevant word categories might be expected to track them. This expectation is borne out to some degree when looking at LIWC's anger and death categories across segments of each text. Figures 1 and 2 show local polynomial regression (LOESS) lines for each text, with the Hitler and Rodger texts showing marked increases in the two categories in their ending segments. It is notable, however, that the "killers" are not the most exaggerated of either category (and are even, at times, among the least). The Hawk and Lawrence texts each use death and anger words at a high frequency, which is fitting with their war-related content. Another comparison with a high anger use frequency is the Beers text, in which anger words mostly appear in the descriptions of treatment in psychiatric hospitals (e.g., ". . . this man was *cruelly assaulted*, and I do not know how many times he suffered *assaults* of less severity."[7]; Beers, 1917).

A slightly more refined, sentiment analytic method accounts for some of this subject matter, but makes much the same characterizations (Figure 3; see Table 2 for correlations between sentiment and LIWC categories). Here, the Douglass text shows up among the lowest in positive sentiment. Much like the Beers text, the Douglass text deals with cruel treatment, this time at the hands of slave owners (Douglass, 1845). In the death category, another comparison with a high use frequency is the Darrow text, in which death words are mostly used in the discussion of murderers and

---

[3]https://www.gutenberg.org

[4]To account for the disparity in word count to some degree, category frequencies were weighted by segment word count: adjusted frequency = frequency * (1 + segment word count * .0001).

[5]https://github.com/miserman/splot

[6]https://osf.io/vwq9p

[7]Italics added in all quotes to show category-relevant words. *Cruel* is part of the anger category, though "cruelly" is not captured by LIWC2015 version 1.3.1.

Author	Word Count	Author	Word Count
Henry Adams	176,320	Adolf Hitler	267,619
George Biddell Airy	67,530	Louis Hughes	44,922
Elizabeth von Arnim	48,410	James Weldon Johnson	51,826
Margot Asquith	86,648	Joseph Rudyard Kipling	53,287
Clifford Beers	63,908	T. E. Lawrence (Lawrence of Arabia)	250,611
Annie Besant	93,289	Karl May	96,350
Samuel Clemens (Mark Twain)	172,895	John Stuart Mill	73,442
William Cody (Buffalo Bill)	81,912	G. E. Morrison	86,406
Henry Coke	105,829	James Nasmyth	120,005
Joseph Conrad	42,456	Dave Ranney	34,870
Theodore L. Cuyler	78,259	Elliot Rodger	108,024
Clarence Darrow	159,665	Theodore Roosevelt	188,915
Charles Darwin	22,455	Catherine Spence	69,264
James John Davis	49,145	William James Stillman	192,375
Richard Harding Davis	125,520	Saint Thérèse of Lisieux	58,349
Fredrick Douglass	34,282	Charles Thomson	21,435
Friedrich Fröbel	36,546	Anthony Trollope	97,838
Benjamin Franklin	63,685	Andrew Dickson White	401,007
Robert Dean Frisbie	90,052	Hale White (Mark Rutherford)	42,168
Philip Gilbert Hamerton	74,632	Paramahansa Yogananda	141,215
Black Hawk	39,850		

Table 1: The authors of all analyzed autobiographies and their total word counts. Mean segment word count = total word count / 100.

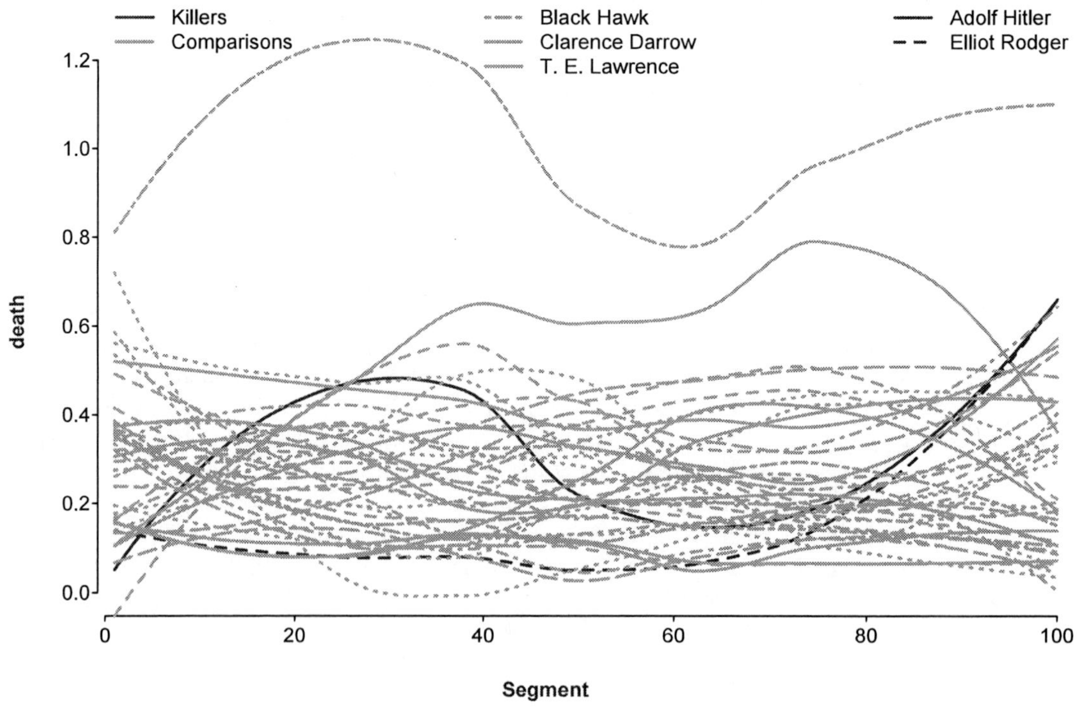

Figure 1: Frequencies of death words through segments of each text. The central legend shows the 3 comparison texts with the highest mean frequencies of death words.

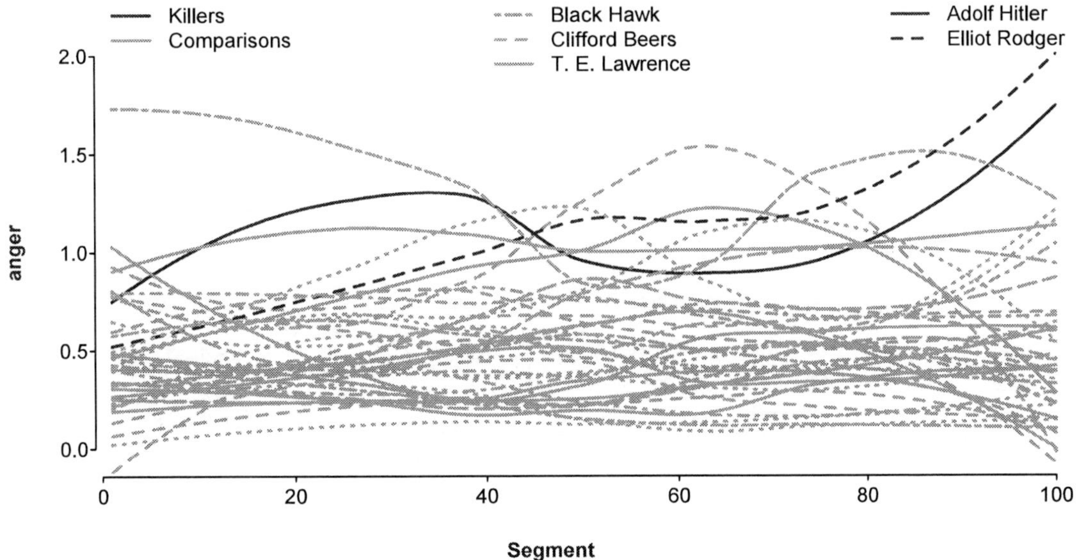

Figure 2: Frequencies of anger words through segments of each text. The central legend shows the 3 comparison texts with the highest mean frequencies of anger words.

	sentiment	neg	anx	ang	sad
negemo	−.45				
anx	−.28	.55			
anger	−.32	.72	.2		
sad	−.22	.55	.21	.12	
posemo	.38	.01	−.01	−.04	.09

Table 2: Correlations between sentiment and LIWC categories. The negemo category contains the anx, anger, and sad categories.

the justice system (e.g., "The *killer's* psychology is not different from that of any other man. Indeed, in a large proportion of the cases the *murderer* had no malice toward the *dead*."; Darrow, 1932).

In both anger and death, the "killers" are similar to their comparisons in that their high use rate of each category is mostly reflective of subject matter. The Hitler text talks of war, which results in high anger and death frequencies, due largely to the words of war, such as *attack, fight, destroy,* and *enemy* in the anger category, and, most notably, *war* in both the death and anger categories[8]. In terms of these LIWC categories, degrees of passion or sentiment may be washed out in discus-

sions of war. The Rodger text often looks similar to the Beers and Douglass texts in its description of cruel treatment (e.g., "I had been rejected, *insulted, humiliated,* cast out, bullied, starved, *tortured,* and *ridiculed* for far too long."; Rodger, 2014), though, particularly with talk of death, it gets more concrete and intentional than other texts (e.g., "When they are *dead,* I will *behead* them and keep their heads in a bag . . ."; Rodger, 2014).

These texts that are high in anger and death word use seem to differ in level of focus—from the grand, collective panorama of war, to the personal, singular experience of cruelty. Considering pronoun use seems to clarify this difference. In a cluster analysis (Figure 4), when i and we are included with anger and death, the killers no longer appear in the same cluster.

Affiliation and Personal Pronouns. Another potential feature of killers is a certain purposiveness, particularly in their drive and planning. Opposing the similarities that showed up in anger and death word usage, here the two killers differ in interesting ways. On initial inspection of LIWC's drive categories (affiliation, achieve, power, reward, and risk), affiliation seemed to have the clearest trend over segments. The affiliation category is something of a hodgepodge of social and organizational terms, including pronouns, so it can

---

[8]We found it useful to see how LIWC was categorizing words in each text, which was helped by our visualization tool: https://www.depts.ttu.edu/psy/liwc

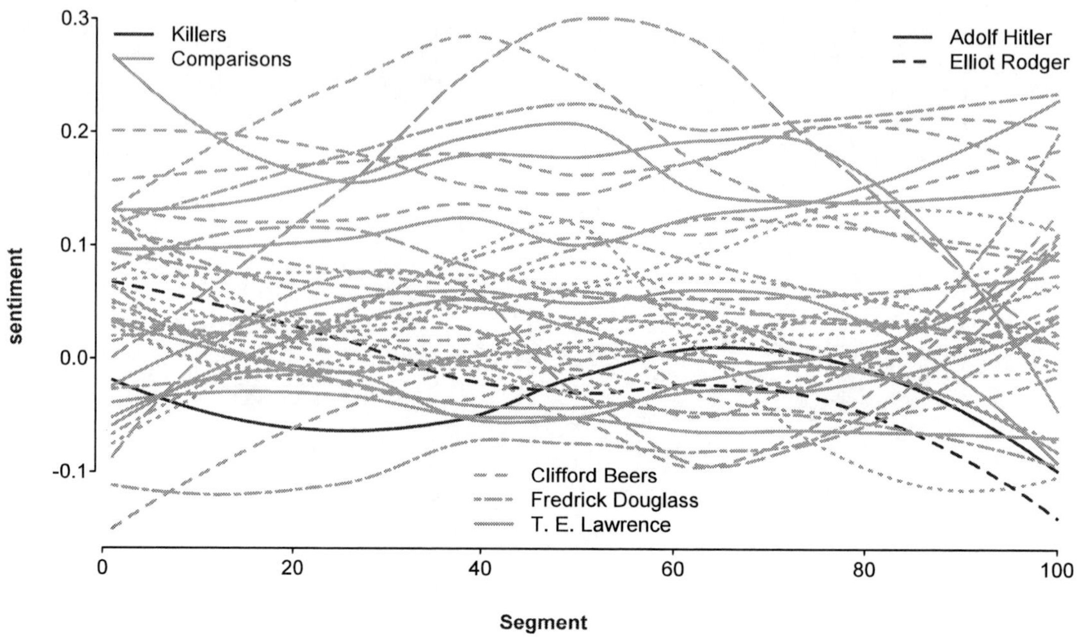

Figure 3: Mean sentence-level polarity scores within segments across each text, with higher scores indicating a more positive sentiment. The central legend shows the 3 comparison texts with the lowest mean polarity scores.

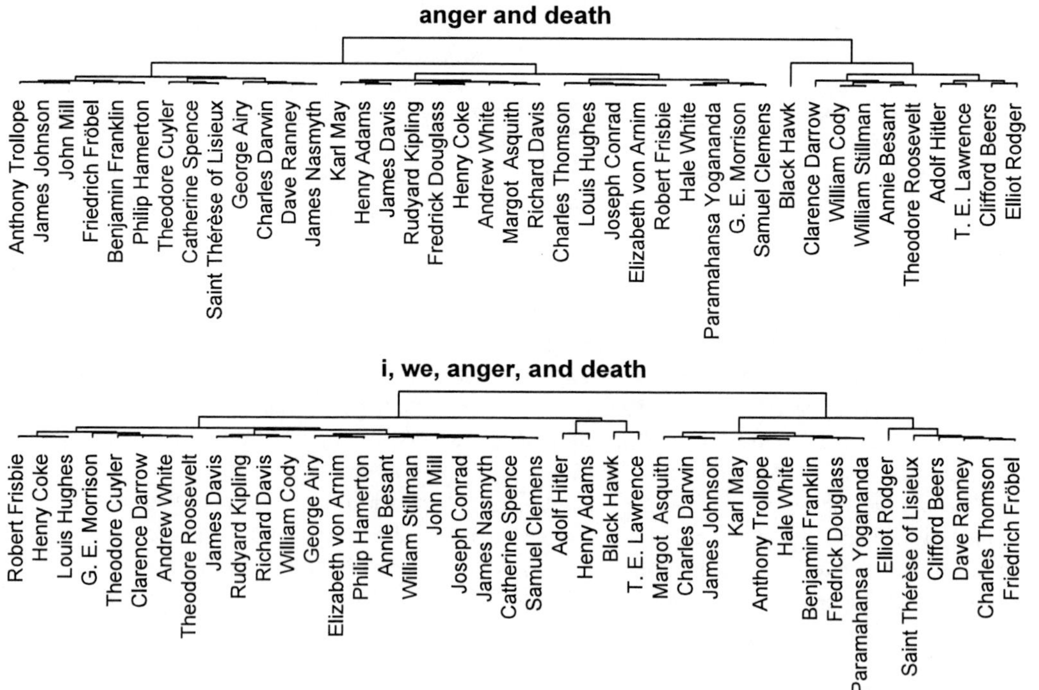

Figure 4: A comparison of hierarchical cluster analyses based on Ward clustering of Euclidean distances between text-mean frequencies, when pronouns are and are not considered along with the anger and death categories.

be difficult to make sense of all together. A look at potentially group-related pronouns on their own (i.e., the they and we categories) offers a somewhat clearer picture of references to affiliation. As Figure 5 depicts, the Hitler text increases in we category use frequency, while they category use remains stable. In contrast, the Rodger text both increases in they and decreases in we usage over its course. These trends in affiliative references track the broader narratives of each text: The Hitler text ramps up to a political point, speaking of the imperatives of a group (e.g., "*We*, National Socialists, must never allow *ourselves* to re-echo the hurrah patriotism of *our* contemporary bourgeois circles."; Hitler, 1939), whereas the Rodger text moves from recounting early experiences with others (e.g., "*We* would play Pokémon on *our* Gameboys, and sometimes *we* would have playdates where *we* played Nintendo 64 games . . ."; Rodger, 2014) to speaking of others as targets (e.g., "*They* deserve it. *They* must be punished."; Rodger, 2014).

Future Orientation. Part of the story told by pronoun usage, particularly in the Rodger text, is to do with temporal orientation—that is, a shifting of focus over time. Looking at LIWC's focusfuture category (Figure 6), a similar trend appears, with references to the future (e.g., *will, soon, going*) regularly increasing through the Rodger text. The clear temporal structure of the Rodger text may be partially due to its length; being so much shorter than the Hitler text, for example, makes for a tighter narrative with a single arc. Another contribution to the clarity of structure in the Rodger text may be its clarity of intent; this text was written expressly to explain the motivations behind carefully planned, near-future events: "I didn't want things to turn out this way, but humanity forced my hand, and this story will explain why." (Rodger, 2014). The Hughes text—which shows a similar clarity of structure in terms of focusfuture—seems to share this clarity of intent: "the narrator presents his story in compliance with the suggestion of friends, and in the hope that it may add something of accurate information regarding the character and influence of an institution . . ." (Hughes, 1897). In contrast, while the Hitler text certainly has its intents, these are broader and hold a longer view, being offered as a description of a movement and its development, a commitment of its doctrine, and the development

of its leader (Hitler, 1939).

Developmental Categories. The Rodger text is in some sense a linear coming of age story, progressing at a steady pace from an idyllic early childhood to a troubled adolescence and homicidal early adulthood. Given this straightforward chronological layout of the autobiography, it should be possible to assess whether Rodger's life (at least as presented) followed typical developmental trajectories over time, or was developmentally aberrant in some way.

Research on child and adolescent development, as well as text analytic studies on associations between language use and age, propose several clear hypotheses of how language use should change as individuals mature from children to young adults. First, children gradually depend on friends more than family to satisfy attachment needs; for example, children tend to start shifting attachment functions of proximity seeking (wanting to be near someone) and safe haven (seeking support during times of stress) from caregivers to friends in early adolescence (Nickerson and Nagle, 2005). Thus, normally developing adolescents should refer less often to family and more often to friends as they mature (Figure 7).

Adolescence is also associated with the often abrupt emergence of sexual desires and a new desire to seek romantic partners in addition to intimate platonic friends (Furman and Buhrmester, 1992). Accordingly, heterosexual adolescents should pay less attention to same-sex peers or friends, and focus more on potential mates of the other sex over the course of their teens and early 20s (Figure 8).

Adolescence is also a time of increasingly intense emotionality, due largely to rapid increases in sex hormones, and stressful physical and social changes, such as emerging secondary sex characteristics and going to college, respectively (Compas et al., 2001; Pennebaker and Stone, 2003). Therefore, typical individuals may use more intense affective language overall and more negative emotion language in particular as they transition from childhood to adolescence (Figure 9).

Perhaps surprisingly, given the fact that Rodger is atypical in many respects—for example, their intense antipathy towards women, homicidal fantasies, and suicidality—the Rodger text follows the predicted trajectories for most of the categories mentioned (Figures 7-9). In becoming more nega-

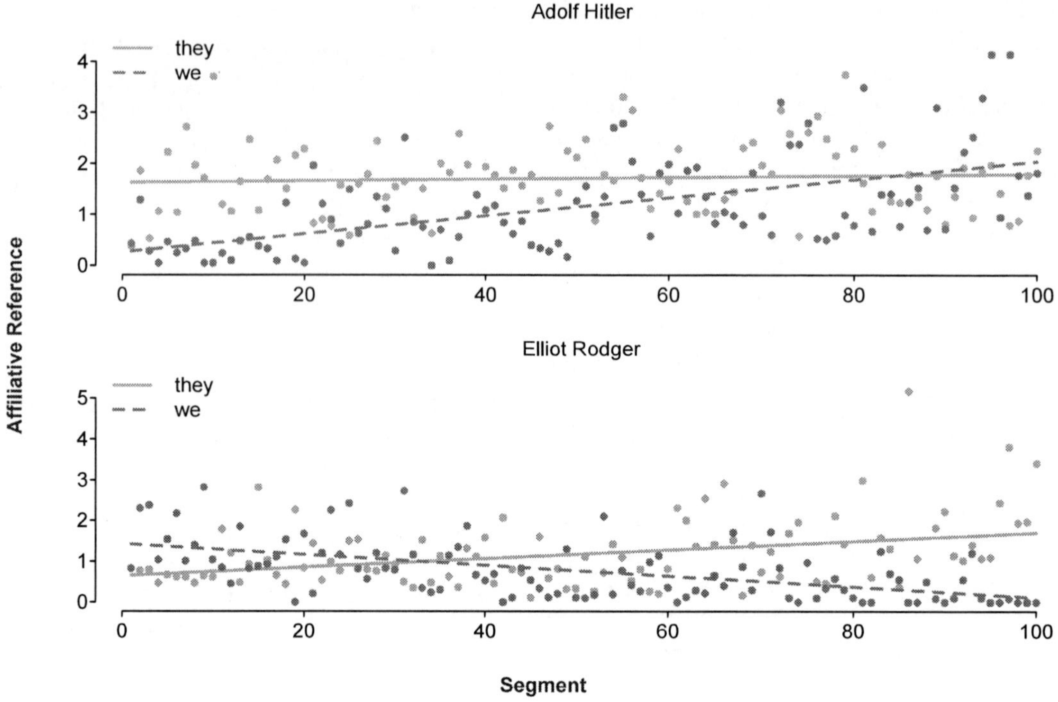

Figure 5: Least squares regression lines fit to frequencies of we and they words through segments of the Hitler and Rodger texts.

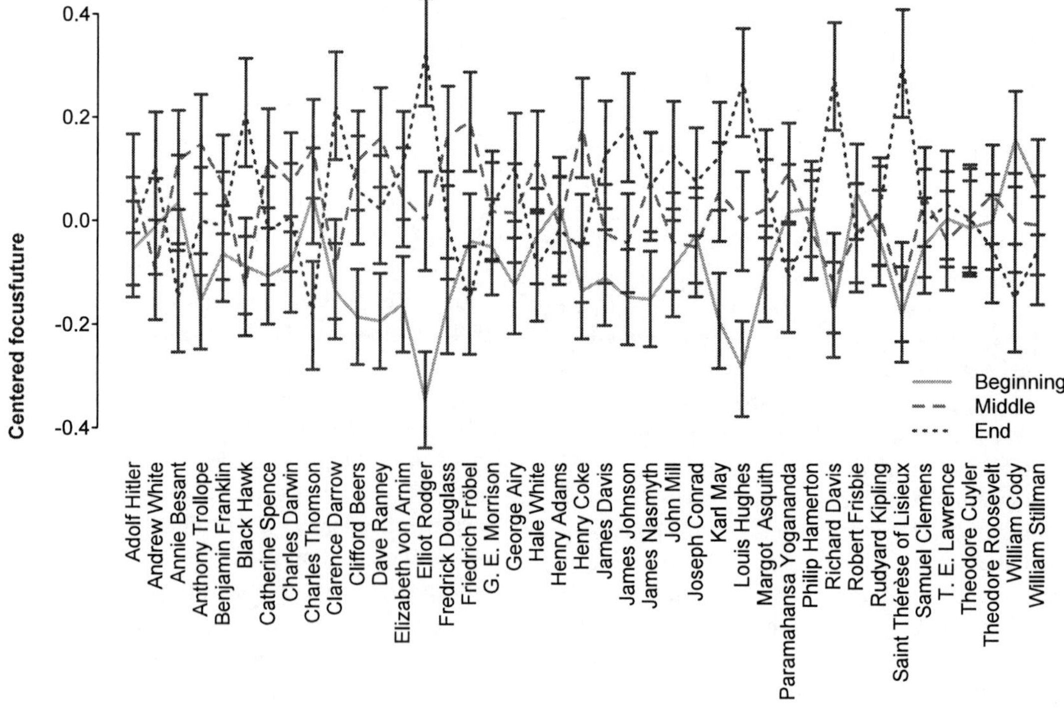

Figure 6: Mean-centered focusfuture within the beginning, middle, and ending segments of each text. Error bars show standard error.

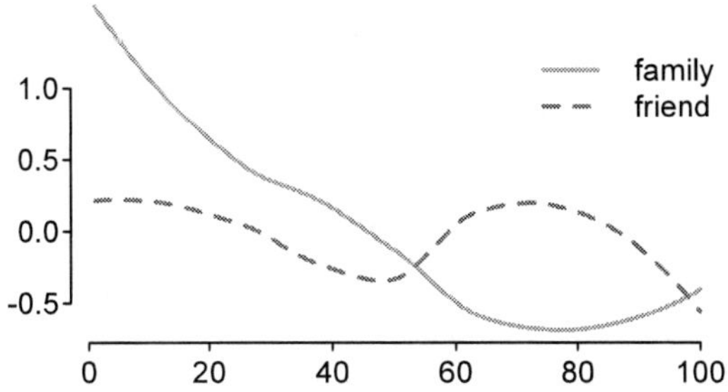

Figure 7: Z-scored frequencies of family and friend words across segments of the Rodger text.

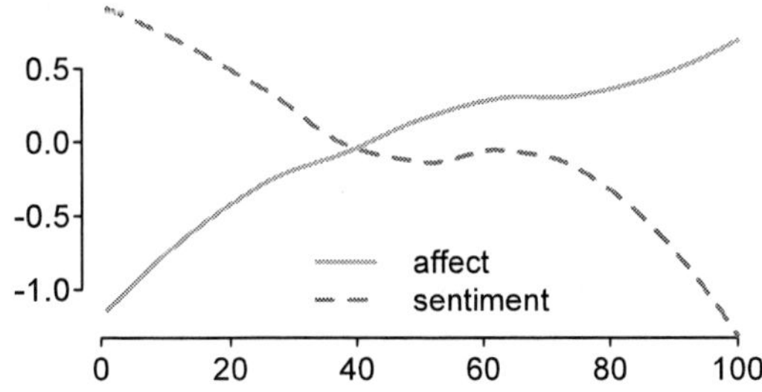

Figure 9: Z-scored frequencies of affect words and sentiment across segments of the Rodger text.

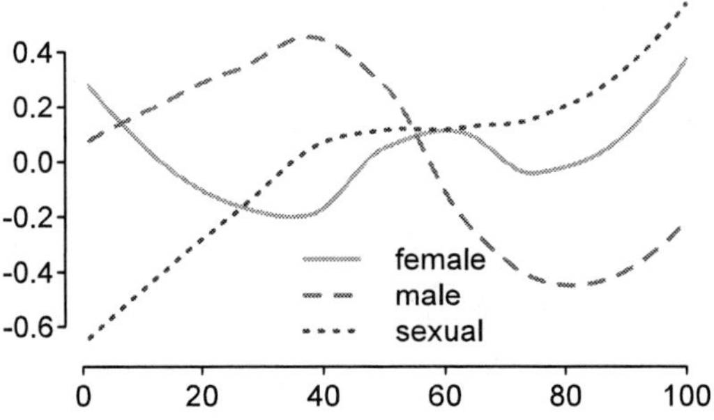

Figure 8: Z-scored frequencies of references to females and males, and sexual words across segments of the Rodger text.

tive in sentiment and using more emotional word, and making fewer references to family and males, and more references to sex through the course of their text, Rodger appears to be a typical young person struggling with the transition from childhood to adulthood. This apparent typicality is consistent with analyses of larger samples of adolescent mass murderers, who often experience depressive symptoms and social rejection, but are only rarely psychotic or diagnosed with severe mental health conditions (Meloy et al., 2001).

4   Limitations and Future Directions

There are several clear limitations in the present analysis and sample, and in this type of research more broadly. First, most of the presented results were of a few intuitively relevant categories that showed both similarities and differences between killers and non-killers. Other categories show similar patterns, but are less clear in their interpretation (such as markedly lower rates of comma use within the killer texts). There are also likely some theoretically interesting categories we did not con-

sider, which show less clear patterns. This report is more interested in thinking about the language use and perspectives of killers than saying anything definitive about them.

Second, very few spree or serial killers have written autobiographies. Most existing autobiographies of killers were written after the fact, looking back and making sense of actions (as in those of Donald Gaskins, Charles Manson, and Dennis Nilsen) rather than ramping up to them, as in the Rodger text. Additionally, few of these texts are publicly or even readily available. Most text written by killers nearer to the time of their actions are short form (as in the journals of Alvaro Castillo, Eric Harris, Dylan Klebold, or Aaron Ybarra; or the suicide notes of Wellington Oliveira, Jose Reyes, or Charles Whitman), are primarily focused on some philosophical or political motivation (as in the manifestos of Pekka-Eric Auvinen, Anders Breivik, Ted Kaczynski, or even Mitchell Heisman—who wrote a substantial, philosophical suicide note, but killed only themself), or are some combination of the two (as in texts left by Christopher Dorner, Jim Adkisson, or Marc Lépine).

Other texts from killers might include social media activity (as in forum posts from T. J. Ready, Jared Loughner, or Kimveer Gill) or creative works (such as writings from Seung-Hui Cho, Kip Kinkel, Jeff Weise, or Luke Woodham). These want for better comparisons than the current autobiographies, due to the disparate forms of each text and to the times in which they were written. Viable comparisons would be time-paired, and might include anything from suicide notes by those who died by suicide but did not kill others, to everyday social media posts by controls matched on key demographic or mental health characteristics.

5 Ethical Caveats

Although killers are increasingly leaving behind linguistic traces of their thought patterns on social media, email, and other forms of internet communication, a larger analytic issue is the base rate of mass murder. The rate of homicide victims per 100,000 citizens is below 4 in nearly all developed countries (3.9 in the United States, 0.9 in Germany; UNODC, 2013), and mass homicides are much rarer (Krouse and Richardson, 2015). As others have noted (Cohen et al., 2014; Fox and Fridel, 2016), with such sparse data it is doubtful that behavioral scientists will ever be able to predict which potential killers will go on to commit homicide, without incorrectly identifying a troubling number of non-violent individuals. False positives become particularly ethically problematic with the prospect of labeling students, employees, or military personnel (for example) as potential or likely murderers. A more realistic model of prevention may be less psychological, and more temporally proximal (e.g., involving weapons procurement near to the time of a planned attack, along the lines of Brynielsson et al., 2013).

A separate ethical concern involves speculation about the mental health of individuals who are not subject to standard diagnostic procedures, such as structured clinical interviews (First and Gibbon, 2004). For over 40 years, the American Psychiatric Association has upheld the so-called Goldwater Rule, stating that it is unethical for professional psychologists to diagnose a public figure they have not personally treated (APA, 2013). Although some have criticized the Goldwater Rule for being overcautious (Kroll and Pouncey, 2016), and argued that exceptions should be made for mass murderers (Knoll and Meloy, 2014; Lake, 2014) or world leaders (Lenzer, 2017), the majority of mental health practitioners today abide by it. Though we are not clinical psychologists or psychiatrists (equally unqualified and unmoved by APA principals), we have limited our comments to the content of the two killers' texts rather than speculating about their reported behavior, or claims about psychotherapeutic treatment they may have received in their lives. That is, this project sought insight into the mindset of killers, and did not set out to diagnose anyone, or suggest anyone was free of mental health conditions, which may well have been present and diagnosable.

6 Conclusion

On something of a flipside to the ethical caveats discussed, the main takeaway from this initial look into the autobiographies of killers and non-killers is that killers are not different in kind than non-killers—as with people in general, these texts are more similar than different. The clearest mark of a killer is what defines them (i.e., killing). This framing leads into two related considerations when conceiving of others. The first is of categorization: When we categorize (label, name, or define), we are modeling the world in terms of kinds. This sort of modeling is useful for the purposes of sense making, but those same sense making forces attempt to realize and rarefy the models they propose. Once a categorization has been made (e.g., "killers" and "non-killers"), the second consideration plays within that model. Part of the work of a category is to add information beyond what is observed. For example, sex might be defined by the reproductive system, but the sex-bases sense of others we have goes far beyond that distinction; sex is seen as essential to the individual, which is realized and reinforces through social and conceptual processes. That is, we classify individuals based on a physiological feature, then fill out those classes with patterns of behavior and ways of being. In the same way, killers are classified by a small set of their actions, which blossom in the mind into monstrous figures with regular, detectable patterns of thought and feeling.

Categorization is neither good nor bad; it is a modeling tool. When and how we should categorize is a pragmatic question, much like classification problems in general. Posed in this way, the limiting influence of a calcified model should be evident; in the parlance of machine learning, it is fully biased and invariant. Calcification in our modeling occurs when we start to believe in the realities suggested by our categorizations. If we are too rigid in our model selection, we may fail to make interesting, alternative model connections (in the present context, rather than killers from non-killers, we may more pragmatically distinguish individual- from group-level focus, as hinted at by Figure 4). If our models themselves are too rigid, we may start to view our data as ununderstandable. That is, if the concept 'killer' rigidly contains the feature 'mentally unwell', we will be unable to even conceive of, much less understand, a mentally well killer.

References

AHD. 2016. *The American Heritage Dictionary of the English language*. Houghton Mifflin Harcourt.

AP. 2017. *Associated Press stylebook and briefing on media law*. Basic Books.

APA. 2013. *The principles of medical ethics: With annotations especially applicable to psychiatry*. American Psychiatric Association.

Clifford Beers. 1917. *A Mind That Found Itself: An Autobiography*. Project Gutenberg. https://www.gutenberg.org/ebooks/11962.

Joel Brynielsson, Andreas Horndahl, Fredrik Johansson, Lisa Kaati, Christian Mårtenson, and Pontus Svenson. 2013. Harvesting and analysis of weak signals for detecting lone wolf terrorists. *Security Informatics* 2(1):11. https://doi.org/10.1186/2190-8532-2-11.

Katie Cohen, Fredrik Johansson, Lisa Kaati, and Jonas Clausen Mork. 2014. Detecting linguistic markers for radical violence in social media. *Terrorism and Political Violence* 26(1):246–256. https://doi.org/10.1080/09546553.2014.849948.

Bruce E. Compas, Jennifer K. Connor-Smith, Heidi Saltzman, Alexandria Harding Thomsen, and Martha E. Wadsworth. 2001. Coping with stress during childhood and adolescence: problems, progress, and potential in theory and research. *Psychological bulletin* 127(1):87. https://doi.org/10.1037/0033-2909.127.1.87.

Clarence Darrow. 1932. *The Story of My Life*. Project Gutenberg. http://gutenberg.net.au/ebooks05/0500951.txt.

Martin Davies, Max Coltheart, Robyn Langdon, and Nora Breen. 2001. Monothematic delusions: Towards a two-factor account. *Philosophy, Psychiatry, & Psychology* 8(2):133–158. https://doi.org/10.1353/ppp.2001.0007.

Frederick Douglass. 1845. *The Narrative of the Life of Frederick Douglass, an American Slave*. Project Gutenberg. https://www.gutenberg.org/ebooks/23.

Paul Feyerabend. 1975. How to defend society against science. *Radical Philosophy* 11(1):3–9.

Michael B. First and Miriam Gibbon. 2004. *The Structured Clinical Interview for DSM-IV Axis I Disorders (SCID-I) and the Structured Clinical Interview for DSM-IV Axis II Disorders (SCID-II).*, John Wiley & Sons Inc, pages 134–143.

James Alan Fox and Emma E Fridel. 2016. The tenuous connections involving mass shootings, mental illness, and gun laws. *Violence and gender* 3(1):14–19. https://doi.org/10.1089/vio.2015.0054.

Wyndol Furman and Duane Buhrmester. 1992. Age and sex differences in perceptions of networks of personal relationships. *Child development* 63(1):103–115. https://doi.org/10.1111/j.1467-8624.1992.tb03599.x.

Dariusz Galasiński. 2017. Context and goals: Suicide notes from a linguistic point of view. *Death Studies* pages 1–2. https://doi.org/10.1080/07481187.2017.1292815.

George Graham. 2013. *The disordered mind: An introduction to philosophy of mind and mental illness*. Routledge.

Adolf Hitler. 1939. *Mein Kampf*. Project Gutenberg. http://gutenberg.net.au/ebooks02/0200601.txt.

Minqing Hu and Bing Liu. 2004. Mining and summarizing customer reviews. In *Proceedings of the Tenth ACM SIGKDD International Conference on Knowledge Discovery and Data Mining*. ACM, New York, NY, USA, KDD '04, pages 168–177. https://doi.org/10.1145/1014052.1014073.

Louis Hughes. 1897. *Thirty Years a Slave*. Project Gutenberg. https://www.gutenberg.org/ebooks/10431.

James L Knoll and J Reid Meloy. 2014. Mass murder and the violent paranoid spectrum. *Psychiatric Annals* 44(5):236–243. https://doi.org/10.3928/00485713-20140502-07.

Jerome Kroll and Claire Pouncey. 2016. The ethics of apas goldwater rule. *J Am Acad Psychiatry Law* 44:226–235. https://www.ncbi.nlm.nih.gov/pubmed/27236179.

William J Krouse and Daniel J Richardson. 2015. Mass murder with firearms: Incidents and victims, 1999-2013. *Congressional Research Service, Library of Congress* https://fas.org/sgp/crs/misc/R44126.pdf.

C Ray Lake. 2014. Psychotic rampage killers: Mania, not schizophrenia—psychiatrys role in prevention. *Psychiatric Annals* 44(5):213–214. https://doi.org/10.3928/00485713-20140502-04.

Jeanne Lenzer. 2017. Do doctors have a "duty to warn" if they believe a leader is dangerously mentally ill? *BMJ* 356:j1087. https://doi.org/10.1136/bmj.j1087.

Dan P. McAdams, Jeffrey Reynolds, Martha Lewis, Allison H. Patten, and Phillip J. Bowman. 2001. When bad things turn good and good things turn bad: Sequences of redemption and contamination in life narrative and their relation to psychosocial adaptation in midlife adults and in students. *Personality and Social Psychology Bulletin* 27(4):474–485. https://doi.org/10.1177/0146167201274008.

J Reid Meloy, Anthony G Hempel, Kris Mohandie, Andrew A Shiva, and B Thomas Gray. 2001. Offender and offense characteristics of a nonrandom sample of adolescent mass murderers. *Journal of the American Academy of Child & Adolescent Psychiatry* 40(6):719–728. https://doi.org/10.1097/00004583-200106000-00018.

Amanda B. Nickerson and Richard J. Nagle. 2005. Parent and peer attachment in late childhood and early adolescence. *The Journal of Early Adolescence* 25(2):223–249. https://doi.org/10.1177/0272431604274174.

Gareth Owen and Robert Harland. 2007. Editor's introduction: Theme issue on phenomenology and psychiatry for the 21st century. taking phenomenology seriously. *Schizophrenia bulletin* 33(1):105. https://doi.org/10.1093/schbul/sbl059.

James W. Pennebaker, Ryan L. Boyd, Kayla Jordan, and Kate Blackburn. 2015. The development and psychometric properties of liwc2015. *UT Faculty/Researcher Works* http://hdl.handle.net/2152/31333.

James W. Pennebaker and Lori D. Stone. 2003. Words of wisdom: language use over the life span. *Journal of personality and social psychology* 85(2):291. https://doi.org/10.1037/0022-3514.85.2.291.

John Pestian, Henry Nasrallah, Pawel Matykiewicz, Aurora Bennett, and Antoon Leenaars. 2010. Suicide note classification using natural language processing: A content analysis. *Biomedical informatics insights* 2010(3):19. https://www.ncbi.nlm.nih.gov/pubmed/21643548.

R Core Team. 2017. *R: A Language and Environment for Statistical Computing*. R Foundation for Statistical Computing, Vienna, Austria. Version 3.4.0. https://www.R-project.org.

Tyler W. Rinker. 2017. *sentimentr: Calculate Text Polarity Sentiment*. Version 1.0.0. https://github.com/trinker/sentimentr.

Elliot Rodger. 2014. *My Twisted World: The Story of Elliot Rodger*. Cryptome. https://cryptome.org/2014/05/elliot-rodger.pdf.

UNODC. 2013. *Global study on homicide 2013: trends, contexts, data*. United Nations.

Small but Mighty: Affective Micropatterns for Quantifying Mental Health from Social Media Language

Kate Loveys
Qntfy
kate@qntfy.com

Patrick Crutchley
Qntfy
patrick@qntfy.com

Emily Wyatt
Qntfy
emily.wyatt@qntfy.com

Glen Coppersmith
Qntfy
glen@qntfy.com

Abstract

Many psychological phenomena occur in small time windows, measured in minutes or hours. However, most computational linguistic techniques look at data on the order of weeks, months, or years. We explore *micropatterns* in sequences of messages occurring over a short time window for their prevalence and power for quantifying psychological phenomena, specifically, patterns in affect. We examine affective micropatterns in social media posts from users with anxiety, eating disorders, panic attacks, schizophrenia, suicidality, and matched controls.

1 Introduction

Mental illness and suicide pose a significant public health problem. Each year approximately 800,000 people will die by suicide, and an estimated 16 million suicide attempts will occur (World Health Organization, 2013). Mental illness is a similarly widespread problem, affecting almost one in four people worldwide during the course of their lifetime (World Health Organization, 2013). Mental illness (including suicide) detrimentally affects quality of life, ranking as the fourth-largest contributor to disability-adjusted life years (Vigo et al., 2016). Moreover, five of the top twenty causes of global disease burden were from mental illness (Vigo et al., 2016). Little progress has been made over the past fifty years in terms of improving these figures (Franklin et al., 2016).

A key step to reducing the global burden of mental illness and suicide deaths is to ensure that early risk detection and intervention occur (Insel, 2009). Current systems of care struggle with scalability and measures of long term efficacy. Given recent advances in many industries by ubiq-uitous technology and data science, many hold out hope that a similar revolution is possible in mental health. *Digital phenotyping*, where data from everyday interactions with digital devices like smartphones and computers can be turned into quantifiable signals of mental health, holds promise for providing the real-time data needed for these advances. Real-time analysis of dispositional and discrete situational factors could help clinicians predict the onset or exacerbation of symptoms or suicidal behaviors (Nelson et al., 2017). This would transcend analysis and open the possibility for data-empowered interventions.

Generally, computational linguistics uses techniques that examine significant portions of a user's data, spanning a long period of time. The few exceptions still only examine subsets of the data on the order of days or weeks (Resnik et al., 2015; Coppersmith et al., 2016; Mitchell et al., 2015). However, there are meaningful psychological phenomena occurring at much smaller time scales that slip past current methods (Nelson et al., 2017). Micropatterns, inspired by Bryan et al. (in press), are intended to focus on this neglected time window on the order of hours, by analyzing consecutive social media posts within such a window.

Here we examine affective micropatterns in language produced by individuals with a self-reported diagnosis of mental illness, a panic attack or suicide history, and neurotypical controls. We evaluate the affective valence of sequences of three consecutive tweets produced by individuals in each user group to identify micropatterns characteristic of each group. We compared suicide, panic attack, and mental illness group micropatterns to those of neurotypical controls. We address two questions:

[1] Are there meaningful signals in affective micropatterns relevant to mental health?

[2] Do micropatterns hold more information than the labels that make up their components?

Proceedings of the Fourth Workshop on Computational Linguistics and Clinical Psychology, pages 85–95,
Vancouver, Canada, August 3, 2017. © 2017 Association for Computational Linguistics

This paper is the first time that affective micropatterns are examined directly, rather than as a component of a more complex learning system. This is also the first time that the relative power of micropatterns is explored beyond suicide risk.

1.1 Why Social Media?

One particularly compelling and rich source of data for digital phenotyping is language. Language provides a window into the perception, cognition, and other psychological processes at work in a person, and thus provides a useful lens through which we can understand, quantify, and eventually improve mental health. Social media, in particular, provides a trove of language data in a form conducive to computational analysis. Critically for this work, it also includes the time that a particular piece of language was authored by the user. Social media is, thus, one data source through which the early signs of mental illness and suicide can be detected (Reece et al., 2016; Coppersmith et al., 2016; Bryan et al., in press). Quantifiable signals for a wide range of behavioral health conditions have been uncovered recently, and this provides a foothold into analysis and intervention empowered by data science. A wide array of conditions have been studied including major depressive disorder (Chung and Pennebaker, 2007; De Choudhury et al., 2013), post-traumatic stress disorder (Coppersmith et al., 2014b, 2015b; Resnik et al., 2015; Preotiuc-Pietro et al., 2015; Pedersen, 2015), schizophrenia (Mitchell et al., 2015), eating disorders (Walker et al., 2015; Chancellor et al., 2016), generalized anxiety disorder, bipolar disorder (Coppersmith et al., 2014a), suicide (Coppersmith et al., 2015c; Kumar et al., 2015; Wood et al., 2016; Kiciman et al., 2016), borderline personality disorder, and others (Coppersmith et al., 2015a).

1.2 Social Media Micropattern Analysis

Micropatterns in short sequences of emotion, cognition, behavior and symptoms relevant to specific psychological states may be evident in social media data, reflecting dynamic shifts in internal situational factors. Many social media users report enough personal information on public feeds to be able to capture brief shifts in behaviors, cognitions, emotions, and symptoms relevant to particular psychological states. This information has been used to assess whether a user is declining into a suicidal state (Bryan et al., in press). Bryan

et al. (in press) found that distinct micropatterns in content of social media posts were predictive of proximity to a suicide death. One month prior to a suicide death, a seesaw-like effect was observed between social media posts about a maladaptive coping behavior and a negative belief, and at one week prior to a suicide death, this negative relationship grows stronger. Bryan et al. (in press) detected micropatterns from human-labeled posts and a complex model informed by dynamic systems theory. Here, we complement this work by adding automation to the labeling and exploring the micropatterns directly, rather than embedded in a larger system. No prior research has evaluated micropatterns in social media post content for psychological disorders other than suicidality.

This technique of looking at short subsequent posts and the psychological phenomena present therein is relatively new, so we aim for simplicity and straightforwardness in our experimental design and features. While there are a number of potentially more interesting avenues of exploration involving fine-grained emotions, psychologically meaningful events, coping mechanisms, and decompensation, we eschew the added complexity in favor of exploring a fundamental unanswered question: Is there meaningful signal in the micropatterns relevant to mental health?

1.3 Symptom Dynamics

Broadly, the motivation for exploring micropatterns and data on the timescale of minutes and hours stems from the importance of temporal information in the assessment of psychological symptoms. Knowledge of symptom co-occurrence over specified time periods can determine whether a mental illness diagnosis is received, as well as inform assessments of treatment responsiveness and relapse (American Psychiatric Association, 2013; Nelson et al., 2017). Temporal information is essential to detecting ongoing fluctuations in psychological symptoms, which may be key to predicting the onset of psychological disorders or increased suicide risk (McGorry and van Os, 2013).

Emotions, behavior, and cognitions fluctuate rapidly as an individual interacts with the environment (van Ockenburg et al., 2015; van Os, 2013). People have tendencies to behave, think, or feel certain ways, however, conditions and interactions fluctuate and one might have a markedly different reaction to the same environment on a different day. These brief shifts in behaviors, emotions, cognitions, and physical symptoms relative to one another in an environment, over the course of seconds to hours, can determine a persons present-moment psychological state (van Os, 2013). The Fluid Vulnerability theory encapsulates this idea, suggesting that daily perturbations in situational factors interact with dispositional factors to trigger present-moment psychological states (Rudd, 2006). Dispositional (or distal) factors establish baseline risk, and are relatively fixed variables such as demographics, trait characteristics, beliefs or life histories, which tend to indicate stable predispositions toward experiencing particular psychological states or disorders. Conversely, situational (or proximal) factors indicate the likelihood that a person experiences a mental illness episode or engages in self-harming behavior at a specific point in time. Examples could include events such as the onset of a troubling thought or an unpleasant social interaction in the workplace. The Fluid Vulnerability theory suggests that for individuals with low baseline risk, even a severe stressor will not elicit suicidality or exacerbations in mental illness symptoms; alternatively, for people with high baseline risk, situational factors conducive to suicidality or mental illness episodes need not be as high for an episode to be triggered (Rudd, 2006). Most work at the intersection of natural language processing and social media has focused on assessing dispositional factors through examination of a large corpus of posts. However, assessing more situational risk factors will require a different set of methods. While existing bag of words approaches evaluate dispositional risk factors, temporal analyses are necessary to detect brief fluctuations in situational risk factors.

2   Data

We briefly explain the data collection method here, but we refer the interested reader with further questions on the methodology to Coppersmith et al. (2016) for the suicide attempt data and Coppersmith et al. (2014a) for all other conditions.

The data for these analyses are Twitter posts collected via two methods. Most of the data come from users who have publicly discussed their mental health conditions. These users are frequently referred to as "self-stated diagnosis" users, as they state publicly something like "I was diagnosed with schizophrenia", or "I'm so thankful to have survived my suicide attempt last year". The data for users with a suicide attempt was supplemented by data from `OurDataHelps.org`, a data donation site where people provide access to their public posts and fill out a short questionnaire about their mental health history. Data are then de-identified and made available to researchers addressing questions of interest to the mental health community. Donors provide consent for their data to be used in mental health research upon sign-up. Of the users who attempted suicide, 146 came from `OurDataHelps.org`.

Specifically, we examine generalized anxiety disorder, eating disorders, panic attacks, schizophrenia, and attempted suicides. These conditions were selected based on the theory that there are important timing aspects to their symptoms – ebbing and flowing of symptoms as treatment is effective (especially schizophrenia), onset and exacerbation of symptoms by external events and stress, and punctuated events in time of psychological symptoms (suicide attempts, panic attacks, and binging/purging behavior with eating disorders).

We use the Twitter streaming API to collect a sample of users who used a series of mental health words or phrases in their tweet text (e.g., 'schizophrenia' or 'suicide attempt'). Each tweet that uses one of these phrases is examined via regular expression to indicate that the user is talking about themselves. Finally, those tweets that pass the regular expression are examined by a human to confirm (to the best of our ability) that their self-statement of diagnosis appears to be genuine.

This results in a dataset with users that have a self-stated diagnosis of generalized anxiety disorder ($n = 2408$), an eating disorder (749), panic attacks (263), schizophrenia (350), or someone who would go on to attempt suicide (423). Some of these users do not exhibit the sort of posting behavior required to create micropatterns (i.e., they rarely post multiple times within a 3 hour time window). We exclude these users from our analysis, which is 5-9% of users for most conditions, with the exception of those with a suicide attempt, where a little over half the users do not exhibit this posting behavior. The resultant dataset used for analyses is: generalized anxiety disorder ($n = 2271$), eating disorders (687), panic attacks (247), schizophrenia (318), suicide attempts (157).

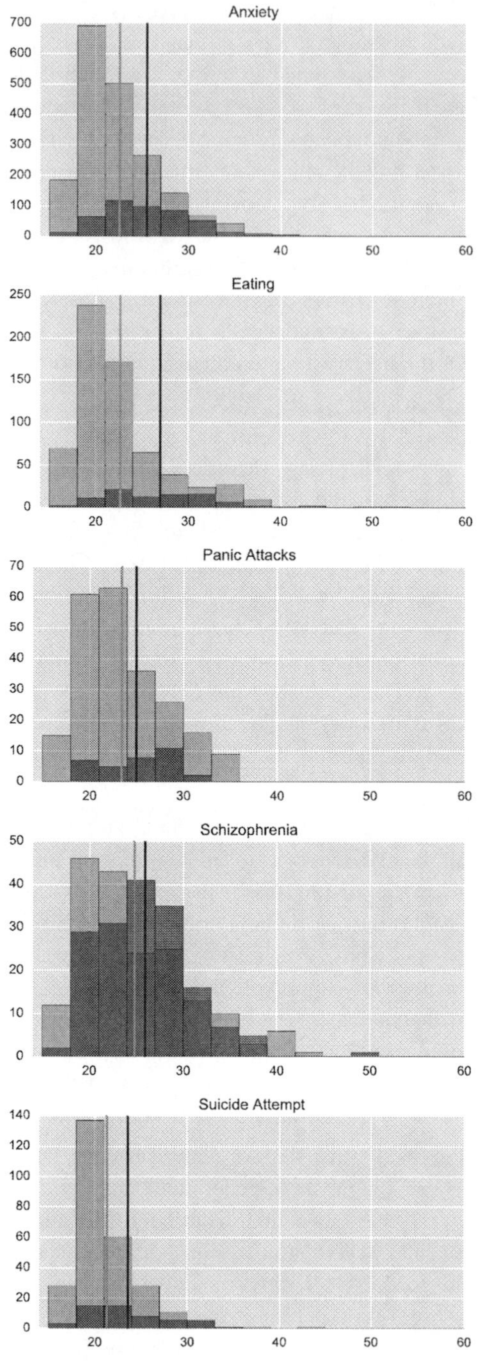

Figure 1: Histograms of age distributions for each condition. Females are in coral and males are in blue. The mean of each gender is denoted by the corresponding vertical line.

In order to allow comparisons of each condition to control users, we gather a random sample of 10,000 Twitter users for whom at least 75% of their posts are identified by Twitter as English. All the users with a self-stated diagnoses and all members of this control population have their age and gender estimated according to Sap et al. (2014). For each user with a self-stated diagnosis, we find a matched control through the following procedure: create a pool of users where the estimated gender matches and the estimated age is within the same 10-year bracket (the suggested accuracy of the age estimator). From that pool of age- and gender- matched users, we select the user whose tweets start and end over the most similar timeframe. We will refer to these age-, gender-, and time-matched controls simply as "matched controls" throughout the rest of this paper.

All tweets were publicly posted by their author (i.e., no users marked at "protected" or "private" were included). On average, users had 2949 tweets. The distribution of estimated age and genders for users with each self-stated condition can be seen in Figure 1. For most conditions, the population skews female, though for schizophrenia the genders are roughly balanced. The average age tends to be in the early-to-mid 20s.

2.1 Caveats

All of the following analysis is subject to a few caveats emergent from the data and how the data were collected. The users with mental health conditions are all found data of one sort or another, so there are some inherent biases. We prefer to express these biases rather than add complexity by attempting to cleverly correct for them. Many of these users talk publicly about their mental health, which given the stigma and discrimination they face, is likely a distinct subpopulation of those with mental health conditions. It is possible that users with a psychological disorder or suicide history who did not publicly disclose this information could have been included in the control group for analyses, which may have the effect of artificially lowering the estimated power of any emergent differences. Users who donated data through `OurDataHelps.org` are likely biased differently, with over representation of altruism, since they are willing to do things for the public good without any obvious self gain. Another consideration is that all users who reported a suicide attempt within our dataset survived. There is a possibility that characteristic differences also exist between individuals who do and do not die by

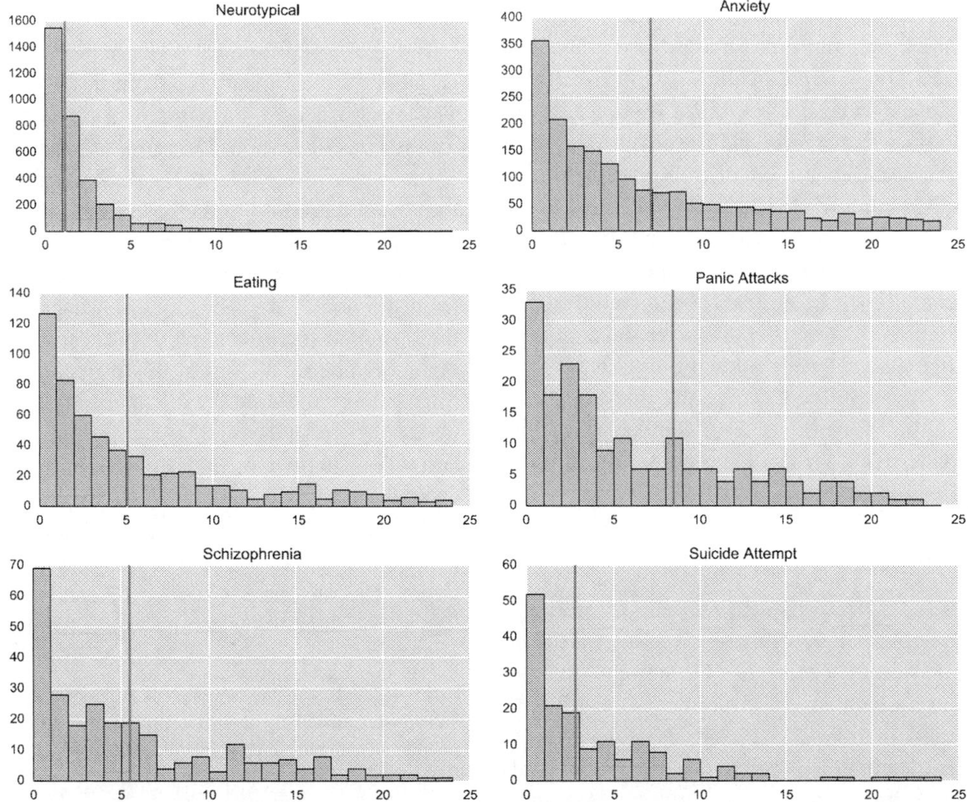

Figure 2: Histograms of micropattern per day average for each condition. The median for each condition is denoted by the vertical blue line. Note that neurotypicals generally generate micropatterns at a rate lower than the mental health conditions, with the exception of users who would go on to attempt suicide.

a suicide attempt. Note that this research was conducted on English-speaking social media users. The content of social media post micropatterns for psychological disorders and suicidality could differ between cultural contexts, due to differences in cross-cultural expressions of mental illness (Chentsova-Dutton et al., 2007). These are active Twitter users, which imparts a demographic skew compared to the rest of the world (in particular, these users skew young). We see more females in our user populations than the rough gender balance observed for general Twitter users (Greenwood et al., 2016). The language data itself is meant for public consumption, and may reflect how the authors wish to be perceived, and not what one would get from a more traditional journal study of internal and private thoughts and feelings. Finally, we **include** users who had a concomittant or comorbid mental health condition. Thus a small number of users appear in more than one category.

3 Methods

This study aimed to examine the prevalence of affective *micropatterns* in social media posts and highlight differences in micropattern occurrence that might be relevant to quantifying mental health. Primarily, we do this through comparison of users with anxiety disorders, eating disorders, schizophrenia, suicide attempt history, and their matched controls.

We use a straightforward and well-understood method for sentiment analysis, VADER (Hutto and Gilbert, 2014), to produce a trinary label for each message: `positive`, `neutral`, or `negative`. VADER outputs a $[0, 1]$ score for each sentiment label; we use the label with the maximum score.

Specifically, we examined trajectories of posted emotional content in three subsequent tweets, no more than three hours from earliest to latest. The same tweet will be counted in more than one overlapping micropattern if more than three tweets occur in the three-hour time window – so if 5 tweets occur in 3 hours, 3 micropatterns will be recorded from those 5 tweets, likewise for 4 tweets, 2 micropatterns will be recorded. The potential overlap exists for both patients and neurotypical users, and subsequent analyses (e.g., classifying users based on proportion of micropatterns) were designed to be robust to this property of overlapping micropattern generation. The number of sequential tweets to examine was chosen to minimize the complexity of the analysis while allowing significant variability to be observed. Critically, we aimed for the resulting dimensions (i.e., number of distinct micropatterns) to be small enough for meaningful interpretation by clinical psychologists.

4 Results

Our results collectively suggest that **(1)** micropatterns are not random **(2)** there are some significant differences in the occurrence of micropatterns between users who have a given mental health condition and their matched controls and **(3)** there is some quantifiable predictive power for separating users with mental health conditions from their matched controls captured by the micropatterns, in excess of what power the labels that underlie the micropattern have alone.

4.1 Micropatterns are not Randomly Distributed

Before any analysis of the differences in micropattern occurrence between users with mental health conditions and their matched controls, we demonstrate that these micropatterns are not randomly distributed, nor are they an artifact of the different base rate of users with mental health conditions expressing negative sentiment more often.

Previous work indicates that there are some expected variability in the proportion of messages from users in each condition, and significantly different from their matched control users (Coppersmith et al., 2015a). Specifically, it has been widely reported that users with certain behavioral health conditions use more words from the LIWC category `Negative Emotion` (Chung and Pennebaker, 2007; Park et al., 2012; De Choudhury et al., 2012; Coppersmith et al., 2015a), which in this case would have the effect of inflating the number and proportion of micropatterns involving `negative` labels, simply because

the prevalence of these labels were higher.

For each condition, we observe the distribution of labels for all messages from each condition. This establishes the base rate of each label occurring for that condition. Using these base rates, we randomly generate a label for each message from each user according to the base rate (i.e., respecting the timestamps of each post, but randomly assigning a label rather than what VADER predicted from the text). We then, for each user, examine the observed micropatterns with these randomly-assigned labels. We repeat this procedure 10,000 times, thus providing a null distribution of what we would expect the number and proportion of micropatterns to be if the underlying sentiment labels were randomly distributed. When we compare the observed value from real data to this randomly-generated population, the differences are stark and large. The observed z-scores for each micropattern's deviation from normal range from 13.3 to 423859.1, with a median of 895.5. Since the significance for a z-score (at the $p < 0.05$ level) is 1.96, we can safely assume that the observed population of labels was not likely the result of a random process. This strongly suggests that the differences observed are not attributable merely to random fluctuations and a different base-rate of the underlying labels.

4.2 Differences in Micropatterns

Figure 3 shows the deviation in each micropattern for users with mental health conditions relative to their matched neurotypical controls. This, taken with significant differences observed in matched-sample t-tests (omitted for brevity), clearly indicates that there are significant differences in micropatterns for a range of mental health conditions. While there are some observed similarities between the changes in micropatterns across conditions, significant differences exist between the various mental health conditions and their deviations from controls.

Note that the vast majority of the micropatterns observed in all conditions ($> 80\%$) are (`neutral, neutral, neutral`). This is likely an overestimate of the number of neutral messages present, due to the closed-vocabulary nature of our lexicon-based labeling approach. Specifically, VADER depends on a lexicon of words and associated scores, and lexicon-based approaches generally provide higher precision

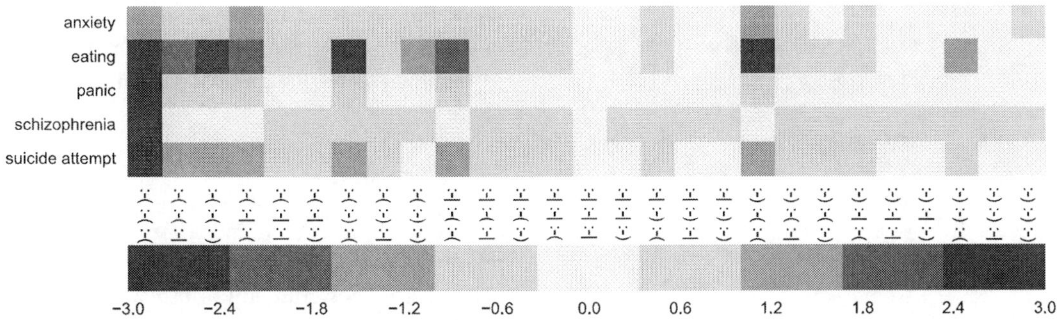

Figure 3: Change in micropattern frequency relative to age-, gender-, and time-matched controls for each condition. Red cells indicate lower frequency in users with a given mental health condition versus neurotypical, blue cells indicate higher frequency in users with a mental health condition versus neurotypical. Emoticons below the columns indicate the patterns in sentiment: far left is `(negative,negative,negative)`, second to left is `(negative,negative,neutral)`, and far right is `(positive,positive,positive)`.

(i.e., fewer false alarms, which means fewer neutral messages tagged as valenced) at the cost of significantly decreased recall (i.e., many valenced messages are tagged as neutral). This is exacerbated by the fact we are scoring individual tweets, which contain relatively few words. Thus, while there are often some parameters to adjust around the sensitivity of classifiers, the combination of the lexicon approach and the short document makes for a very sparse set of features to score from. In turn, this tends to create more `neutral` labeled messages.

Some observed deviations line up with current psychological literature, providing some face-validity to this approach. First, all mental health conditions show an increase in the number of `(negative,negative,negative)` affect micropatterns. This is consistent with the widely-found phenomenon that those with mental health conditions tend to experience greater negative affect (Chung and Pennebaker, 2007; Park et al., 2012; De Choudhury et al., 2012; Coppersmith et al., 2015a). This does suggest, though, that these are not necessarily randomly distributed negative posts, but in fact they are more likely to have concentrated and subsequent strings of negative posts. Second, users with schizophrenia were less likely than neurotypicals to show affect or affective variability between posts. This reflects research suggesting that individuals with schizophrenia display deficits in affective expression; a common negative symptom triggered by both disease pathophysiology and use of

antipsychotic medication (Messinger et al., 2011). Third, we see increases in affective volatility by users prior to a suicide attempt (as evidenced by `(positive,negative,positive)` and `(negative,positive,negative)` micropatterns, consistent with many as-of-yet unpublished findings from the Jelenik Summer Workshop at Johns Hopkins University (Hollingshead et al., in prep.). Fourth, users with an anxiety disorder were less likely than neurotypical controls to post consecutive positively-valenced tweets. This may be reflective of a negative attentional bias often associated with anxious emotion (Bar-Haim et al., 2007).

4.3 Separating Users

We also aim to understand if micropatterns convey some additional information about mental health and mental health status, above and beyond the labels that go into the micropattern (in this case, `positive`, `negative`, and `neutral` sentiment labels). Ideally, we would examine how well micropatterns could predict meaningful psychological events, but we lack significant data to do this more than anecdotally. Instead, we continue in line with previous work and compare performance on a binary prediction task. The task is to separate users with mental health conditions from their matched controls. Rather than examining absolute performance of this task as if it were a real world scenario, we aim to examine the *relative* performance of the micropatterns, the underlying sentiment labels, and a combination of the two, as a

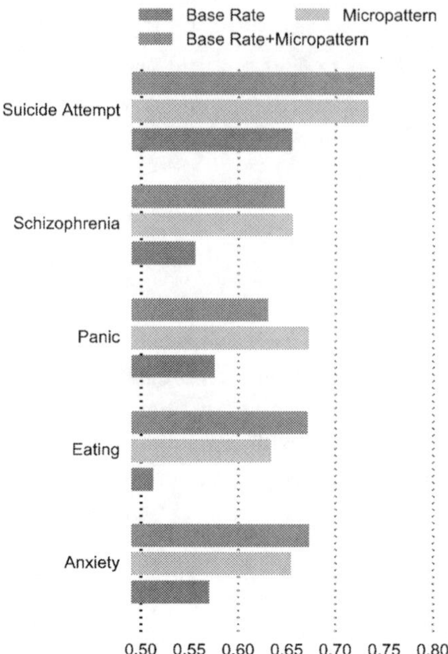

Figure 4: Prediction accuracy for separating users with mental health conditions from their matched controls by base rate occurrence of sentiment labels alone (blue) and occurrence of micropatterns alone (green) and both features together (coral). Chance is 0.5 and is denoted by a black dotted vertical line.

way of assessing how much unique information the micropatterns themselves impart[1].

For each user, we created a feature vector where each entry was the proportion of micropatterns that a particular micropattern made up. Similarly, we made a feature vector for the proportion of sentiment labels that each sentiment label made up (the base rate). Figure 4 shows the accuracy results of a 10-fold cross validation binary classification experiment (balanced samples) using a random forest classifier. In all cases, the micropatterns outperform the base rate, which is often little better than chance. In most cases, using both signals together (by concatenating the feature vectors) provides no significant gain in performance over either one alone. This suggests that for most conditions, most of the information from the sentiment labels are captured as part of the micropat-

---

[1]From an information theoretic perspective, it may be more appropriate to say how much information is lost by ignoring the ordering of the labels (in going from the micropatterns to simply the sentiment labels).

terns, but not all of it. Thus, we are led to conclude that micropatterns do provide additional information over the base rate of the sentiment labels alone.

5 Discussion

This paper presents foundational analysis of a relatively novel computational linguistic method that incorporates temporal information over short durations. Micropattern analysis provides information about common shifts in language content which may be useful for helping to distinguish between people with and without a psychological disorder or suicide risk. This study demonstrated that micropatterns in social media posts hold some power to distinguish between users who have a mental health condition or a history of suicide attempts or panic attacks from their matched controls.

Despite potential limitations, this study provides promising evidence in support of using micropattern analysis to detect progressions in suicide risk and symptoms of psychological disorders in future research. While the present study demonstrated that differences in micropatterns exist between users with and without a particular psychological disorder, information was not gathered on whether specific micropatterns can indicate the severity of a psychological disorder. We also did not assess whether micropatterns can distinguish between clinical conditions, and this is a likely next step for future research.

While there are a number of potentially more interesting avenues of exploration involving more fine-grained emotions, psychologically meaningful events, sleep disturbance, physical symptoms, coping mechanisms, decompensation, and their interplay, these bring with them an exponential complexity. We have done some preliminary examination of more fine-grained emotional labels, and found that interpretation and assessment was unwieldy and too complex for a reasonable human to undertake – 27 possible micropatterns are observed here (three labels, observed over three subsequent messages: $3^3 = 27$). Extending this to the emotion classifier from Coppersmith et al. (2016), for example, would bring this to $8^3 = 512$ micropatterns. Careful thought is required for analysis as the depth of possible labels grows.

Many avenues for future work seem apparent, as the veritable panoply of labels to augment the straightforward VADER sentiment labels opens up. However, first and foremost of those possibilities is to directly replicate the work of Bryan et al. (in press) and extend it to non-military populations, and populations of different demographics to assess generalizability. This paper strongly suggests that micropatterns hold power for a wide range of mental health conditions, not just suicide risk. Specifically, including some of the known-relevant psychological phenomena that can be inferred from explicit self-reports seem a worthwhile next step, including: cognitive symptoms, physical symptoms, sleep disturbance, coping behavior, and suicidal thoughts and behavior.

Ultimately, technology is only a small part of the solution, since humans, workflows, and incentives that make up the existing system of care will need to integrate these technological solutions into their processes.

5.1 Ethics and Privacy

We gave careful consideration to the ethics and privacy surrounding this work, and employed the ethical guidelines from Benton et al. (2017), and used social media data donated with consent for use in mental health research from `OurDataHelps.Org`. We strongly encourage researchers interested in working in this space to consider the ethical implications from the outset, both of the research itself and also for the possible resultant technology. Recently, Mikal et al. (2016) conducted focus groups around their perception of this vein of work, which has greatly informed our work, and we heartily recommend it for informing ethical discussions.

6 Conclusion

We present evidence that quantifiable information relevant to mental health can be found in examining subsequent posts in relatively short order (so-called *micropatterns*). Furthermore, we demonstrate that even with a simple and straightforward lexicon approach, signficant deviations in micropatterns can be found between users who have mental health conditions and their matched controls. While some of the observable differences have face validity and align with existing psychological literature, some remain unexplained. Moreover, micropatterns hold more predictive power than the sentiment labels that they rely upon, which suggests that they are capturing

important information not captured by the sentiment of the message alone. The results here were presented on simple and straightforward lexicon-based linguistic analysis, but the evidence strongly suggests that increasing the variety of psychologically meaningful (e.g., life changing events, coping mechanisms, decompensation) will lead to additional fruitful insights. Challenges remain about the sheer dimensionality of these more complex micropatterns, and how they should be best interpreted for synthesis with the psychological literature. While there is significant future work to understand why these micropatterns emerge and what value they hold for psychological understanding and intervention, we see this as a promising step, and a worthy avenue of future study.

Acknowledgments

The authors would like ackowledge the support of the 2016 Jelinek Memorial Workshop on Speech and Language Technology, at Johns Hopkins University, for providing the concerted time to perform this research. The authors would like to especially thank Craig and Annabelle Bryan for the inspiration for this work and the generosity with which they shared their time to mutually explore results. Finally and more importantly, the authors would like to thank the people who donated their data at `OurDataHelps.org` to support this and other research endeavors at the intersection of data science and mental health.

References

American Psychiatric Association. 2013. *Diagnostic and Statistical Manual of Mental Disorders (5th Edition)*. Arlington, VA: American Psychiatric Publishing.

Yair Bar-Haim, Dominique Lamy, Lee Pergamin, Marian J Bakermans-Kranenburg, and Marinus H Van Ijzendoorn. 2007. Threat-related attentional bias in anxious and nonanxious individuals: a meta-analytic study. *Psychological bulletin* 133(1):1.

Adrian Benton, Glen Coppersmith, and Mark Dredze. 2017. Ethical research protocols for social media health research. *EACL 2017* page 94.

C. J. Bryan, J. E. Butner, S. Sinclair, A. O. Bryan, C. M. Hesse, and A. E. Rose. in press. Predictors of emerging suicide death among military personnel on social media networks. *Suicide and Life-Threatening Behavior* .

Stevie Chancellor, Tanushree Mitra, and Munmun De Choudhury. 2016. Recovery amid pro-anorexia: Analysis of recovery in social media. In *Proceedings of the 2016 CHI Conference on Human Factors in Computing Systems*. ACM, pages 2111–2123.

Yulia E. Chentsova-Dutton, Joyce P Chu, Jeanne L Tsai, Jonathan Rottenberg, James J Gross, and Ian H Gotlib. 2007. Depression and emotional reactivity: variation among Asian Americans of East Asian descent and European Americans. *Journal of Abnormal Psychology* 116(4):776–785. https://doi.org/10.1037/0021-843X.116.4.776.

Cindy Chung and James Pennebaker. 2007. The psychological functions of function words. *Social Communication* .

Glen Coppersmith, Mark Dredze, and Craig Harman. 2014a. Quantifying mental health signals in Twitter. In *Proceedings of the ACL Workshop on Computational Linguistics and Clinical Psychology*.

Glen Coppersmith, Mark Dredze, Craig Harman, and Kristy Hollingshead. 2015a. From ADHD to SAD: Analyzing the language of mental health on Twitter through self-reported diagnoses. In *Proceedings of the Workshop on Computational Linguistics and Clinical Psychology: From Linguistic Signal to Clinical Reality*. North American Chapter of the Association for Computational Linguistics, Denver, Colorado, USA.

Glen Coppersmith, Mark Dredze, Craig Harman, Kristy Hollingshead, and Margaret Mitchell. 2015b. CLPsych 2015 shared task: Depression and PTSD on Twitter. In *Proceedings of the Shared Task for the NAACL Workshop on Computational Linguistics and Clinical Psychology*.

Glen Coppersmith, Craig Harman, and Mark Dredze. 2014b. Measuring post traumatic stress disorder in Twitter. In *Proceedings of the 8th International AAAI Conference on Weblogs and Social Media (ICWSM)*.

Glen Coppersmith, Ryan Leary, Eric Whyne, and Tony Wood. 2015c. Quantifying suicidal ideation via language usage on social media. In *Joint Statistics Meetings Proceedings, Statistical Computing Section*. JSM.

Glen Coppersmith, Kim Ngo, Ryan Leary, and Tony Wood. 2016. Exploratory data analysis of social media prior to a suicide attempt. In *Proceedings of the Workshop on Computational Linguistics and Clinical Psychology: From Linguistic Signal to Clinical Reality*. North American Chapter of the Association for Computational Linguistics, San Diego, California, USA.

Munmun De Choudhury, Michael Gamon, and Scott Counts. 2012. Happy, nervous or surprised? Classification of human affective states in social media. In *Proceedings of the 6th International AAAI Conference on Weblogs and Social Media (ICWSM)*.

Munmun De Choudhury, Michael Gamon, Scott Counts, and Eric Horvitz. 2013. Predicting depression via social media. In *Proceedings of the 7th International AAAI Conference on Weblogs and Social Media (ICWSM)*.

Joseph C Franklin, Jessica D Ribeiro, Kathryn R Fox, Kate H Bentley, Evan M Kleiman, Xieyining Huang, Katherine M Musacchio, Adam C Jaroszewski, Bernard P Chang, and Matthew K Nock. 2016. Risk factors for suicidal thoughts and behaviors: A meta-analysis of 50 years of research. .

S Greenwood, A Perrin, and M Duggan. 2016. Social media update 2016: Facebook usage and engagement is on the rise, while adoption of other platforms holds steady.

Kristy Hollingshead, H Andrew Schwartz, Glen Coppersmith, Fatemeh Almoradasi, Adrian Benton, Jeff Craley, Patrick Crutchley, Dirk Hovy, Molly Ireland, Bu Sun Kim, Leo Kim, Raina Merchant, Margaret Mitchell, Phillip Resnik, Masoud Rouhizadeh, and Lyle Ungar. in prep. Detecting risk and protective factors of mental health using social media. *Center for Language and Speech Processing Technical Reports* .

Clayton J Hutto and Eric Gilbert. 2014. Vader: A parsimonious rule-based model for sentiment analysis of social media text. In *Eighth International AAAI Conference on Weblogs and Social Media*.

Thomas R Insel. 2009. Translating scientific opportunity into public health impact: a strategic plan for research on mental illness. *Archives of General Psychiatry* 66(2):128–133.

Emre Kiciman, Mrinal Kumar, Glen Coppersmith, Mark Dredze, and Munmun De Choudhury. 2016. Discovering shifts to suicidal ideation from mental health content in social media. In *Proceedings of the SIGCHI Conference on Human Factors in Computing Systems*. ACM.

Mrinal Kumar, Mark Dredze, Glen Coppersmith, and Munmun De Choudhury. 2015. Detecting changes in suicide content manifested in social media following celebrity suicides. In *Proceedings of the 26th ACM conference on Hypertext and hypermedia*. ACM.

Patrick McGorry and Jim van Os. 2013. Redeeming diagnosis in psychiatry: timing versus specificity. *The Lancet* 381(9863):343–345.

Julie W. Messinger, Fabien Trémeau, Daniel Antonius, Erika Mendelsohn, Vasthie Prudent, Arielle D. Stanford, and Dolores Malaspina. 2011. Avolition and expressive deficits capture negative symptom phenomenology: Implications for DSM-5 and schizophrenia research. *Clinical Psychology Review* 31(1):161–168. https://doi.org/10.1016/j.cpr.2010.09.002.

Jude Mikal, Samantha Hurst, and Mike Conway. 2016. Ethical issues in using twitter for population-level depression monitoring: a qualitative study. *BMC medical ethics* 17(1):1.

Margaret Mitchell, Kristy Hollingshead, and Glen Coppersmith. 2015. Quantifying the language of schizophrenia in social media. In *Proceedings of the Workshop on Computational Linguistics and Clinical Psychology: From Linguistic Signal to Clinical Reality*. North American Chapter of the Association for Computational Linguistics, Denver, Colorado, USA.

Barnaby Nelson, Patrick D McGorry, Marieke Wichers, Johanna TW Wigman, and Jessica A Hartmann. 2017. Moving from static to dynamic models of the onset of mental disorder: A review. *JAMA psychiatry* .

Minsu Park, Chiyoung Cha, and Meeyoung Cha. 2012. Depressive moods of users portrayed in Twitter. In *Proceedings of the ACM SIGKDD Workshop on Healthcare Informatics (HI-KDD)*.

Ted Pedersen. 2015. Screening Twitter users for depression and PTSD with lexical decision lists. In *Proceedings of the Workshop on Computational Linguistics and Clinical Psychology: From Linguistic Signal to Clinical Reality*. North American Chapter of the Association for Computational Linguistics, Denver, Colorado, USA.

Daniel Preotiuc-Pietro, Maarten Sap, H. Andrew Schwartz Schwartz, and Lyle Ungar. 2015. Mental illness detection at the World Well-Being Project for the CLPsych 2015 shared task. In *Proceedings of the Workshop on Computational Linguistics and Clinical Psychology: From Linguistic Signal to Clinical Reality*. North American Chapter of the Association for Computational Linguistics, Denver, Colorado, USA.

Andrew G. Reece, Andrew J. Reagan, Katharina L. M. Lix, Peter Sheridan Dodds, Christopher M. Danforth, and Ellen J. Langer. 2016. Forecasting the onset and course of mental illness with Twitter data. *arXiv:1608.07740 [physics]* ArXiv: 1608.07740. http://arxiv.org/abs/1608.07740.

Philip Resnik, William Armstrong, Leonardo Claudino, Thang Nguyen, Viet-An Nguyen, and Jordan Boyd-Graber. 2015. The University of Maryland CLPsych 2015 shared task system. In *Proceedings of the Workshop on Computational Linguistics and Clinical Psychology: From Linguistic Signal to Clinical Reality*. North American Chapter of the Association for Computational Linguistics, Denver, Colorado, USA.

M. David Rudd. 2006. Fluid Vulnerability Theory: A Cognitive Approach to Understanding the Process of Acute and Chronic Suicide Risk. In Thomas E. Ellis, editor, *Cognition and suicide: Theory, research, and therapy.*, American Psychological Association,

Washington, pages 355–368. DOI: 10.1037/11377-016. http://content.apa.org/books/11377-016.

Maarten Sap, Greg Park, Johannes C. Eichstaedt, Margaret L. Kern, David J. Stillwell, Michal Kosinski, Lyle H. Ungar, and H. Andrew Schwartz. 2014. Developing age and gender predictive lexica over social media. In *Proceedings of the Conference on Empirical Methods in Natural Language Processing (EMNLP)*. pages 1146–1151.

Sonja L. van Ockenburg, Sanne H. Booij, Harri?tte Riese, Judith G. M. Rosmalen, and Karin A. M. Janssens. 2015. How to assess stress biomarkers for idiographic research? *Psychoneuroendocrinology* 62:189–199. https://doi.org/10.1016/j.psyneuen.2015.08.002.

Jim van Os. 2013. The dynamics of subthreshold psychopathology: implications for diagnosis and treatment.

Daniel Vigo, Graham Thornicroft, and Rifat Atun. 2016. Estimating the true global burden of mental illness. *The Lancet Psychiatry* 3(2):171–178. https://doi.org/10.1016/S2215-0366(15)00505-2.

Morgan Walker, Laura Thornton, Munmun De Choudhury, Jaime Teevan, Cynthia M Bulik, Cheri A Levinson, and Stephanie Zerwas. 2015. Facebook use and disordered eating in college-aged women. *Journal of Adolescent Health* 57(2):157–163.

Anthony Wood, Jessica Shiffman, Ryan Leary, and Glen Coppersmith. 2016. Discovering shifts to suicidal ideation from mental health content in social media. In *Proceedings of the SIGCHI Conference on Human Factors in Computing Systems*. ACM.

World Health Organization. 2013. *Mental health action plan 2013-2020*. Geneva: World Health Organization.

Author Index

Association for Computational Linguistics
209 N. Eighth Street
Stroudsburg, Pennsylvania 18360

ISBN 978-1-5108-4581-7